Selected
Readings

Introducing
Sociology

Selected Readings

Introducing Sociology

Edited by
James M. Henslin

THE FREE PRESS
A Division of Macmillan Publishing Co., Inc.

NEW YORK

THE FREE PRESS
A Division of Macmillan Publishing Co., Inc.
866 Third Avenue, New York, N.Y. 10022

Collier–Macmillan Canada Ltd.

Library of Congress Catalog Card Number: 74–16903

Printed in the United States of America

printing number
1 2 3 4 5 6 7 8 9 10

Library of Congress Cataloging in Publication Data

Henslin, James M   comp.
  Introducing sociology.

  CONTENTS: Mills, C. W. The task and the promise.--
Mosca, G. The structure of dominance.--Horton, J.
Time and cool people. [etc.]
  1. Sociology--Addresses, essays, lectures. I. Title.
HM51.H3977   301   74-16903
ISBN 0-02-914650-X

**To my parents—
to whom I owe so much.**

Contents

Preface

This volume contains twenty carefully selected articles on sociological theory and research that offer in uncomplicated language sophisticated summaries of major sociological ideas. The professional training of the authors covers a broad range, including not only sociology but also anthropology, history, law, political science, and psychiatry.

Part 1 sets the framework for the book by introducing the student to the basic ideas of the sociological imagination. Part 2 directly builds on this foundation by analyzing major class divisions in society, the role of culture and subculture in influencing life styles and orientations to life, the significance of language in the formation of culture and the perception of reality, and cultural influences on morality. Part 3 discusses the role of society in the origin and the maintenance of the self, dramaturgical aspects of everyday life, and the political construction of reality. Major sociological theories as they are applied to homosexuality, mental illness, and juvenile delinquency are also covered here. The section concludes with an article that presents a contrasting and complementary perspective on human behavior, that of social exchange theory. The readings in Part 4 investigate the social institutions of law, politics, and slavery; the relationship between racism and poverty in contemporary society; the social bases for the current rise in women's liberation activities; and the development and tactics of social movements. Part 5 concludes the volume by dealing with the basic question of what keeps pluralistic societies from separating into warring factions. The focus here is on the role of ideology in maintaining the social order.

I have written introductions to each article, as well as to each Part. With their supplementary materials, these introductions are intended to analytically complement the selections and to integrate them by emphasizing their continuity of thought.

It is my pleasure to express my appreciation to Linda Henslin and Art Iamele for their contributions to this book.

James M. Henslin

Selected Readings

Introducing Sociology

1 The Sociological Imagination

The first section of this book consists of but a single article. Quite properly, it is a selection from Mills' seminal writing on the sociological imagination. In this selection, Mills argues the need for what he calls a quality of mind, a form of self-consciousness. By these terms he is referring to an orientation towards the world by which an individual places what happens to people into the broader context of what is happening in society and history. The thinking of someone who gains this perspective transcends the immediate locales of work, friends, and family: He comes to view many events of life in terms of what is happening both in his own society and in other societies around the world.

Being sensitized to drawing out this interconnection between biography, social structure, and historical events is the "quality of mind" that Mills refers to in his discussion of the sociological imagination. Understanding people from an historical context is a clear enough idea. Though we follow this approach only too rarely, we can certainly see that living in a time of economic "boom" rather than depression will certainly influence one's outlook on life, as well as one's opportunities. It is similarly the case with times of war versus times of peace, or an era of rapid transportation and communication that joins communities around the globe versus an era in which transportation is primarily by foot or by horse and communication is primarily limited to face-to-face speech.

It is, however, not as easy initially to grasp what Mills means by the interplay between biography and social structure. How can an understanding of social structure lead an individual to a different view of his situation in life?

This approach assumes that one's life experiences are not due simply to individuated or isolated circumstances. It assumes, rather, that they are intimately related to the way society is structured. All of us are located in some particular part of society. We are, for example, members of social class and occupational groups. We are reacted to by others on the basis of these memberships, as well as our memberships and activities in other large groupings such as age, sex, and religion. Experiences in the various groups to which we belong lead to certain patternings in our lives which differ from those that characterize persons located in other parts of the social structure. We not only either possess or lack opportunities on the basis of where we are located in society, but we are also exposed to certain ideas, attitudes, and orientations rather than others. Because of our location in society we learn certain sets of attitudes, goals, aspirations, ideas of what we can legitimately hope for in life, and other basic ways of orienting ourselves to the world. Many contrary sets also exist in our society, but we do not learn them because our location in the social structure serves as a filter, allowing certain ones to pass through and become part of our lives while keeping others from being influential in our orientation to life.

Our social location, then, along with the historical period in which we live, greatly determines the type of persons we become. Understanding human behavior by placing it within the context of history and the structure of society lies at the root of the sociological imagination.

1

C. Wright Mills

The Task and the Promise

The *task* which Mills indicates is to learn to think sociologically, that is, to place what happens to people into its relevant social-historical context. In this selection Mills emphasizes that none of us lives in a social or historical vacuum. We are all affected, and drastically so, by what is occurring within the larger bounds of our own society and by world history. Our lives are written bold in these terms. Note the events that Mills lists in this selection which so greatly affect us all: industrialization, changes in the relationships between the social classes, economic depressions and booms, conflicts among nations, the enlarging scope of violence, and the threat of World War III. To see how our lives are affected because such characteristics mark our age is to apply the sociological imagination. It is to link individual lives to history and social structure.

The *promise* is that the sociological imagination will yield a different and profitable understanding of both others and the self. Placing what happens to individuals in a social-historical context will provide a different interpretation of life experiences. Personal troubles, for example, will take on a different meaning. Although we usually perceive events in our lives in much smaller terms, what we personally experience is intricately linked to larger events in society and history. Changing ideas about marriage, about child-bearing, and about child-rearing, for example, take on a different interpretation when they are seen as part of sweeping changes occurring throughout the country and throughout the world. Though they are experienced on the individual level, often painfully, they derive from sources of which we are usually not even aware. A growing awareness of the effect of social structure and history on our lives, resulting in a deepened understanding of both society and what we personally experience, is the outcome or promise of the sociological imagination.

☐ Nowadays men often feel that their private lives are a series of traps. They sense that within their everyday worlds, they cannot overcome their troubles, and in this feeling, they are often quite correct: What ordinary men are directly aware of and what they try to do are bounded by the private orbits in which they live; their visions and their powers are limited to the close-up scenes of job, family, neighborhood; in other milieux, they move vicariously and remain spectators. And the more aware they become, however vaguely, of ambitions and of threats which transcend their immediate locales, the more trapped they seem to feel.

Underlying this sense of being trapped are seemingly impersonal changes in the very structure of continent-wide societies. The facts of contemporary history are also facts about the success and the failure of individual men and women. When a society is industrialized, a peasant becomes a worker; a feudal lord is liquidated or becomes a businessman. When classes rise or fall, a man is employed or unemployed; when the rate of investment goes up or down, a man takes new heart or goes broke. When wars happen, an insurance salesman becomes a rocket launcher; a store clerk, a radar man; a wife lives alone; a child grows up without a father. Neither the life of an individual nor the history of a society can be understood without understanding both.

Yet men do not usually define the troubles they endure in terms of historical change and institutional contradiction. The well-being they enjoy, they do not usually impute to the big ups and downs of the societies in which they live. Seldom aware of the intricate connection between the patterns of their own lives and the course of world history, ordinary men do not usually know what this connection means for the kinds of men they are becoming and for the kinds of history-making in which they might take part. They do not possess the quality of mind essential to grasp the interplay of man and society, of biography and history, of self and world. They cannot cope with their personal troubles in such ways as to control the structural transformations that usually lie behind them.

Surely it is no wonder. In what period have so many men been so totally exposed at so fast a pace to such earthquakes of change? That Americans have not known such catastrophic changes as have the men and women of other societies is due to historical facts that are now quickly becoming "merely history." The history that now affects every man is world history. Within this scene and this period, in the course of a single generation, one sixth of mankind is transformed from all that is feudal and backward into all that is modern, advanced, and fearful. Political colonies are freed; new and less visible forms of imperialism installed. Revolutions occur; men feel the intimate grip of new kinds of authority. Totalitarian societies rise, and are smashed to bits—or succeed fabulously. After two centuries of ascendancy, capitalism is shown up as only one way to make society into an industrial apparatus. After two centuries of hope, even formal democracy is restricted to a quite small portion of mankind. Everywhere in the underdeveloped world, ancient ways of life are broken up and vague expectations become urgent demands. Everywhere in the overdeveloped world, the means of authority and of violence become total in scope and bureaucratic in form. Humanity itself now lies before us, the super-nation at either pole concentrating its most co-ordinated and massive efforts upon the preparation of World War Three.

The very shaping of history now outpaces the ability of men to orient themselves in accordance with cherished values. And which values? Even when they do not panic, men often sense that older ways of feeling and thinking have collapsed and that newer beginnings are ambiguous to the point of moral stasis. Is it any wonder that ordinary men feel they cannot cope with the larger worlds with which they are so suddenly confronted? That they cannot understand the meaning of their epoch for their own lives? That—in defense of selfhood—they become morally insensible, trying to remain altogether private men? Is it any wonder that they come to be possessed by a sense of the trap?

It is not only information that they need—in this Age of Fact, information often dominates their attention and overwhelms their capacities to assimilate it. It is not only the skills of reason that they need—although their struggles to acquire these often exhaust their limited moral energy.

What they need, and what they feel they need, is a quality of mind that will help them to use information and to develop reason in order to achieve lucid summations of what is going on in the world and of what may be happening within themselves. It is this quality, I am going to contend, that journalists and scholars, artists and publics, scientists and editors are coming to expect of what may be called the sociological imagination.

The sociological imagination enables its possessor to understand the larger historical scene in terms of its meaning for the inner life and the external career of a variety of individuals. It enables him to take into account how individuals, in the welter of their daily experience, often become falsely conscious of their social positions. Within that welter, the framework of modern society is sought, and within that framework the psychologies of a variety of men and women are formulated. By such means the personal uneasiness of individuals is focused upon explicit troubles and the indifference of publics is transformed into involvement with public issues.

The first fruit of this imagination—and the first lesson of the social science that embodies it—is the idea that the individual can understand his own experience and gauge his own fate only by locating himself within his period, that he can know his own chances in life only by becoming aware of those of all individuals in his circumstances. In many ways it is a terrible lesson; in many ways a magnificent one. We do not know the limits of man's capacities for supreme effort or willing degradation, for agony or glee, for pleasurable brutality or the sweetness of reason. But in our time we have come to know that the limits of "human nature" are frighteningly broad. We have come to know that every individual lives, from one generation to the next, in some society; that he lives out a biography, and that he lives it out within some historical sequence. By the fact of his living he contributes, however minutely, to the shaping of this society and to the course of its history, even as he is made by society and by its historical push and shove.

The sociological imagination enables us to grasp history and biography and the relations between the two within society. That is its task and its promise. To recognize this task and this promise is the mark of the classic social analyst. It is characteristic of Herbert Spencer—turgid, polysyllabic, comprehensive; of E. A. Ross—graceful, muckraking, upright; of Auguste Comte and Emile Durkheim; of the intricate and subtle Karl Mannheim. It is the quality of all that is intellectually excellent in Karl Marx; it is the clue to Thorstein Veblen's brilliant and ironic insight, to Joseph Schumpeter's many-sided constructions of reality; it is the basis of the psychological sweep of W. E. H. Lecky no less than of the profundity and clarity of Max Weber. And it is the signal of what is best in contemporary studies of man and society.

No social study that does not come back to the problems of biography, of history and of their intersections within a society has completed its intellectual journey. Whatever the specific problems of the classic social analysts, however limited or however broad the features of social reality they have examined, those who have been imaginatively aware of the promise of their work have consistently asked three sorts of questions:

1. What is the structure of this particular society as a whole? What are its essential components, and how are they related to one another?

How does it differ from other varieties of social order? Within it, what is the meaning of any particular feature for its continuance and for its change?

2. Where does this society stand in human history? What are the mechanics by which it is changing? What is its place within and its meaning for the development of humanity as a whole? How does any particular feature we are examining affect, and how is it affected by, the historical period in which it moves? And this period—what are its essential features? How does it differ from other periods? What are its characteristic ways of history-making?

3. What varieties of men and women now prevail in this society and in this period? And what varieties are coming to prevail? In what ways are they selected and formed, liberated and repressed, made sensitive and blunted? What kinds of "human nature" are revealed in the conduct and character we observe in this society in this period? And what is the meaning for "human nature" of each and every feature of the society we are examining?

Whether the point of interest is a great power state or a minor literary mood, a family, a prison, a creed—these are the kinds of questions the best social analysts have asked. They are the intellectual pivots of classic studies of man in society—and they are the questions inevitably raised by any mind possessing the sociological imagination. For that imagination is the capacity to shift from one perspective to another—from the political to the psychological; from examination of a single family to comparative assessment of the national budgets of the world; from the theological school to the military establishment; from considerations of an oil industry to studies of contemporary poetry. It is the capacity to range from the most impersonal and remote transformations to the most intimate features of the human self—and to see the relations between the two. Back of its use there is always the urge to know the social and historical meaning of the individual in the society and in the period in which he has his quality and his being.

That, in brief, is why it is by means of the sociological imagination that men now hope to grasp what is going on in the world, and to understand what is happening in themselves as minute points of the intersections of biography and history within society. In large part, contemporary man's self-conscious view of himself as at least an outsider, if not a permanent stranger, rests upon an absorbed realization of social relativity and of the transformative power of history. The sociological imagination is the most fruitful form of this self-consciousness. By its use men whose mentalities have swept only a series of limited orbits often come to feel as if suddenly awakened in a house with which they had only supposed themselves to be familiar. Correctly or incorrectly, they often come to feel that they can now provide themselves with adequate summations, cohesive assessments, comprehensive orientations. Older decisions that once appeared sound now seem to them products of a mind unaccountably dense. Their capacity for astonishment is made lively again. They acquire a new way of thinking, they experience a transvaluation of values; in a word, by their reflection and by their sensibility, they realize the cultural meaning of the social sciences.

Perhaps the most fruitful distinction with which the sociological imagination works is between "the personal troubles of milieu" and "the public issues of social structure." This distinction is an essential tool of the sociological imagination and a feature of all classic work in social science.

Troubles occur within the character of the individual and within the range of his immediate relations with others; they have to do with his self and with those limited areas of social life of which he is directly and personally aware. Accordingly, the statement and the resolution of troubles properly lie within the individual as a biographical entity and within the scope of his immediate milieu—the social setting that is directly open to his personal experience and to some extent his willful activity. A trouble is a private matter: values cherished by an individual are felt by him to be threatened.

Issues have to do with matters that transcend these local environments of the individual and the range of his inner life. They have to do with the organization of many such milieux into the institutions of an historical society as a whole, with the ways in which various milieux overlap and interpenetrate to form the larger structure of social and historical life. An issue is a public matter: some value cherished by publics is felt to be threatened. Often there is a debate about what that value really is and about what it is that really threatens it. This debate is often without focus if only because it is the very nature of an issue, unlike even widespread trouble, that it cannot very well be defined in terms of the immediate and everyday environments of ordinary men. An issue, in fact, often involves a crisis in institutional arrangements, and often too it involves what Marxists call "contradictions" or "antagonisms."

In these terms, consider unemployment. When, in a city of 100,000, only one man is unemployed, that is his personal trouble, and for its relief we properly look to the character of the man, his skills, and his immediate opportunities. But when in a nation of 50 million employees, 15 million men are unemployed, that is an issue, and we may not hope to find its solution within the range of opportunities open to any one individual. The very structure of opportunities has collapsed. Both the correct statement of the problem and the range of possible solutions require us to consider the economic and political institutions of the society, and not merely the personal situation and character of a scatter of individuals.

Consider war. The personal problem of war, when it occurs, may be how to survive it or how to die in it with honor; how to make money out of it; how to climb into the higher safety of the military apparatus; or how to contribute to the war's termination. In short, according to one's values, to find a set of milieux and within it to survive the war or make one's death in it meaningful. But the structural issues of war have to do with its causes; with what types of men it throws up into command; with its effects upon economic and political, family and religious institutions, with the unorganized irresponsibility of a world of nation-states.

Consider marriage. Inside a marriage a man and a woman may experience personal troubles, but when the divorce rate during the first four years of marriage is 250 out of every 1,000 attempts, this is an indication of a structural issue having to do with the institutions of marriage and the family and other institutions that bear upon them.

Or consider the metropolis—the horrible, beautiful, ugly, magnificent sprawl of the great city. For many upper-class people, the personal solution to "the problem of the city" is to have an apartment with private garage under it in the heart of the city, and forty miles out, a house by Henry Hill, garden by Garrett Eckbo, on a hundred acres of private land. In these two controlled environments—with a small staff at each end and a private helicopter connection—most people could solve many of the problems of personal milieux caused by the facts of the city. But all this, however splendid, does not solve the public issues that the structural fact of the city poses. What should be done with this wonderful monstrosity? Break it all up into scattered units, combining residence and work? Refurbish it as it stands? Or, after evacuation, dynamite it and build new cities according to new plans in new places? What should those plans be? And who is to decide and to accomplish whatever choice is made? These are structural issues; to confront them and to solve them requires us to consider political and economic issues that affect innumerable milieux.

In so far as an economy is so arranged that slumps occur, the problem of unemployment becomes incapable of personal solution. In so far as war is inherent in the nation-state system and in the uneven industrialization of the world, the ordinary individual in his restricted milieu will be powerless—with or without psychiatric aid—to solve the troubles this system or lack of system imposes upon him. In so far as the family as an institution turns women into darling little slaves and men into their chief providers and unweaned dependents, the problem of a satisfactory marriage remains incapable of purely private solution. In so far as the overdeveloped megalopolis and the overdeveloped automobile are built-in features of the overdeveloped society, the issues of urban living will not be solved by personal ingenuity and private wealth.

What we experience in various and specific milieux, I have noted, is often caused by structural changes. Accordingly, to understand the changes of many personal milieux we are required to look beyond them. And the number and variety of such structural changes increase as the institutions within which we live become more embracing and more intricately connected with one another. To be aware of the idea of social structure and to use it with sensibility is to be capable of tracing such linkages among a great variety of milieux. To be able to do that is to possess the sociological imagination.

What are the major issues for publics and the key troubles of private individuals in our time? To formulate issues and troubles, we must ask what values are cherished yet threatened, and what values are cherished and supported, by the characterizing trends of our period. In the case both of threat and of support we must ask what salient contradictions of structure may be involved.

When people cherish some set of values and do not feel any threat to them, they experience *well-being*. When they cherish values but *do* feel them to be threatened, they experience a crisis—either as a personal trouble or as a public issue. And if all their values seem involved, they feel the total threat of panic.

But suppose people are neither aware of any cherished values nor experience any threat? That is the experience of *indifference*, which, if it seems to involve all their values, becomes apathy. Suppose, finally, they are unaware of any cherished values, but still are very much aware of a threat? That is the experience of *uneasiness*, of anxiety, which, if it is total enough, becomes a deadly unspecified malaise.

Ours is a time of uneasiness and indifference—not yet formulated in such ways as to permit the work of reason and the play of sensibility. Instead of troubles—defined in terms of values and threats—there is often the misery of vague uneasiness; instead of explicit issues there is often merely the beat feeling that all is somehow not right. Neither the values threatened nor whatever threatens them has been stated; in short, they have not been carried to the point of decision. Much less have they been formulated as problems of social science.

In the 'thirties there was little doubt, except among certain deluded business circles, that there was an economic issue which was also a pack of personal troubles. In these arguments about "the crisis of capitalism," the formulations of Marx and the many unacknowledged reformulations of his work probably set the leading terms of the issue, and some men came to understand their personal troubles in these terms. The values threatened were plain to see and cherished by all; the structural contradictions that threatened them also seemed plain. Both were widely and deeply experienced. It was a political age.

But the values threatened in the era after World War Two are often neither widely acknowledged as values nor widely felt to be threatened. Much private uneasiness goes unformulated; much public malaise and many decisions of enormous structural relevance never become public issues. For those who accept such inherited values as reason and freedom, it is the uneasiness itself that is the trouble; it is the indifference itself that is the issue. And it is this condition, of uneasiness and indifference, that is the signal feature of our period.

All this is so striking that it is often interpreted by observers as a shift in the very kinds of problems that need now to be formulated. We are frequently told that the problems of our decade, or even the crises of our period, have shifted from the external realm of economics and now have to do with the quality of individual life—in fact with the question of whether there is soon going to be anything that can properly be called individual life. Not child labor but comic books, not poverty but mass leisure, are at the center of concern. Many great public issues as well as many private troubles are described in terms of "the psychiatric"—often, it seems, in a pathetic attempt to avoid the large issues and problems of modern society. Often this statement seems to rest upon a provincial narrowing of interest to the Western societies, or even to the United States—thus ignoring two-thirds of mankind; often, too, it arbitrarily divorces the individual life from the larger institutions within which that life is enacted, and which on occasion bear upon it more grievously than do the intimate environments of childhood.

Problems of leisure, for example, cannot even be stated without considering problems of work. Family troubles over comic books cannot be formulated as problems without considering the plight of the contemporary family in its new relations with the newer institutions of the social structure. Neither leisure nor its debilitating uses can be understood as problems without recognition of the extent to which malaise and indifference now form the social and personal climate of contemporary American society. In this climate, no problems of "the private life" can be stated and solved without recognition of the crisis of ambition that is part of the very career of men at work in the incorporated economy.

It is true, as psychoanalysts continually point out, that people do often have "the increasing sense of being moved by obscure forces within themselves which they are unable to define." But it is *not* true, as Ernest Jones asserted, that "man's chief enemy and danger is his own unruly nature and the dark forces pent up within him." On the contrary: "Man's chief danger" today lies in the unruly forces of contemporary society itself, with its alienating methods of production, its enveloping techniques of political domination, its international anarchy—in a word, its pervasive transformations of the very "nature" of man and the conditions and aims of his life.

It is now the social scientist's foremost political and intellectual task— for here the two coincide—to make clear the elements of contemporary uneasiness and indifference. It is the central demand made upon him by other cultural workmen—by physical scientists and artists, by the intellectual community in general. It is because of this task and these demands, I believe, that the social sciences are becoming the common denominator of our cultural period, and the sociological imagination our most needed quality of mind.

2
The Culture Context

The first selection by Mills presented the need of viewing people's lives within their structural context. It also held forth the promise of gaining a transforming understanding of society and one's place in it. The articles in this second part of the book are designed to aid the growth of the sociological imagination. They illustrate some of the far-reaching effects culture has on what people become.

The type of person we become is the result of our experiences within culture. By growing up in a particular culture, we learn certain sets of attitudes, certain ideas of right and wrong, and particular ways of looking at the self in relationship to others. If we had grown up in some other culture, we would have learned different ways of viewing the world, of looking at ourselves, and of acting towards others. These different ways might have been complementary or highly contrasting, depending on how the cultures are related. Regardless of the particulars, however, it is learning within a cultural context which makes us the type of person we become. Consequently, we cannot sufficiently understand either ourselves or others without understanding the culture in which we or they grow up. Understanding the pervasive influences of culture on people's lives is a first major step in attaining the sociological imagination.

In the opening essay of this section Mosca traces some of the major strands in the historical development of the major cleavage in society, that between those who do the ruling and those who are the ruled. Being born into one or the other of these broad social categories obviously makes a world of difference for what a person becomes. In addition to these major divisions, however, there are much finer distinctions in social rank which also greatly influence people's thoughts, actions, and basic orientations to the world.

The second article in this section picks up this idea. Just as there are a variety of social classes within what Mosca calls "the ruled," each exerting different effects on its members, so there are a variety of subtypes of the general category of "lower class." They vary from migrant workers to janitors, from gas station attendants to farmers, from Appalachian whites to Texan Chicanos, from those who are third-generation welfare recipients to the poor who go hungry rather than accept "government handouts." Each has its own subculture, differing in major respects from others who are also broadly classified as "lower class." In the second article of this section Horton examines one such subculture, that of streetcorner blacks. As he analyzes their interactions, he emphasizes their conception of time. He indicates how their temporal orientation differs from that of the dominant culture and how this affects the ways members of this street culture order their lives.

In the third selection, Hertzler analyzes the significance of language in personal and social life. She emphasizes that language is essential to our learning culture, that it is, indeed, our utilization of language which allows culture to exist. She also indicates how language allows us to apprehend the social divisions of time and space, how language is the vehicle by which the past is transmitted and rules and basic expectations are taught, and how our language both frees and constrains us.

In the final selection, Margaret Mead describes some of the sexual customs of Samoa. She presents their norms or rules regarding premarital sexual relations and contrasts these ideals with the Samoan's actual behavior. Like other social groups, the Samoan's norms and behavior do not quite coincide. Mead also analyzes "patterned evasions" of the norms, that is, violations general enough to be acknowledged as normal but still considered violations. Even though these violations are fairly general, they bring down penalties upon anyone who is caught. The particulars of the Samoans' expectations concerning premarital sex, marriage, and divorce certainly vary from ours, but in a similar manner our norms and behavior also conflict.

2

Gaetano Mosca

The Structure of Dominance

In every society people are characterized by inequalities of some sort, and criteria are established for ranking the members of that society. The bases for social ranking differ widely around the world, ranging from ancestry to courage and from birth order to birthmarks. That people rank one another appears to be an inevitable characteristic of social life. But no system of social ranking is inevitable or natural. Rather, all systems of ranking are contrived and arbitrary.

The major system of social ranking, or social stratification, used by members of industrialized societies is the possession of wealth. Wealth can serve as the basis for social stratification only if a society has both economic surplus and the private ownership of property, two major characteristics of industrialized societies. In addition to wealth or income, members of industrialized societies also rank one another by type of occupation and amount of education. These are the three major factors, or variables, which go into the make-up of contemporary social classes in industrialized societies. Income, or wealth, however, is by far the most important variable.

When sociologists study social class membership, they pay particular attention to the effects class membership has on life chances, the fate a person can expect in life. Social class affects almost every aspect of life, from one's chance of survival in childbirth to the chance one will become a physician or a garbage collector, from the type of food one will eat to the type of recreation one will enjoy. The life chances due to social class membership follow an individual from birth to death. It can hardly be otherwise in a society where social class membership is primarily determined by the amount of money possessed, and where that amount of money determines who gets what.

In this selection Mosca points out that society always consists of those who do the ruling and those who are being ruled, the minority and the majority. He indicates that this basic division of society into the rulers and the ruled first came about through the development of a warrior class. The warriors were established for the protection of those who worked the land. But the warriors gradually appropriated for themselves first the fruits of the land, then the land itself. Class antagonisms were then established which, Mosca would say, remain with us today.

The Concept of the Ruling Class

In all societies—from societies that are very meagerly developed and have barely attained the dawnings of civilization, down to the most advanced and powerful societies—two classes of people appear, a class that rules and a class that is ruled. The first class, always the less numerous, performs all the political functions, monopolizes power, and enjoys the advantages that power brings. The second, the more numerous class, is directed and controlled by the first, in a manner that is now more-or-less legal, now more-or-less arbitrary and violent; it supplies the first class, in appearance at least, with material means of subsistence and with the instrumentalities that are essential to the vitality of the political organism.

In practical life we all recognize the existence of this ruling class. We all know that, in our own country, whichever it may be, the management of public affairs is in the hands of a minority of influential persons, to which, willingly or unwillingly, the majority defers. We know that the same thing goes on in neighboring countries, and in fact we should be hard put to it to conceive of a real world otherwise organized—a world in which all men would be directly subject to a single person without relationships of superiority or subordination, or in which all men would share equally in the direction of political affairs. If we reason otherwise in theory, that is due partly to inveterate habits that we follow in our thinking and partly to the exaggerated importance that we attach to two political facts that loom far larger in appearance than they are in reality.

The first of these facts—and one has only to open one's eyes to see it—is that in every political organism there is one individual who is chief among the leaders of the ruling class as a whole and stands, as we say, at the helm of the state. That person is not always the person who holds supreme power according to law. At times, alongside of the hereditary king or emperor, there is a prime minister or a major-domo who wields an actual power that is greater than the sovereign's. At other times, in place of the elected president, the influential politician who has procured the president's election will govern. Under special circumstances, there may be, instead of a single person, two or three who discharge the functions of supreme control.

The second fact, too, is readily discernible. Whatever the type of political organization, pressures arising from the discontent of the masses who are governed, from the passions by which they are swayed, exert a certain amount of influence on the policies of the ruling, political class.

But the man who is at the head of the state would certainly not be able to govern without the support of a numerous class to enforce respect for his orders and to have them carried out; and granting that he can make one individual, or indeed many individuals, in the ruling class feel the weight of his power, he certainly cannot be at odds with the class as a whole or do away with it. Even if that were possible, he would at once be forced to create another class, without the support of which action on his part would be completely paralyzed. On the other hand, granting that the discontent of the masses might succeed in deposing a ruling class, inevitably, as we shall later show, there would have to be another organized minority within the masses themselves to discharge the functions of a ruling class. Otherwise all organization and the whole social structure would be destroyed.

From the point of view of scientific research the real superiority of the concept of the ruling, or political, class lies in the fact that the varying structure of ruling classes has a preponderant importance in determining the political type, and also the level of civilization, of the different peoples.

. . . We think it may be desirable . . . to reply at this point to an objection which might very readily be made to our point of view. If it is easy to understand that a single individual cannot command a group without finding within the group a minority to support him, it is rather difficult to grant, as a constant and natural fact, that minorities rule majorities, rather than majorities minorities. But that is one of the points—so numerous in all the other sciences—where the first impression one has of things is contrary to what they are in reality. In reality the dominion of an organized minority, obeying a single impulse, over the unorganized majority, is inevitable. The power of any minority is irresistible as against each single individual in the majority, who stands alone before the totality of the organized minority. At the same time, the minority is organized for the very reason that it is a minority. A

hundred men acting uniformly in concert, with a common understanding, will triumph over a thousand men who are not in accord and
can therefore be dealt with one by one. Meanwhile, it will be easier for
the former to act in concert and have a mutual understanding, simply
because they are a hundred and not a thousand. It follows that the
larger the political community, the smaller will the proportion of the
governing minority to the governed majority be and the more difficult
will it be for the majority to organize for reaction against the minority.

However, in addition to the great advantage accruing to them from
the fact of being organized, ruling minorities are usually so constituted
that the individuals who make them up are distinguished from the
mass of the governed by qualities that give them a certain material, intellectual or even moral superiority; or else they are the heirs of individuals who possessed such qualities. In other words, members of a
ruling minority regularly have some attribute, real or apparent, which
is highly esteemed and very influential in the society in which they live.

From the Warriors to the Wealthy

In primitive societies that are still in the early stages of organization,
military valor is the quality that most readily opens access to the ruling
or political class. In societies of advanced civilization, war is the exceptional condition. It may be regarded as virtually normal in societies that
are in the initial stages of their development; and the individuals who
show the greatest ability in war easily gain supremacy over their fellows, the bravest becoming chiefs. The fact is constant, but the forms it
may assume in one set of circumstances or another vary considerably.

As a rule, the dominance of a warrior class over a peaceful multitude
is attributed to a superposition of races, to the conquest of a relatively
unwarlike group by an aggressive one. Sometimes that is actually the
case: we have examples in India after the Aryan invasions, in the
Roman Empire after the Germanic invasions and in Mexico after the
Aztec conquest. But more often, under certain social conditions, we
note the rise of a warlike ruling class in places where there is absolutely
no trace of a foreign conquest. As long as a horde lives exclusively by
the chase, all individuals can easily become warriors. There will of
course be leaders who will rule over the tribe, but we will not find a
warrior class rising to exploit, and at the same time to protect, another
class that is devoted to peaceful pursuits. As the tribe emerges from the
hunting stage and enters the agricultural and pastoral stage, then,
along with an enormous increase in population and a greater stability

in the means of exerting social influence, a more-or-less cleancut division into two classes will take place, one class being devoted exclusively to agriculture, the other class to war. In this event, it is inevitable that the warrior class should little by little acquire such ascendancy over the other as to be able to oppress it with impunity.

Poland offers a characteristic example of the gradual metamorphosis of a warrior class into an absolutely dominant class. Originally the Poles had the same organization by rural villages as prevailed among all the Slavic peoples. There was no distinction between fighters and farmers—in other words, between nobles and peasants. But after the Poles came to settle on the broad plains that are watered by the Vistula and the Niemen, agriculture began to develop among them. However, the necessity of fighting with warlike neighbors continued, so that the tribal chiefs, or voivodes, gathered about themselves a certain number of picked men whose special occupation was the bearing of arms. These warriors were distributed among the various rural communities. They were exempt from agricultural duties, yet they received their share of the produce of the soil along with the other members of the community. In early days their position was not considered very desirable, and country dwellers sometimes waived exemption from agricultural labor in order to avoid going to war. But gradually as this order of things grew stabilized, as one class became habituated to the practice of arms and military organization while the other hardened to the use of the plow and the spade, the warriors became nobles and masters, and the peasants, once companions and brothers, became villeins and serfs. Little by little, the warrior lords increased their demands, to the point where the share they took as members of the community came to include the community's whole produce, minus what was absolutely necessary for subsistence on the part of the cultivators; and when the latter tried to escape such abuses, they were constrained by force to stay bound to the soil, their situation taking on all the characteristics of serfdom pure and simple.

In the course of this evolution, around the year 1333, King Casimir the Great tried vainly to curb the overbearing insolence of the warriors. When peasants came to complain of the nobles, he contented himself with asking whether they had no sticks and stones. Some generations later, in 1537, the nobility forced all tradesmen in the cities to sell such real estate as they owned, and landed property became a prerogative of nobles only. At the same time the nobility exerted pressure upon the king to open negotiations with Rome, to the end that thenceforward only nobles should be admitted to holy orders in Poland. That barred townsmen and peasants almost completely from honorific positions, and stripped them of any social importance whatever.

Everywhere—in Russia and Poland, in India and medieval Europe—the ruling warrior classes acquire almost exclusive ownership of the land. Land, as we have seen, is the chief source of production and wealth in countries that are not very far advanced in civilization. But as civilization progresses, revenue from land increases proportionately. With the growth of population there is, at least in certain periods, an increase in rent, in the Ricardian sense of the term, largely because great centers of consumption arise, such at all times have been the great capitals and other large cities, ancient and modern. Eventually, if other circumstances permit, a very important social transformation occurs. Wealth rather than military valor comes to be the characteristic feature of the dominant class: the people who rule are the rich rather than the brave.

The condition that in the main is required for this transformation is that social organization shall have concentrated and become perfected to such an extent that the protection offered by public authority is considerably more effective than the protection offered by private force. In other words, private property must be so well protected by the practical and real efficacy of the laws as to render the power of the proprietor himself superfluous. This comes about through a series of gradual alterations in the social structure whereby a type of political organization, which we shall call the "feudal state," is transformed into an essentially different type, which we shall term the "bureaucratic state." We are to discuss these types at some length hereafter, but we may say at once that the evolution here referred to is as a rule greatly facilitated by progress in pacific manners and customs and by certain moral habits which societies contract as civilization advances.

Once this transformation has taken place, wealth produces political power, just as political power has been producing wealth. In a society already somewhat mature—where, therefore, individual power is curbed by the collective power—if the powerful are as a rule the rich, to be rich is to become powerful. And in truth, when fighting with the mailed fist is prohibited whereas fighting with pounds and pence is sanctioned, the better posts are inevitably won by those who are better supplied with pounds and pence.

There are, to be sure, states of a very high level of civilization which in theory are organized on the basis of moral principles of such a character that they seem to preclude this overbearing assertiveness on the part of wealth. But this is a case—and there are many such—where theoretical principles can have no more than a limited application in real life. In the United States all powers flow directly or indirectly from popular elections, and suffrage is equal for all men and women in all the states of the union. What is more, democracy prevails not only in institutions, but to a certain extent also in morals. The rich ordinarily feel a certain aversion to entering public life, and the poor a certain aversion to choosing the rich for elective office. But that does not prevent a rich man from being more influential than a poor man, since he can use pressure upon the politicians who control public administration. It does not prevent elections from being carried on to the music of clinking dollars. It does not prevent whole legislatures and considerable numbers of national congressmen from feeling the influence of powerful corporations and great financiers.

In all countries of the world, those other agencies for exerting social influence—personal publicity, good education, specialized training, high rank in church, public administration, and army—are always readier of access to the rich than to the poor. The rich invariably have a considerably shorter road to travel than the poor, to say nothing of the fact that the stretch of road that the rich are spared is often the roughest and most difficult.

The Ruling Class in Periods of Renovation and Crystallization

. . . As soon as there is a shift in the balance of political forces—when, that is, a need is felt that capacities different from the old should assert themselves in the management of the state, when the old capacities therefore lose some of their importance or changes in their distribution occur—then the manner in which the ruling class is constituted changes also. If a new source of wealth develops in a society, if the practical importance of knowledge grows, if an old religion declines or a new one is born, if a new current of ideas spreads, then, simultaneously, far-reaching dislocations occur in the ruling class. One might say, indeed, that the whole history of civilized mankind comes down to a conflict between the tendency of dominant elements to monopolize political power and transmit possession of it by inheritance, and the tendency toward a dislocation of old forces and an insurgence of new forces; and this conflict produces an unending ferment of endosmosis and exosmosis between the upper classes and certain portions of the lower. Ruling classes decline inevitably when they cease to find scope for the capacities through which they rose to power, when they can no longer render the social services which they once rendered, or when their talents and the services they render lose in importance in the social environment in which they live. So the Roman aristocracy declined when it was no longer the exclusive source of higher officers for the army, of administrators for the commonwealth, of governors for the provinces. So the Venetian aristocracy declined when its nobles ceased to command the galleys and no longer passed the greater part of their lives in sailing the seas and in trading and fighting.

In inorganic nature we have the example of our air, in which a tendency to immobility produced by the force of inertia is continuously in conflict with a tendency to shift about as the result of inequalities in the distribution of heat. The two tendencies, prevailing by turn in various regions on our planet, produce now calm, now wind and storm. In much the same way in human societies, there prevails now the tendency that produces closed, stationary, crystallized ruling classes, now the tendency that results in a more or less rapid renovation of ruling classes.

The oriental societies which we consider stationary have in reality not always been so, for otherwise, as we have already pointed out, they could not have made the advances in civilization of which they have left irrefutable evidence. It is much more accurate to say that we came to know them at a time when their political forces and their political classes were in a period of crystallization. The same thing occurs in what we commonly call "aging" societies, where religious beliefs, scientific knowledge, methods of producing and distributing wealth have for centuries undergone no radical alteration and have not been disturbed in their everyday course by infiltrations of foreign elements, material or intellectual. In such societies political forces are always the same, and the class that holds possession of them holds a power that is undisputed. Power is therefore perpetuated in certain families, and the inclination to immobility becomes general through all the various strata in that society.

So in India we see the caste system become thoroughly entrenched after the suppression of Buddhism. The Greeks found hereditary castes in ancient Egypt, but we know that in the periods of greatness and renaissance in Egyptian civilization political office and social status were not hereditary. We possess an Egyptian document that summarizes the life of a high army officer who lived during the period of the expulsion of the Hyksos. He had begun his career as a simple soldier. Other documents show cases in which the same individual served successively in the army, civil administration, and priesthood.

The best known and perhaps the most important example of a society tending toward crystallization is the period in Roman history that used to be called the Low Empire. There, after several centuries of almost complete social immobility, a division between two classes grew sharper and sharper, the one made up of great landowners and high officials, the other made up of slaves, farmers and urban plebeians. What is even more striking, public office and social position became hereditary by custom before they became hereditary by law, and the trend was rapidly generalized during the period mentioned.

On the other hand it may happen in the history of a nation that commerce with foreign peoples, forced emigrations, discoveries, wars, create new poverty and new wealth, disseminate knowledge of things that were previously unknown, or cause infiltrations of new moral, intellectual and religious currents. Or again—as a result of such infiltrations, or through a slow process of inner growth, or from both causes—it may happen that a new learning arises, or that certain elements of an old, long forgotten learning return to favor, so that new ideas and new beliefs come to the fore and upset the intellectual habits on which the obedience of the masses has been founded. The ruling class may also be vanquished and destroyed in whole or in part by foreign invasions, or, when the circumstances just mentioned arise, it may be driven from power by the advent of new social elements who are strong in fresh political forces. Then, naturally, there comes a period of renovation, or, if one prefers, of revolution, during which individual energies have free play and certain individuals, more passionate, more energetic, more intrepid or merely shrewder than others, force their way from the bottom of the social ladder to the topmost rungs.

Once such a movement has set in, it cannot be stopped immediately. The example of individuals who have started from nowhere and reached prominent positions fires new ambitions, new greeds, new energies; and this molecular rejuvenation of the ruling class continues vigorously until a long period of social stability slows it down again. We need hardly mention examples of nations in such periods of renovation. In our age that would be superfluous. Rapid restocking of ruling classes is a frequent and very striking phenomenon in countries that have been recently colonized. When social life begins in such environments, there is no ready-made ruling class, and while such a class is in process of formation, admittance to it is gained very easily. Monopolization of land and other agencies of production is, if not quite impossible, at any rate more difficult than elsewhere. That is why, at least during a certain period, the Greek colonies offered a wide outlet for all Greek energy and enterprise. That is why, in the United States, where the colonizing of new lands continued through the whole nineteenth century and new industries were continually springing up, examples of men who started with nothing and have attained fame and wealth are still frequent—all of which helps to foster in the people of that country the illusion that democracy is a fact.

Suppose now that a society gradually passes from its feverish state to calm. Since the human being's psychological tendencies are always the same, those who belong to the ruling class will begin to acquire a group spirit. They will become more and more exclusive and learn better and better the art of monopolizing to their advantage the qualities and capacities that are essential to acquiring power and holding it. Then, at last, the force that is essentially conservative appears—the force of habit. Many people become resigned to a lowly station, while the members of certain privileged families or classes grow convinced that they have almost an absolute right to high station and command.

From Feudalism to Bureaucracy

Before we proceed any further, it might be wise to linger briefly on the two types into which, in our opinion, all political organisms may be classified, the feudal and the bureaucratic.

This classification, it should be noted, is not based upon essential, unchanging criteria. It is not our view that there is any psychological law peculiar to either one of the two types and therefore alien to the other. It seems to us, rather, that the two types are just different manifestations, different phases, of a single constant tendency whereby human societies become less simple, or, if one will, more complicated in political organization, as they grow in size and are perfected in civilization. Level of civilization is, on the whole, more important in this regard than size, since, in actual fact a literally huge state may once have been feudally organized. At bottom, therefore, a bureaucratic state is just a feudal state that has advanced and developed in organization and so grown more complex; and a feudal state may derive from a once bureaucratized society that has decayed in civilization and reverted to a simpler, more primitive form of political organization, perhaps falling to pieces in the process.

By "feudal state" we mean that type of political organization in which all the executive functions of society—the economic, the judicial, the administrative, the military—are exercised simultaneously by the same individuals, while at the same time the state is made up of small social aggregates, each of which possesses all the organs that are required for self-sufficiency. The Europe of the Middle Ages offers the most familiar example of this type of organization—that is why we have chosen to designate it by the term "feudal"; but as one reads the histories of other peoples or scans the accounts of travelers of our own day, one readily perceives that the type is widespread.

In the bureaucratic state, not all the executive functions need to be concentrated in the bureaucracy and exercised by it. One might even declare that so far in history that has never been the case. The main characteristic of this type of social organization lies, we believe, in the fact that, wherever it exists, the central power conscripts a considerable portion of the social wealth by taxation, and uses it first to maintain a military establishment and then to support a more-or-less extensive number of public services. The greater the number of officials who perform public duties and receive their salaries from the central government or from its local agencies, the more bureaucratic a society becomes.

Feudalism introduced . . . the political supremacy of an exclusively warrior class. . . . Another characteristic of the feudal system was the centralization of all administrative functions and all social influence in the local military leader, who at the same time was master of the land—virtually the one instrument for the production of wealth which still existed.

Feudalism, finally, created a new type of sovereignty that was intermediate between the central, coordinating organ of the state and the individual. Once their position had become hereditary, the more important local leaders bound lesser leaders to themselves by subgrants of land, and these lesser chiefs were tied by oaths of feudal homage and fidelity to the man who made the grant. They had, therefore, no direct relations with the head of the feudal confederation as a whole, the king. In fact, they felt obliged to fight the king if the leader to whom they were directly bound was at war with him. This, certainly, was the main cause of the long resistance which the feudal system offered to the continuous efforts of the central power to destroy it.

. . . Down to the fourteenth century, the memory of the old unity of all civilized and Christian peoples, guided in religious matters by the Roman pontiff, who little by little gained recognition as supreme hierarch of the universal church, and in temporal matters by the successor of the ancient Roman emperor, lingered alive and vigorous in the intellectual classes, the clergy and the doctors of the law. Unless such memories had been very much alive, we should be at a loss to explain the attempt to restore the Empire that took place under Charlemagne and Pope Leo III in the year 800, or another somewhat more successful attempt that was made by Otto I of Saxony in 962.

A name and an idea may exercise a great moral influence, but they are not enough to restore a centralized, coordinated political system once that system has fallen to pieces. In order to effect such a restoration, they have to have a material organization at their disposal, and in

order to have such an organization the agencies required for establishing it must be available. Such agencies Charlemagne's successors
and the Germanic emperors lacked. They had neither a sound financial organization nor a regular bureaucracy nor, finally, a standing
army that was capable of enforcing obedience to imperial edicts.

In Charlemagne's day, the old Germanic band still furnished a fairly
well-disciplined militia for the Frankish armies, and the local lords were
not yet omnipotent. For the same reason the emperors of the House of
Saxony, and the first two emperors of the House of Franconia, could
count on the cooperation of the German military class, which was not
yet solidly grouped about a few leaders. Imperial and regal power attained its maximum efficiency in Germany under Henry III of Franconia. That emperor managed for some time to keep a few of the principal duchies unfilled, or to have them occupied by relatives of the
reigning house. He held the duchy of Franconia and, for a time, the
duchy of Swabia under his personal dominion and further retained the
exclusive right to name the holders of the great ecclesiastical fiefs,
bishoprics and abbacies, which were not hereditary and which covered
almost half of the territory of Germany. Henry III died an untimely
death. Henry IV at that moment was a minor, and he was personally
weak. His struggles with the papacy permitted the higher German nobility to regain the ground it had lost.

But the moment the feudal system had taken a strong hold in Germany, the military base of the empire became shaky. Then the struggle
between the Empire and the Church gave the local sovereignties the
support of a great moral force in their clash with imperial authority.
The effort to reestablish the worldwide political unity of Christian peoples, which Charlemagne had made and which Otto I of Saxony had
repeated, may be considered a complete and final failure with the
death of Frederick II of Hohenstaufen.

But the state of semibarbarism which characterized the darkest
period of the Middle Ages in central and western Europe was not to be
eternal. Civilization was to rise again. The process of reabsorbing local
powers into the central organ of the state had, therefore, to start anew
under a different form; and, in fact, what the representative of the ancient Roman Empire had been unable to do became the task of the
various national monarchies.

Meantime, from about the year 1000 on, another sort of local sovereignty had begun to rise alongside of the fief: the medieval town, the
commune. The commune was a federation of guilds, neighborhood organizations and trade corporations—all the various associations of people who were neither nobles nor subject vassals—which were organized
in the more troublous periods of feudal anarchy, in order that those

who belong to them might enjoy a certain measure of personal security through mutual defense. The communes became powerful first in northern Italy, then in Germany and Flanders and in those countries they were among the greatest obstacles to the growth of the power of the . . . emperors. They achieved more modest positions in France, England, the Iberian kingdoms and southern Italy. In those countries they supported the crown against feudalism.

In general, the national monarchies claimed historical connections with the old barbarian monarchies which the invading Germans had set up on the ruins of the ancient Roman Empire. But after the period of political dissolution that occurred under Charlemagne's first successors, they began to take shape again following geographic and linguistic lines rather than historic traditions. The France of St. Louis, for instance, did not correspond to the old territory of the Franks. In one direction it embraced ancient Septimania, which the Visigoths had formerly controlled. In the other it withdrew from Flanders, Franconia and the Rhineland, which were all Germanic territories and were eventually attracted into the orbit of the Holy Roman Empire.

Furthermore, though his title might derive officially from the titles with which the old barbarian kings had adorned their persons, the national king was at first only the head, and sometimes the nominal head, of a federation of great barons—first among them, but first among peers. Hugh Capet and Philip Augustus were looked upon in just that way in France. King John of England appears in that guise in the text of the Magna Charta, and so do the kings of Aragon in the oath which they were obliged to take before the Cortes. As is well known, the barons of Aragon, in council assembled, invited the new king to swear that he would keep all the old agreements. Before enumerating them, they repeated a declaration: "We, who one by one are your equals and all united are more than your equals, name you our king on the following conditions." And when the conditions had been read, they concluded: "And otherwise not."

More than six centuries of struggle and slow but constant ferment were needed for the feudal king to develop into the absolute king, the feudal hierarchy into a regular bureaucracy, and the army made up of the nobles in arms and their vassals into a regular standing army. During those six hundred years, there were periods when feudalism was able to take advantage of critical moments that country and crown chanced to be passing through and regain some of its lost ground. But in the end victory rested with centralized monarchy. The kings little by little succeeded in gathering into their hands assemblages of material agencies that were greater than the feudal nobility could match. They also made shrewd use of the support of the communes and of powerful and constant moral forces, such as the widespread belief that reigning dynasties had been divinely appointed to rule, or a theory of the doctors of law that the king, like the ancient Roman Emperor, was the sovereign will that created law and the sovereign power that enforced it.

The process by which feudal monarchy evolved into an absolute bureaucratic monarchy might be called typical or normal, since it was followed in France and in a number of other countries in Europe. Nevertheless, there were other processes which led, or might have led, to the same results. The commune of Milan, for instance, in the valley of the Po, developed first into a signoria, or tyranny, and then into a duchy. In the first half of the fifteenth century it subjected many other communes and acquired a fairly extensive territory. It might easily have become a modern national kingdom. Elsewhere great feudatories enlarged their domains and transformed them into kingdoms. That was the case with the margraves of Brandenburg, who became kings of Prussia and then emperors of Germany, and with the dukes of Savoy, who became kings of Sardinia and finally of Italy.

Economic causes seem to have exercised very little influence on the transformation of the feudal state into the bureaucratic state, and that evolution certainly is one of the events that have most profoundly modified the history of the world. Systems of economic production did not undergo any very radical changes between the fourteenth century and the seventeenth, expecially if we compare them with the changes that took place after bureaucratic absolutism was founded. On the other hand, between the end of the fifteenth century and the second half of the seventeenth—in other words, during the period when the feudal system was losing ground every day and was being permanently tamed—a farreaching revolution was taking place in military art and organization, owing to improvements in firearms and their wider and wider use. The baronial castle could easily and rapidly be battered down as soon as cannon became common weapons. The heavy cavalry had been made up of nobles, the only ones who could find time for long training and money for the expensive knightly equipment. But cavalry ceased to be the arm that decided battles, once the arquebus had been perfected and the infantry had generally adopted it.

The absolute bureaucratic state may be regarded as permanently established and fully developed in France at the beginning of the personal reign of Louis XIV—in 1661, that is. At the same time, or soon after, the strengthening of central authority and the absorption of local sovereignties became more or less completely generalized throughout Europe. The few states, such as Poland or Venice, that would not, or could not, move with the times and transform their constitutions, lost power and cohesion, and disappeared before the end of the eighteenth century.

Thus the origins of absolute monarchy are relatively recent. Inside it, and under its wing, new ruling forces, new intellectual, moral and economic conditions, rapidly grew up, so that in less than a century and a half its transformation into the modern representative state became inevitable. The rapidity of that evolution strikes us as one of the most interesting phenomena in history.

3

John Horton

Time and Cool People

When we are born, we are unsocialized (or unacculturated). That is, we have none of the ideas, beliefs, or other orientations to life that characterize the human group into which we are born. Our growing up in a human group involves an intricate process by which we become similar to those around us as we learn the attitudes and ways of life deemed acceptable by our group.

Because we grow up in the American culture, we learn certain things in common with almost every other member of this society. We learn ways of sitting, standing, walking, looking at others, giving expressions of dismay, alarm, shock, happiness, surprise, fear, and so on, which are quite close to what most members of this culture learn. In common with others, we also learn the English language. We are, however, born of parents who occupy a particular corner in American society. Consequently, we learn some values, attitudes, and ways of doing things which characterize our particular subgroup but differ from the dominant culture.

Such subcultural differences lead to contrasting perspectives on life and to differing ways of evaluating the self and others. Whether they differ sharply or slightly, what we learn to value as worthwhile in life depends, like the acquisition of language, on the groups into which we become socialized.

In this selection Horton provides us with an analysis of street culture. He analyzes the culture of the unemployed ghetto male, wherein hustling, or illegal activity, provides the basic means of survival. In the circumstances in which they find themselves, these men cannot depend upon jobs for their livelihoods. Rather, a large proportion of their incomes comes from living off the street, by conning others, by stealing, gambling, selling drugs, and being supported by women. A value system almost antithetical to the one dominant in American culture operates in this subculture.

As Horton analyzes it, members of this street culture even operate within a temporal orientation different from that of members of other social classes. It is not the clock which dictates time for them, but the pattern and flow of money and people. A sense of rhythm develops out of daily life, a patterning of high and low points from which yesterday flows into today and tomorrow gradually unfolds. Street people live in a much more existential present than do members of the other social classes. But it is a temporal orientation which, though perhaps intrinsically rewarding, nonetheless helps guarantee that these people must continue the hustle in order to survive.

As this selection makes abundantly clear, the group into which we are born is of the utmost significance in influencing the type of person we become, in shaping our orientations to life. Had we been born of parents who were members of the street culture and been exposed only or almost exclusively to that culture, we would obviously be different people than we are today. Our ideas about the world, our ideas about what is worthwhile in life, our ideas about what we want out of life, our perception of time, our speech, our mannerisms, our ways of relating to others, whom we trust and whom we hate—all would have been different.

The Variety of Time [An Introductory Note by John Horton]

Time in industrial society is clock time. It seems to be an external, objective regulator of human activities. But for the sociologist, time is not an object existing independent of man, dividing his day into precise units. Time is diverse; it is always social and subjective. A man's sense of time derives from his place in the social structure and his lived experience.

The diversity of time perspectives can be understood intellectually—but it is rarely tolerated socially. A dominant group reifies and objectifies its time; it views all other conceptions of time as subversive—as indeed they are.

Thus, today in the dominant middle class stereotype, standard American time is directed to the future; it is rational and impersonal. In contrast, time for the lower class is directed to the present, irrational and personal. Peasants, Mexican-Americans, Negroes, Indians, workers are "lazy"; they do not possess the American virtues of ambition and striving for success. Viewed solely from the dominant class norm of rationality, their presumed orientation to present time is seen only as an irrational deviation, something to be controlled and changed. It is at best an epiphenomenon produced in reaction to the "real, objective" phenomenon of middle class time.

Sociologists have not been completely exempt from this kind of reified thinking. When they universalize the middle class value of rational action and future time and turn it into a "neutral" social fact, they reinforce a negative stereotype: Lower classes are undependable in organized work situations (they seek immediate rewards and cannot defer gratification); in their political action, they are prone to accept immediate, violent, and extreme solutions to personal problems; their sense of time is dysfunctional to the stability of the economic and political orders. For example, Seymour Martin Lipset writes in a paper significantly entitled "Working Class Authoritarianism":

> This emphasis on the immediately perceivable and concern with the personal and concrete is part and parcel of the short time perspective and the inability to perceive the complex possibilities and consequences of action which often results in a general readiness to support extremist political and religious movements, and generally lower level of liberalism on noneconomic questions.

To examine time in relation to the maintenance or destruction of the dominant social order is an interesting political problem, but it is not a sociology of time; it is a middle class sociology of order or change in its time aspect. Surely, a meaningful sociology of time should take into account the social situation in which time operates and the actor's as well as the observer's perspective. The sociologist must at least entertain the idea that lower class time may be a phenomenon in and of itself, and quite functional to the life problems of that class.

Of course, there are dangers in seeking the viewpoint of a minority: The majority stereotypes might be reversed. For example, we might find out that no stereotype is more incorrect than that which depicts the lower classes as having no sense of future time. As Max Weber has observed, it is the powerful and not the powerless who are present-oriented. Dominant groups live by maintaining and expanding their present. Minority groups survive in this present, but their survival is nourished by a dream of the future. In "Ethnic Segregation and Caste" Weber says:

> The sense of dignity that characterizes positively privileged status groups is natural to their "being" which does not transcend itself, that is, to their beauty and excellence. Their kingdom is of this world. They live for the present by exploiting the great past. The sense of dignity of the negatively privileged strata naturally refers to

a future lying beyond the present whether it is of this life or another. In other words it must be nurtured by a belief in a providential "mission" and by a belief in a specific honor before God.

It is time to re-examine the meaning of time, the reality of the middle class stereotype of itself, as well as the middle class stereotype of the lower class. In this article I explore the latter: the meaning of time among a group most often stereotyped as having an irrational, present sense of time—the sporadically unemployed young Negro street corner population. I choose the unemployed because they live outside of the constraints of industrial work time; Negroes because they speak some of the liveliest street language, including that of time; young males because the street culture of the unemployed and the hustler is young and masculine.

To understand the meaning of street time was to discover "what's happening" in the day-to-day and week-to-week activities of my respondents. Using the middle class stereotype of lower class time as a point of departure, I asked myself the following questions:

In what sense is street time personal (not run by the clock) and present oriented?

What kind of future orientation, if any, exists?

Are street activities really irrational in the sense that individuals do not use time efficiently in the business of living?

I have attempted to answer the questions in the language and from the experience of my respondents.

Time and Cool People [The Essay Proper]

Street culture exists in every low income ghetto. It is shared by the hustling elements of the poor, whatever their nationality or color. In Los Angeles, members of such street groups sometimes call themselves "street people," "cool people," or simply "regulars." Whatever the label, they are known the world over by outsiders as hoods or hoodlums, persons who live on and off the street. They are recognizable by their own fashions in dress, hair, gestures, and speech. The particular fashion varies with time, place, and nationality. For example, in 1963 a really sharp Los Angeles street Negro would be "conked to the bone" (have processed hair) and "togged-out" in "continentals." Today "natural" hair and variations of mod clothes are coming in style.

Street people are known also by their activities—"duking" (fighting or at least looking tough), "hustling" (any way of making money outside the "legitimate" world of work), "gigging" (partying)—and by their apparent nonactivity, "hanging" on the corner. Their individual roles are defined concretely by their success or failure in these activities. One either knows "what's happening" on the street, or he is a "lame," "out of it," "not ready" (lacks his diploma in street knowledge), a "square."

There are, of course, many variations. Negroes, in particular, have contributed much to the street tongue which has diffused into both the more hip areas of the middle class and the broader society. Such expressions as "a lame," "taking care of righteous business," "getting down to the nitty-gritty," and "soul" can be retraced to Negro street life.

The more or less organized center of street life is the "set"—meaning both the peer group and the places where it hangs out. It is the stage and central market place for activity, where to find out what's happening. My set of Negro street types contained a revolving and sometimes disappearing (when the "heat," or police pressure, was on) population of about 45 members ranging in age from 18 to 25. These were the local "dudes," their term meaning not the fancy city slickers but simply "the boys," "fellas," the "cool people." They represented the hard core of street culture, the role models for younger teenagers. The dudes could be found when they were "laying dead"—hanging on the corner, or shooting pool and "jiving" ("goofing" or kidding around) in a local community project. Isolated from "the man" (in this context the man in power—the police, and by extension, the white man), they lived in a small section of Venice outside the central Los Angeles ghetto and were surrounded by a predominantly Mexican and Anglo population. They called their black "turf" "Ghost-town"—home of the "Ghostmen," their former gang. Whatever the origin of the word, Ghost-town was certainly the home of socially "invisible" men.

The Street Set

In 1965 and 1966 I had intensive interviews with 25 set members. My methods emerged in day to day observations. Identified as white, a lame, and square, I had to build up an image of being at least "legit" (not working for police). Without actually living in the area, this would have been impossible without the aid of a key field worker, in this case an outsider who could be accepted inside. This field worker, Cowboy, was a white dude of 25. He had run with "Paddy" (white), "Chicano"

(Mexican), and "Blood" (Negro) sets since the age of 12 and was highly respected for having been president of a tough gang. He knew the street, how to duke, move with style, and speak the tongue. He made my entry possible. I was the underprivileged child who had to be taught slowly and sympathetically the common-sense features of street life.

Cowboy had the respect and I the toleration of several set leaders. After that, we simply waited for the opportunity to "rap." Although sometimes used synonymously with street conversation, "rap" is really a special way of talking—repartee. Street repartee at its best is a lively way of "running it down," or of "jiving" (attempting to put someone on), of trying "to blow another person's mind," forcing him "to lose his cool," to give in or give up something. For example, one needs to throw a lively rap when he is "putting the make on a broad."

Sometimes we taped individuals, sometimes "soul sessions." We asked for life histories, especially their stories about school, job, and family. We watched and asked about the details of daily surviving and attempted to construct street time schedules. We probed beyond the past and present into the future in two directions—individual plans for tomorrow and a lifetime, and individual dreams of a more decent world for whites and Negroes.

The set can be described by the social and attitudinal characteristics of its members. To the observer, these are expressed in certain realities of day to day living: not enough skill for good jobs, and the inevitable trouble brought by the problem of surviving. Of the 25 interviewed, only four had graduated from high school. Except for a younger set member who was still in school, all were dropouts, or perhaps more accurately kicked-outs. None was really able to use or write formal language. However, many were highly verbal, both facile and effective in their use of the street tongue. Perhaps the art of conversation is most highly developed here where there is much time to talk, perhaps too much—an advantage of the *lumpen*-leisure class.

Their incomes were difficult to estimate, as "bread" or "coins" (money) came in on a very irregular basis. Of the 17 for whom I have figures, half reported that they made less than $1,400 in the last year, and the rest claimed income from $2,000–4,000 annually. Two-thirds were living with and partially dependent on their parents, often a mother. The financial strain was intensified by the fact that although 15 of 17 were single, eight had one or more children living in the area. (Having children, legitimate or not, was not a stigma but proof of masculinity.)

At the time of the interview, two-thirds of them had some full- or part-time employment—unskilled and low-paid jobs. The overall pattern was one of sporadic and—from their viewpoint—often unsatisfactory work, followed by a period of unemployment compensation, and petty hustling whenever possible and whenever necessary.

When I asked the question, "When a dude needs bread, how does he get it?" the universal response was "the hustle." Hustling is, of course, illegitimate from society's viewpoint. Street people know it is illegal, but they view it in no way as immoral or wrong. It is justified by the necessity of surviving. As might be expected, the unemployed admitted that they hustled and went so far as to say that a dude could make it better on the street than on the job: "There is a lot of money on the street, and there are many ways of getting it," or simply, "This has always been my way of life." On the other hand, the employed, the part-time hustlers, usually said, "A dude could make it better on the job than on the street." Their reasons for disapproving of hustling were not moral. Hustling meant trouble. "I don't hustle because there's no security. You eventually get busted." Others said there was not enough money on the street or that it was too difficult to "run a game" on people.

Nevertheless, hustling is the central street activity. It is the economic foundation for everyday life. Hustling and the fruit of hustling set the rhythm of social activities.

What are the major forms of hustling in Ghost-town? The best hustles were conning, stealing, gambling, and selling dope. By gambling, these street people meant dice; by dope, peddling "pills" and "pot." Pills are "reds" and "whites"—barbiturates and benzedrine or dexedrine. Pot is, of course, marijuana—"grass" or "weed." To "con" means to put "the bump" on a "cat," to "run a game" on somebody, to work on his mind for goods and services.

The "woman game" was common. As one dude put it. "If I have a good lady and she's on County, there's always some money to get." In fact, there is a local expression for getting county money. When the checks come in for child support, it's "mother's day." So the hustler "burns" people for money, but he also "rips off" goods for money; he thieves, and petty thieving is always a familiar hustle. Pimping is often the hustler's dream of the good life, but it was almost unknown here among the small-time hustlers. That was the game of the real professional and required a higher level of organization and wealth.

Hustling means bread and security but also trouble, and trouble is a major theme in street life. The dudes had a "world of trouble" (a popular song about a hustler is "I'm in a World of Trouble")—with school, jobs, women, and the police. The intensity of street life could be gauged in part by the intensity of the "heat" (police trouble). The hotter the street, the fewer the people visible on the street. On some days the set was empty. One would soon learn that there had been a "bust" (an arrest). Freddy had run amok and thrown rocks at a police car. There had been a leadership struggle; "Big Moe" had been cut up, and the "fuzz" had descended. Life was a succession of being picked up on suspicion of assault, theft, possession, "suspicion of suspicion" (an expression used by a respondent in describing his life). This was an ordinary experience for the street dude and often did lead to serious trouble. Over half of those interviewed claimed they had felony convictions.

The Structure of Street Time

Keeping cool and out of trouble, hustling bread, and looking for something interesting and exciting to do created the structure of time on the street. The rhythm of time is expressed in the high and low points in the day and week of an unemployed dude. I stress the pattern of the unemployed and full-time hustler because he is on the street all day and night and is the prototype in my interviews. The sometimes employed will also know the pattern, and he will be able to hit the street whenever released from the bondage of jail, work, and the clock. Here I describe a typical time schedule gleaned through interviews and field observation.

Characteristically the street person gets up late, hits the street in the late morning or early afternoon, and works his way to the set. This is a place for relaxed social activity. Hanging on the set with the boys is the major way of passing time and waiting until some necessary or desirable action occurs. Nevertheless, things do happen on the set. The dudes "rap" and "jive" (talk), gamble, and drink their "pluck" (usually a cheap, sweet wine). They find out what happened yesterday, what is happening today, and what will hopefully happen on the weekend—the perpetual search for the "gig," the party. Here peer socialization and reinforcement also take place. The younger dude feels a sense of pride when he can be on the set and throw a rap to an older dude. He is learning how to handle himself, show respect, take care of business, and establish his own "rep."

On the set, yesterday merges into today, and tomorrow is an emptiness to be filled in through the pursuit of bread and excitement. Bread makes possible the excitement—the high (getting loaded with wine, pills, or pot), the sharp clothes, the "broad," the fight, and all those good things which show that one knows what's happening and has "something going" for himself. The rhythm of time—of the day and of the week—is patterned by the flow of money and people.

Time is "dead" when money is tight, when people are occupied else-where—working or in school. Time is dead when one is in jail. One is "doing dead time" when nothing is happening, and he's got nothing going for himself.

Time is alive when and where there is action. It picks up in the evening when everyone moves on the street. During the regular school year it may pick up for an hour in the afternoon when the "broads" leave school and meet with the set at a corner taco joint. Time may pick up when a familar car cruises by and a few dudes drive down to Johnny's for a "process" (hair straightening and styling). Time is low on Monday (as described in the popular song, "Stormy Monday"), Tuesday, Wednesday, when money is tight. Time is high on Friday nights when the "eagle flies" and the "gig" begins. On the street, time has a personal meaning only when something is happening, and something is most likely to happen at night—especially on Friday and Saturday nights. Then people are together, and there may be bread—bread to take and bread to use.

Human behavior is rational if it helps the individual to get what he wants whether it is success in school or happiness in the street. Street people sometimes get what they want. They act rationally in those situations where they are able to plan and choose because they have control, knowledge, and concern, irrationally where there are barriers to their wants and desires.

When the street dude lacks knowledge and power to manipulate time, he is indeed irrational. For the most part, he lacks the skills and power to plan a move up and out of the ghetto. He is "a lame" in the middle class world of school and work; he is not ready to operate effectively in unfamiliar organizations where his street strengths are his visible weaknesses. Though irrational in moving up and out of the street, he can be rational in day to day survival in the street. No one survives there unless he knows what's happening (that is, unless he knows what is available, where to get what he can without being burned or busted). More euphemistically, this is "taking advantage of opportunities," exactly what the rational member of the middle class does in his own setting.

To know what's happening is to know the goods and the bads, the securities, the opportunities, and the dangers of the street. Survival requires that a hustling dude know who is cool and uncool (who can be trusted); who is in power (the people who control narcotics, fences, etc.); who is the "duker" or the fighter (someone to be avoided or someone who can provide protection). When one knows what's happening he can operate in many scenes, providing that he can "hold his mud," keep cool, and out of trouble.

With his diploma in street knowledge, a dude can use time efficiently and with cunning in the pursuit of goods and services—in hustling to eat and yet have enough bread left over for the pleasures of pot, the chicks, and the gig. As one respondent put it, "The good hustler has the know-how, the ambition to better himself. He conditions his mind and must never put his guard too far down, to relax, or he'll be taken." This is street rationality. The problem is not a deficient sense of time but deficient knowledge and control to make a fantasy future and a really better life possible.

The petty hustler more fully realizes the middle class ideal of individualistic rationality than does the middle class itself. When rationality operates in hustling, it is often on an individual basis. In a world of complex organization, the hustler defines himself as an entrepreneur; and indeed, he is the last of the competitive entrepreneurs.

The degree of organization in hustling depends frequently on the kind of hustling. Regular pimping and pushing require many trusted contacts and organization. Regular stealing requires regular fences for hot goods. But in Ghost-town when the hustler moved, he usually moved alone and on a small scale. His success was on him. He could not depend on the support of some benevolent organization. Alone, without a sure way of running the same game twice, he must continually recalculate conditions and people and find new ways of taking or be taken himself. The phrase "free enterprise for the poor and socialism for the rich" applies only too well in the streets. The political conservative should applaud all that individual initiative.

Clock Time vs. Personal Time

Negro street time is built around the irrelevance of clock time, white man's time, and the relevance of street values and activities. Like anyone else, a street dude is on time by the standard clock whenever he wants to be, not on time when he does not want to be and does not have to be.

When the women in school hit the street at the lunch hour and he wants to throw them a rap, he will be there then and not one hour after they have left. But he may be kicked out of high school for truancy or lose his job for being late and unreliable. He learned at an early age that school and job were neither interesting nor salient to his way of life. A regular on the set will readily admit being crippled by a lack of formal education. Yet school was a "bum kick." It was not his school. The teachers put him down for his dress, hair, and manners. As a human being he has feelings of pride and autonomy, the very things most threatened in those institutional situations where he was or is the underdeveloped, unrespected, illiterate, and undeserving outsider. Thus whatever "respectable" society says will help him, he knows oppresses him, and he retreats to the streets for security and a larger degree of personal freedom. Here his control reaches a maximum, and he has the kind of autonomy which many middle class males might envy.

In the street, watches have a special and specific meaning. Watches are for pawning and not for telling time. When they are worn, they are decorations and ornaments of status. The street clock is informal, personal, and relaxed. It is not standardized nor easily synchronized to other clocks. In fact, a street dude may have almost infinite toleration for individual time schedules. To be on time is often meaningless, to be late an unconsciously accepted way of life. "I'll catch you later," or simply "later," are the street phrases that mean business will be taken care of, but not necessarily now.

Large areas of street life run on late time. For example, parties are not cut off by some built-in alarm clock of appointments and schedules. At least for the unemployed, standard time neither precedes nor follows the gig. Consequently, the action can take its course. It can last as long as interest is sustained and die by exhaustion or by the intrusion of some more interesting event. A gig may endure all night and well into another day. One of the reasons for the party assuming such time dimensions is purely economic. There are not enough cars and enough money for individual dates, so everyone converges in one place and takes care of as much business as possible there, that is, doing whatever is important at the time—sex, presentation of self, hustling.

Colored People's Time

Events starting late and lasting indefinitely are clearly street and class phenomena, not some special trait of Afro-Americans. Middle class Negroes who must deal with the organization and coordination of activities in church and elsewhere will jokingly and critically refer to a lack of standard time sense when they say that Mr. Jones arrived "CPT" (colored people's time). They have a word for it, because being late is a problem for people caught between two worlds and confronted with the task of meshing standard and street time. In contrast, the street dudes had no self-consciousness about being late; with few exceptions they had not heard the expression CPT. (When I questioned members of a middle class Negro fraternity, a sample matched by age to the street set, only three of the 25 interviewed could not define CPT. Some argued vehemently that CPT was the problem to be overcome.)

Personal time as expressed in parties and other street activities is not simply deficient knowledge and use of standard time. It is a positive adaption to generations of living whenever and wherever possible outside of the sound and control of the white man's clock. The personal clock is an adaptation to the chance and accidental character of events on the street and to the very positive value placed on emotion and feeling. (For a discussion of CPT which is close to some of the ideas presented here, see Jules Henry, "White People's Time, Colored People's Time," *Trans-action*, March/April 1965.)

Chance reinforces personal time. A dude must be ready on short notice to move "where the action is." His internal clock may not be running at all when he is hanging on the corner and waiting for something to do. It may suddenly speed up by chance: Someone cruises by in a car and brings a nice "stash" of "weed," a gig is organized and he looks forward to being well togged-out and throwing a rap to some "boss chick," or a lame appears and opens himself to a quick "con." Chance as a determinant of personal time can be called more accurately *uncertain predictability*. Street life is an aggregate of relatively independent events. A dude may not know exactly what or when something will happen, but from past experience he can predict a range of possibilities, and he will be ready, in position, and waiting.

In white middle class stereotypes and fears—and in reality—street action is highly expressive. A forthright yet stylized expression of emotion is positively evaluated and most useful. Street control and communication are based on personal power and the direct impingement of one individual on another. Where there is little property, status in the set is determined by personal qualities of mind and brawn.

The importance of emotion and expression appears again and again in street tongue and ideology. When asked, "How does a dude make a rep on the set?" over half of the sample mentioned "style," and all could discuss the concept. Style is difficult to define as it has so many referents. It means to carry one's self well, dress well, to show class. In the ideology of the street, it may be a way of behaving. One has style if he is able to dig people as they are. He doesn't put them down for what they do. He shows toleration. But a person with style must also show respect. That means respect for a person as he is, and since there is power in the street, respect for another's superior power. Yet one must show respect in such a way that he is able to look tough and inviolate, fearless, secure, "cool."

Style may also refer to the use of gestures in conversation or in dance. It may be expressed in the loose walk, the jivey or dancing walk, the slow cool walk, the way one "chops" or "makes it" down the street. It may be the loose, relaxed hand rap or hand slap, the swinger's greeting which is used also in the hip middle class teen sets. There are many refined variations of the hand rap. As a greeting, one may simply extend his hand, palm up. Another slaps it loosely with his finger. Or, one person may be standing with his hand behind and palm up. Another taps the hand in passing, and also pays his respect verbally with the conventional greeting "What's happening, Brother." Or, in conversation, the hand may be slapped when an individual has "scored," has been "digging," has made a point, has got through to the person.

Style is a comparatively neutral value compared to "soul." Soul can be many things—a type of food (good food is "soul food," a "bowl of soul"), music, a quality of mind, a total way of acting (in eating, drinking, dancing, walking, talking, relating to others, etc.). The person who acts with soul acts directly and honestly from his heart. He feels it and tells it "like it is." One respondent identified soul with ambition and drive. He said the person with soul, once he makes up his mind, goes directly to the goal, doesn't change his mind, doesn't wait and worry about messing up a little. Another said soul was getting down to the nitty-gritty, that is, moving directly to what is basic without guise and disguise. Thus soul is the opposite of hypocrisy, deceit, and phoniness, the opposite of "affective neutrality," and "instrumentality." Soul is simply whatever is considered beautiful, honest, and virtuous in men.

Most definitions tied soul directly to Negro experience. As one hustler put it, "It is the ability to survive. We've made it with so much less. Soul is the Negro who has the spirit to sing in slavery to overcome the monotony." With very few exceptions, the men interviewed argued that soul was what Negroes had and whites did not. Negroes were "soul brothers," warm and emotional—whites cold as ice. Like other oppressed minorities these street Negroes believed they had nothing except their soul and their humanity, and that this made them better than their oppressors.

The Personal Dream

Soul is anchored in a past and present of exploitation and deprivation, but are there any street values and activities which relate to the future? The regular in the street set has no providential mission; he lives personally and instrumentally in the present, yet he dreams about the day when he will get himself together and move ahead to the rewards of a good job, money, and a family. Moreover, the personal dream coexists with a nascent political nationalism, the belief that Negroes can and will make it as Negroes. His present-future time is a combination of contradictions and developing possibilities. Here I will be content to document without weighing two aspects of his orientation: *fantasy personal future* and *fantasy collective future*. I use the word fantasy because street people have not yet the knowledge and means and perhaps the will to fulfill their dreams. It is hard enough to survive by the day.

When the members of the set were asked, "What do you really want out of life?" their responses were conventional, concrete, seemingly realistic, and—given their skills—rather hopeless. Two-thirds of the sample mentioned material aspirations—the finer things in life, a home, security, a family. For example, one said, in honest street language, "I want to get things for my kids and to make sure they have a father." Another said, jokingly, "a good future, a home, two or three girls living with me." Only one person didn't know, and the others deviated a little from the material response. They said such things as "for everyone to be on friendly terms—a better world . . . then I could get all I wish," "to be free," "to help people."

But if most of the set wanted money and security, they wanted it on their own terms. As one put it, "I don't want to be in a middle class bag, but I would like a nice car, home, and food in the icebox." He wanted the things and the comforts of middle class life, but not the hypocrisy, the venality, the coldness, the being forced to do what one does not want to do. All that was in the middle class bag. Thus the home and the money may be ends in themselves, but also fronts, security for carrying on the usual street values. Street people believed that they already had something that was valuable and looked down upon the person who made it and moved away into the middle class world. For the observer, the myths are difficult to separate from the truths—here where the truths are so bitter. One can only say safely that street people dream of a high status, and they really do not know how to get it.

The Collective Future

The Negro dudes are political outsiders by the usual poll questions. They do not vote. They do not seek out civil rights demonstrations. They have very rudimentary knowledge of political organization. However, about the age of 18, when fighting and being tough are less important than before, street people begin to discuss their position in society. Verbally they care very much about the politics of race and the future of the Negro. The topic is always a ready catalyst for a soul session.

The political consciousness of the street can be summarized by noting those interview questions which attracted at least a 75 percent rate of agreement. The typical respondent was angry. He approves of the Watts incident, although from his isolated corner of the city he did not actively participate. He knows something about the history of discrimination and believes that if something isn't done soon America can expect violence: "What this country needs is a revolutionary change." He is more likely to praise the leadership of Malcolm X than Lyndon Johnson, and he is definitely opposed to the Vietnam war. The reason for this opposition is clear: Why fight for a country which is not mine, when the fight is here?

Thus his racial consciousness looks to the future and a world where he will not have to stand in the shadow of the white man. But his consciousness has neither clear plan nor political commitment. He has listened to the Muslims, and he is not a black nationalist. True, the Negro generally has more soul than the white. He thinks differently, his women may be different, yet integration is preferable to separatism. Or, more accurately, he doesn't quite understand what all these terms mean. His nationalism is real as a folk nationalism based on experience with other Negroes and isolation from whites.

The significance of a racial future in the day to day consciousness of street people cannot be assessed. It is a developing possibility dependent on unforeseen conditions beyond the scope of their skill and imagination. But bring up the topic of race and tomorrow, and the dreams come rushing in—dreams of superiority, dreams of destruction, dreams of human equality. These dreams of the future are salient. They are not the imagination of authoritarian personalities, except from the viewpoint of those who see spite lurking behind every demand for social change. They are certainly not the fantasies of the hipster living philosophically in the present without hope and ambition. One hustler summarized the Negro street concept of ambition and future time when he said:

> The Negro has more ambition than the whites. He's got farther to go. "The man" is already there. But we're on your trail, daddy. You still have smoke in our eyes, but we're catching up.

4

Joyce O. Hertzler

The Influence of Language

Language is one of the basic things of life we take for granted. What is there to analyze about language? We all speak. We all know that language is important because we all depend on it every day. We issue commands, are given orders, whisper words of love, shout words of disgust or anger, declare our intentions, and otherwise use language as a regular part of our everyday lives in order to influence others, to be influenced, and to communicate our thoughts and desires. Certainly we all know language is important.

But how important? Language is more important than most of us would imagine. It should be abundantly clear from the preceding selection that what we become depends upon the group or groups into which we are socialized. The culture we learn determines the way we look at the world and our own place in the world. We gain our attitudes, ideas, ideals, motivations, evaluations, orientations, and ways of behaving towards others through our exposure to human culture.

But human culture could not exist without language. This is the sociological significance of language: It is language which allows human experience to become cumulative. In the absence of language, humans could transmit only an iota of information across generational lines. Each human would be forced to begin life from scratch. The level of our development would be perhaps slightly superior to that of the apes, but not by much.

Information and experiences would not only fail to be cumulative, preventing us from building on the experiences of others, but our communications would also be extremely rudimentary, primarily limited to the present. We would have no tools to discuss the past, and, lacking conceptualization, we would probably be unable to conceive of a future. We would consequently be unable to come to shared understandings regarding our experience, and shared understandings are the essence of culture.

When we learn our native tongue, we are also learning our group's ways of classifying the world of experience. The countless generations who have lived before us have crystallized their experiences into words or concepts. These concepts are a major part of our social inheritance, embodying the ways people in previous generations divided up, or conceptualized, their world of experience. When we learn these concepts, we also learn their ways of conceptualizing the world. The orientations of not only our contemporaries but also those long since dead become ours through the acquisition of language.

Language in the Personal and Social Life of the Individual

The Acquisition of Language by the Child

. . . The infant and child live in all-encompassing physical and sociocultural environments. A fundamental aspect of the latter is the "verbal environment." [1] As he learns to speak, he grows into the language world around him; by means of it, he discovers himself and becomes a full-fledged socialized and encultured being. Since he does not have language facility at birth, however, and without it his humanness is at first only partial, he is for some time relatively unsocialized.

The earliest noises made by the infant are simple crying and screaming sounds, mainly of a reflex nature, and involving purely affective conditions. They are sounds uttered largely in response to conditions of comfort and discomfort, especially the latter, as products of stomach contractions, wetness, fatigue, pain, and so on. These sounds are relatively undifferentiated during the first few days, but soon differences can be distinguished—for example, a cry of hunger as against one caused by a pinprick. These simple cries are supplemented, usually by the third month, by cooing, gurgling, and babbling; this continues until the end of the first year. The latter are expressive sounds, uttered for their own sake, as play. They show some phonetic variation—vowel sounds at first; then a little later consonants—and evidence considerable experimentation.

This early activity appears to be largely "random" in character. During the second six months—in some cases earlier—the child becomes responsive to vocal stimuli, shows some discrimination and, what is of special importance, begins to imitate sounds from his environment, especially those made by his parents and siblings. As time passes, the imitation of sounds becomes surer and more exact, and intonational imitation grows more certain and more precisely articulated. Near the end of his first year, he shows verbal understanding, as he associates sound, act and object through repeated experience. At about this time, he begins to respond in specific ways to conventional speech, and to utter conventional words as a means of dealing with specific situations. Because of the reactions of associates, especially parents, to his utterances, his own sounds begin to contain "meaning" for him; they take on a social character. Usually early in his second year, he begins to produce verbal utterances which involve more or less standard vocal patterns and sound variations, in order to express himself and to communicate specific messages to others.

The child's first spoken words are usually syllables or repeated syllables such as *mama, wawa, dada;* the use of other words soon follows. For the most part, the infant's first words are employed as sentences, rather than as single words; they do service as one-word sentences ("ball" may mean "there is the ball," "where is the ball?," "I want the ball," depending on the intonation). The development of sentences and phrases follows. During the second and third years of life, the child learns the grammatical, syntactical, and stylistic rules of his language. He now has a by no means final, but at least fair, degree of language proficiency. This development of linguistic facility puts the child in a position to receive and to carry forward his historical and continually changing culture. He is also prepared to act as a socialized human being, one fully participant in his various groups and relationships. What are some of the signal early effects in these respects?

The Role of Language in the Enculturation of the Individual

The enculturation of the individual consists primarily of his acquisition of an intellectual and behavioral orientation in his physical and social universe. This, in turn, consists in his attainment of identifications, categorizations, working concepts, and the standard meanings of all manner of things, events and situations, before he can act appropriately. However, the first significant enculturating effect on the child as he acquires his language flows from his use of words, especially when he makes the momentous discovery that things have names. The very act of naming designates an object or attribute or relationship as a specific and restricted part of some whole. He discovers that these words more or less correspond to aspects of the real world around him; they carry the meanings of the items that he has experienced or that have been pointed out to him. The word-stock also provides him with indicators of the categories of things, their different kinds and qualities. Thus he becomes conscious of scope and variation in the nature of things. For him, now as a child and later throughout his life, language has ceased to be a chain of sound; it has become the representative, the surrogate of reality. By means of it, the objective world has been created for him; he has awareness of things in their specific modes of existence, their specific qualities and their relational characteristics.

. . . The words of his language not only mobilize the individual's attention toward the world around him, but also provide him with frames or guides for perception. The different combinations of words and distinctions between words provide him with the diverse meanings of things. They function as the key agencies in the development and conduct of his conceptual thinking, and in the growth and maintenance of his powers of specific description, objective reference, assignment and refinement of meaning, interpretation and generalization, and abstraction.

To revert more specifically to the child: by means of language he becomes conscious of the actuality and distinctions of time and space—very important aspects of advance in the life of the child. He refers first to the present, and then to the past and the future. He becomes aware of such spatial distinctions as large and small, long and short, near and far. With regard to time and space, he comes to be able to conceptualize the extent of each, to explore the part played by people and activity in each, and to project his own thinking into the past and the future, in real and imagined objects, places and events near and far. With language he also takes on such critical categories as those of number, action and quality. These comprehensions he utilizes throughout his life.

By means of the questions he asks, the child not only satisfies his needs and obtains action on his behalf, but becomes able to deal with absent and imaginary situations, to obtain information and satisfy his curiosity about that which he experiences—not only the names of things, but also the why and how of things, their purposes and goals and ends.

In sum, it is in talking about his world—in verbalizing reality—that the individual achieves a full consciousness of it—that is to say, learns about it; in this way explains his experience with it. The world's properties and conditions become part of the schematic framework in which he lives. He comes to terms of some sort with the world, which thus becomes more or less manageable by him. Especially significant in connection with enculturation is the fact that, as the individual's experience is verbalized in the form of standard language forms, it comes into accord with established schemata of his group—that is, the principles whereby experience is organized into knowledge.

. . . It is by means of its own language, with its particular structure and its own unique body of meanings, that *the society indoctrinates the individual with its "history" and its basic operational principles and rules*. He thus acquires the accepted facts, as well as the beliefs and myths, about its career in time—items which it is expected he will accept, exemplify and continue as a member. Through language, the essential knowledge for social behavior is gained and the characteristic mental habits and social interests are inculcated. By means of it, the social values, attitudes, ideas, traditions, ideals, ideologies and goals are defined and made conceivable for the individual, and internalized by him. . . .

Language is *a potent social instrument used by the individual in his relations with his associates*. The child early becomes aware of that fact. He finds that, by the use of certain sounds, words, phrases and sentences, he can declare himself, he can bring upon himself types of attention from others. Some vocalizations enable him to bring about some changes in his environment that are desired by him; others, he discovers, result in unwanted types of reaction. He becomes aware of his ability to direct and manipulate others, and he uses language to do so. As his language facility develops he gains new insights into himself and acquires increasing control over his own behavior—especially the ability to direct it in conformity with learned social standards by conversing with himself about it. By way of the expressions of others, he develops sensitivity to the approval and disapproval of others, and responds more coherently and consistently to the expectations of others.

Language plays an important part in *the assumption of social roles by the individual, and in his performance of these roles*. While he may not be conscious of that fact, he acquires in specific verbal form the definitions and specifications of the roles for the different types of social situations in which he is involved. He outlines verbally his behavior in each role, and imagines the response (of either an approving or a critical nature) of possible others. He thus "rounds out" his conception of his various roles and at the same time internalizes them.

By means of language, the individual *obtains information regarding the social organization of his society*, especially its institutions and the functions they require of him.

By means of language, the individual *learns about the system of social rank of his society, and his place in it*. Through it, he not only acquires the manners, mores, rituals, and economic traits of his own social class; being immersed in the "special" language of his class, he acquires *its* vocabulary, accent, pronunciation, idiom and metaphor.

The very use of the common language of his group has a socializing effect upon him: it binds him to his co-speakers. Furthermore, as was noted in an earlier chapter, the speech community, by contrast with other communities, has a certain *esprit de corps,* which enhances the feeling of "belongingness" of the individual and favors actions valued by the community.

In general, it is only through language that the individual can live with other people, do their bidding, influence them to do his bidding and engage in teamwork with them.

The Part of Language in the Orientation and Range of the Individual in Time

Not only does the individual become aware—as a child—of the actuality of time, and acquire the verbal means of distinguishing its phases; throughout his life, language is the means whereby he orients himself toward the past, present, and future of the stream of time—something that subhuman creatures cannot do. He relates and locates himself with respect to the life of his ancestors and other predecessors, which has been preserved for him in traditions, legends, and written records. It is, of course, by language that he adjusts to and cooperates with his contemporaries. He relates himself to his children, even to his remote descendants, as the culture he has learned (and possibly augmented in some measure) is projected into the future by linguistic instruments. He can achieve a sort of sociocultural immortality through the remembrances and recordings of others, including later generations, about him. As he formulates eschatological doctrines and religious beliefs, he achieves some orientation with eternity.[2]

Language as a Means of the Freedom and the Enslavement of the Individual

The individual is ensured a considerable degree of freedom by means of the possession of language. First and foremost, it gives him the means to express himself—which is of immeasurable value in the development of human personality. Language also frees him, in part, from his own instincts; he can draw on the accumulated knowledge of his civilization, as he lives his life more or less consciously. He can profit by the experience of others, past and present. He does not have to solve anew every problem that was ever faced by his ancestors. Language can free him to some degree from engulfment in complete uniformity: by means of it, each man can specialize. Furthermore, language provides a variety of channels through which the individual may develop his manner of expression; he can do so in an uncommon, fresh, even eccentric manner—a manner individual and proper to him as a particular person.

At the same time, his language to some extent enslaves the individual. While any individual use of language is in some measure an outcome of individual conditions and behavior, and may in some part be an act of original creation, the language is that of his speech community, and his actual language performance is basically a matter of conditioning. He may have much individual "flair" and "style," but he uses an institutionalized medium, which has conditioned not only his speech behavior but also his intellectual behavior. He cannot avoid drawing upon the vast body of established words and structures—which may have a stultifying effect on him. Departure from established expressional forms may be regarded as eccentric. There is always the possibility that the individual sees the world of the past and the world around him "through a screen of linguistic stereotypes." [3]

Furthermore, through linguistically recorded knowledge, the individual is bound by the experience and conclusions of others; he is forced into a sort of experiential and cultural straitjacket. The language couches in somewhat fixed forms the representations of things, events, relations. It also binds him by ancient and sanctified phrases to the ideological attitudes of his group and his society. It not only integrates him with his society as it is, but ties him to it as it is. The individual is by no means an entirely free agent in speech matters.[4]

5

Margaret Mead

Coming of Age in /amoa

As we emphasized in the preceding readings of this section, the type of people we become is dependent upon our culture, upon such things as the social ranking our family has, the values we learn, and the native tongue to which we are introduced. So it is with socialization into morality.

What we think is right and wrong is such a central part of us that we sometimes overlook its social origins. Yet what we feel is right or wrong about any aspect of life, including sex, represents learned feelings and attitudes. Similar to the language we speak and our other orientations to life, if we had been raised within a different culture our ideas and behaviors regarding sexual morality would also be different.

In all human groups, people establish social order. People determine the ways they think things ought to be, and they develop mechanisms for making certain that others follow these expectations. A central activity around which elaborate or highly formalized rules are developed is the human sex drive. In each culture are developed rules concerning who is able to cohabit with or marry whom. The particulars vary markedly from culture to culture, but each culture develops these basic expectations or rules.

The reason each culture is concerned about how their people satisfy the sex drive is because so much else in social life is usually connected to sexual relations. Through rules concerning long-term cohabition, the group exerts control over marriage. Through marriage, control is exerted over the formation of new family units, the birth and socialization of children, the granting of status,

Reprinted by permission of William Morrow & Company, Inc. from *Coming of Age in Samoa* [pp. 86–109] by Margaret Mead. Copyright © 1928, 1955, 1961 by Margaret Mead.

socialization into identity, the division of labor, and the acquisition and inheritance of property. Much of the social order, then, depends upon channeling satisfactions of the sex drive into ways considered culturally appropriate.

Because of the importance of sex in society, social scientists also study the sexual practices of people. In this selection, Margaret Mead details some of the sexual orientations of the Samoans. She did field work among the Samoans to gather her data, learning their language, their customs, and the Samoans' basic approach to the world. The sexual customs of the Samoans documented in this selection provide illustrative contrast with our own.

☐ The first attitude which a little girl learns towards boys is one of avoidance and antagonism. She learns to observe the brother and sister taboo towards the boys of her relationship group and household, and together with the other small girls of her age group she treats all other small boys as enemies elect. After a little girl is eight or nine years of age she has learned never to approach a group of older boys. This feeling of antagonism towards younger boys and shamed avoidance of older ones continues up to the age of thirteen or fourteen, to the group of girls who are just reaching puberty and the group of boys who have just been circumcised. These children are growing away from the age-group life and the age-group antagonisms. They are not yet actively sex-conscious. And it is at this time that relationships between the sexes are least emotionally charged. Not until she is an old married woman with several children will the Samoan girl again regard the opposite sex so quietly. When these adolescent children gather together there is a good-natured banter, a minimum of embarrassment, a great deal of random teasing which usually takes the form of accusing some little girl of a consuming passion for a decrepit old man of eighty, or some small boy of being the father of a buxom matron's eighth child. Occasionally the banter takes the form of attributing affection between two age mates and is gaily and indignantly repudiated by both. Children at this age meet at informal *siva* parties, on the outskirts of more formal occasions, at community reef fishings (when many yards of reef have been enclosed to make a great fish trap) and on torch-fishing excursions. Good-natured tussling and banter and co-operation in common activities are the keynotes of these occasions. But unfortunately these contacts are neither frequent nor sufficiently prolonged to teach the girls co-operation or to give either boys or girls any real appreciation of personality in members of the opposite sex.

Two or three years later this will all be changed. The fact that little girls no longer belong to age groups makes the individual's defection less noticeable. The boy who begins to take an active interest in girls is also seen less in a gang and spends more time with one close companion. Girls have lost all of their nonchalance. They giggle, blush, bridle, run away. Boys become shy, embarrassed, taciturn, and avoid the society of girls in the daytime and on the brilliant moonlit nights for which they accuse the girls of having an exhibitionistic preference. Friendships fall more strictly within the relationship group. The boy's need for a trusted confidant is stronger than that of the girl, for only the most adroit and hardened Don Juans do their own courting. There are occasions, of course, when two youngsters just past adolescence, fearful of ridicule, even from their nearest friends and relatives, will slip away alone into the bush. More frequently still an older man, a widower or a divorced man, will be a girl's first lover. And here there is no need for an ambassador. The older man is neither shy nor frightened, and furthermore there is no one whom he can trust as an intermediary; a younger man would betray him, an older man would not take his amours seriously. But the first spontaneous experiment of adolescent children and the amorous excursions of the older men among the young girls of the village are variants on the edge of the recognised types of relationships; so also is the first experience of a young boy with an older woman. But both of these are exceedingly frequent occurrences, so that the success of an amatory experience is seldom jeopardised by double ignorance. Nevertheless, all of these occasions are outside the recognised forms into which sex relations fall. The little boy and girl are branded by their companions as guilty of *tautala lai titi* (presuming above their ages) as is the boy who loves or aspires to love an older woman, while the idea of an older man pursuing a young girl appeals strongly to their sense of humour; or if the girl is very young and naïve, to their sense of unfitness. "She is too young, too young yet. He is too old," they will say, and the whole weight of vigorous disapproval fell upon a *matai* who was known to be the father of the child of Lotu, the sixteen-year-old feeble-minded girl on Olesega. Discrepancy in age or experience always strikes them as comic or pathetic according to the degree. The theoretical punishment which is meted out to a disobedient and runaway daughter is to marry her to a very old man, and I have heard a nine-year-old giggle contemptuously over her mother's preference for a seventeen-year-old boy. Worst among these unpatterned deviations is that of the man who makes love to some young and dependent woman of his household, his adopted child or his wife's younger sister. The cry of incest is raised against him and sometimes feeling runs so high that he has to leave the group.

Besides formal marriage there are only two types of sex relations which receive any formal recognition from the community—love affairs between unmarried young people (this includes the widowed) who are very nearly of the same age, whether leading to marriage or merely a passing diversion; and adultery.

Between the unmarried there are three forms of relationship: the clandestine encounter, "under the palm trees," the published elopement, *Avaga*, and the ceremonious courtship in which the boy "sits before the girl"; and on the edge of these, the curious form of surreptitious rape, called *moetotolo*, sleep crawling, resorted to by youths who find favour in no maiden's eyes.

In these three relationships, the boy requires a confidant and ambassador whom he calls a *soa*. Where boys are close companions, this relationship may extend over many love affairs, or it may be a temporary one, terminating with the particular love affair. The *soa* follows the pattern of the talking chief who makes material demands upon his chief in return for the immaterial services which he renders him. If marriage results from his ambassadorship, he receives a specially fine present from the bridegroom. The choice of a *soa* presents many difficulties. If the lover chooses a steady, reliable boy, some slightly younger relative devoted to his interests, a boy unambitious in affairs of the heart, very likely the ambassador will bungle the whole affair through inexperience and lack of tact. But if he chooses a handsome and expert wooer who knows just how "to speak softly and walk gently," then as likely as not the girl will prefer the second to the principal. This difficulty is occasionally anticipated by employing two or three *soas* and setting them to spy on each other. But such a lack of trust is likely to inspire a similar attitude in the agents, and as one overcautious and disappointed lover told me ruefully, "I had five *soas*, one was true and four were false."

Among possible *soas* there are two preferences, a brother or a girl. A brother is by definition loyal, while a girl is far more skilful for "a boy can only approach a girl in the evening, or when no one is by, but a girl can go with her all day long, walk with her and lie on the mat by her, eat off the same platter, and whisper between mouthfuls the name of the boy, speaking ever of him, how good he is, how gentle and how true, how worthy of love. Yes, best of all is the *soafafine*, the woman ambassador." But the difficulties of obtaining a *soafafine* are great. A boy may not choose from his own female relatives. The taboo forbids him ever to mention such matters in their presence. It is only by good chance that his brother's sweetheart may be a relative of the girl upon whom he has set his heart; or some other piece of good fortune may throw him into contact with a girl or woman who will act in his interests. The most violent antagonisms in the young people's groups are not between ex-lovers, arise not from the venom of the deserted nor the smarting pride of the jilted, but occur between the boy and the *soa* who has betrayed him, or a lover and the friend of his beloved who has in any way blocked his suit.

In the strictly clandestine love affair the lover never presents himself at the house of his beloved. His *soa* may go there in a group or upon some trumped-up errand, or he also may avoid the house and find opportunities to speak to the girl while she is fishing or going to and from the plantation. It is his task to sing his friend's praise, counteract the girl's fears and objections, and finally appoint a rendezvous. These affairs are usually of short duration and both boy and girl may be carrying on several at once. One of the recognised causes of a quarrel is the resentment of the first lover against his successor of the same night, "for the boy who came later will mock him." These clandestine lovers make their rendezvous on the outskirts of the village. "Under the palm trees" is the conventionalised designation of this type of intrigue. Very often three or four couples will have a common rendezvous, when either the boys or the girls are relatives who are friends. Should the girl ever grow faint or dizzy, it is the boy's part to climb the nearest palm and fetch down a fresh cocoanut to pour on her face in lieu of *eau de cologne*. In native theory, barrenness is the punishment of promiscuity; and, *vice versa*, only persistent monogamy is rewarded by conception. When a pair of clandestine experimenters whose rank is so low that their marriages are not of any great economic importance become genuinely attached to each other and maintain the relationship over several months, marriage often follows. And native sophistication distinguishes between the adept lover whose adventures are many and of short duration and the less skilled man who can find no better proof of his virility than a long affair ending in conception.

Often the girl is afraid to venture out into the night, infested with ghosts and devils, ghosts that strangle one, ghosts from far-away villages who come in canoes to kidnap the girls of the village, ghosts who leap upon the back and may not be shaken off. Or she may feel that it is wiser to remain at home, and if necessary, attest her presence vocally. In this case the lover braves the house; taking off his *lavalava*, he greases his body thoroughly with cocoanut oil so that he can slip through the fingers of pursuers and leave no trace, and stealthily raises the blinds and slips into the house. The prevalence of this practice gives point to the familiar incident in Polynesian folk tales of the ill fortune that falls the luckless hero who "sleeps until morning, until the rising sun reveals his presence to the other inmates of the house." As perhaps a dozen or more people and several dogs are sleeping in the house, a due regard for silence is sufficient precaution. But it is this habit of domestic rendezvous which lends itself to the peculiar abuse of the *moetotolo*, or sleep crawler.

The *moetotolo* is the only sex activity which presents a definitely abnormal picture. Ever since the first contact with white civilisation, rape, in the form of violent assault, has occurred occasionally in Samoa. It is far less congenial, however, to the Samoan attitude than *moetotolo*, in which a man stealthily appropriates the favours which are meant for another. The need for guarding against discovery makes conversation impossible, and the sleep crawler relies upon the girl's expecting a lover or the chance that she will indiscriminately accept any comer. If the girl suspects and resents him, she raises a great outcry and the whole household gives chase. Catching a *moetotolo* is counted great sport, and the women, who feel their safety endangered, are even more active in pursuit than the men. One luckless youth in Luma neglected to remove his *lavalava*. The girl discovered him and her sister succeeded in biting a piece out of his *lavalava* before he escaped. This she proudly exhibited the next day. As the boy had been too dull to destroy his *lavalava*, the evidence against him was circumstantial and he was the laughing stock of the village; the children wrote a dance song about it and sang it after him wherever he went. The *moetotolo* problem is complicated by the possibility that a boy of the household may be the offender and may take refuge in the hue and cry following the discovery. It also provides the girl with an excellent alibi, since she has only to call out "*moetotolo*" in case her lover is discovered. "To the family and the village that may be a *moetotolo*, but it is not so in the hearts of the girl and the boy."

Two motives are given for this unsavoury activity, anger and failure in love. The Samoan girl who plays the coquette does so at her peril. "She will say, 'Yes, I will meet you tonight by that old cocoanut tree just besides the devilfish stone when the moon goes down.' And the boy will wait and wait and wait all night long. It will grow very dark; lizards will drop on his head; the ghost boats will come into the channel. He will be very much afraid. But he will wait there until dawn, until his hair is wet with dew and his heart is very angry and still she does not come. Then in revenge he will attempt a *moetotolo*. Especially will he do so if he hears that she has met another that night." The other set explanation is that a particular boy cannot win a sweetheart by any legitimate means, and there is no form of prostitution, except guest prostitution in Samoa. As some of the boys who were notorious *moetotolos* were among the most charming and good-looking youths of the village, this is a little hard to understand. Apparently, these youths, frowned upon in one or two tentative courtships, inflamed by the loudly proclaimed success of their fellows and the taunts against their own inexperience, cast established wooing procedure to the winds and attempt a *moetotolo*. And once caught, once branded, no girl will ever pay any attention to them again. They must wait until as older men, with position and title to offer, they can choose between some weary and bedraggled wanton or the unwilling young daughter of ambitious and selfish parents. But years will intervene before this is possible, and shut out from the amours in which his companions are engaging, a boy makes one attempt after another, sometimes successfully, sometimes only to be caught and beaten, mocked by the village, and always digging the pit deeper under his feet. Often partially satisfactory solutions are relationships with men. There was one such pair in the village, a notorious *moetotolo*, and a serious-minded youth who wished to keep his heart free for political intrigue. The *moetotolo* therefore complicates and adds zest to the surreptitious love-making which is conducted at home, while the danger of being missed, the undesirability of chance encounters abroad, rain and the fear of ghosts, complicate "love under the palm trees."

Between these strictly *sub rosa* affairs and a final offer of marriage there is an intermediate form of courtship in which the girl is called upon by the boy. As this is regarded as a tentative move towards matrimony, both relationship groups must be more or less favourably inclined towards the union. With his *soa* at his side and provided with a basket of fish, an octopus or so, or a chicken, the suitor presents himself at the girl's home before the late evening meal. If his gift is accepted, it is a sign that the family of the girl are willing for him to pay his addresses to her. He is formally welcomed by the *matai*, sits with reverently bowed head throughout the evening prayer, and then he and his *soa* stay for supper. But the suitor does not approach his beloved. They say: "If you wish to know who is really the lover, look then not at the boy who sits by her side, looks boldly into her eyes and twists the flowers in her necklace around his fingers or steals the hibiscus flower from her hair that he may wear it behind his ear. Do not think it is he who whispers softly in her ear, or says to her, 'Sweetheart, wait for me to-night. After the moon has set, I will come to you,' or who teases her by saying she has many lovers. Look instead at the boy who sits far off, who sits with bent head and takes no part in the joking. And you will see that his eyes are always turned softly on the girl. Always he watches her and never does he miss a movement of her lips. Perhaps she will wink at him, perhaps she will raise her eyebrows, perhaps she will make a sign with her hand. He must always be wakeful and watching or he will miss it." The *soa* meanwhile pays the girl elaborate and ostentatious court and in undertones pleads the cause of his friend.

After dinner, the centre of the house is accorded the young people to play cards, sing or merely sit about, exchanging a series of broad pleasantries. This type of courtship varies from occasional calls to daily attendance. The food gift need not accompany each visit, but is as essential at the initial call as is an introduction in the West. The way of such declared lovers is hard. The girl does not wish to marry, nor to curtail her amours in deference to a definite betrothal. Possibly she may also dislike her suitor, while he in turn may be the victim of family ambition. Now that the whole village knows him for her suitor, the girl gratifies her vanity by avoidance, by perverseness. He comes in the evening, she has gone to another house; he follows her there, she immediately returns home. When such courtship ripens into an accepted proposal of marriage, the boy often goes to sleep in the house of his intended bride and often the union is surreptitiously consummated. Ceremonial marriage is deferred until such time as the boy's family have planted or collected enough food and other property and the girl's family have gotten together a suitable dowry of tapa and mats.

In such manner are conducted the love affairs of the average young people of the same village, and of the plebeian young people of neighbouring villages. From this free and easy experimentation, the *taupo* is excepted. Virginity is a legal requirement for her. At her marriage, in front of all the people, in a house brilliantly lit, the talking chief of the bridegroom will take the tokens of her virginity.* In former days should she prove not to be a virgin, her female relatives fell upon and beat her with stones, disfiguring and sometimes fatally injuring the girl who had shamed their house. The public ordeal sometimes prostrated the girl for as much as a week, although ordinarily a girl recovers from first intercourse in two or three hours, and women seldom lie abed more than a few hours after childbirth. Although this virginity-testing ceremony was theoretically observed at weddings of people of all ranks, it was simply ignored if the boy knew that it was an idle form, and "a wise girl who is not a virgin will tell the talking chief of her husband, so that she be not shamed before all the people."

The attitude towards virginity is a curious one. Christianity has, of course, introduced a moral premium on chastity. The Samoans regard this attitude with reverent but complete scepticism and the concept of celibacy is absolutely meaningless to them. But virginity definitely adds to a girl's attractiveness, the wooing of a virgin is considered far more of a feat than the conquest of a more experienced heart, and a really successful Don Juan turns most of his attention to their seduction. One

---

* This custom is now forbidden by law, but is only gradually dying out.

youth who at twenty-four married a girl who was still a virgin was the laughing stock of the village over his freely related trepidation which revealed the fact that at twenty-four, although he had had many love affairs, he had never before won the favours of a virgin.

The bridegroom, his relatives and the bride and her relatives all receive prestige if she proves to be a virgin, so that the girl of rank who might wish to forestall this painful public ceremony is thwarted not only by the anxious chaperonage of her relatives but by the boy's eagerness for prestige. One young Lothario eloped to his father's house with a girl of a high rank from another village and refused to live with her because, said he, "I thought maybe I would marry that girl and there would be a big *malaga* and a big ceremony and I would wait and get credit for marrying a virgin. But the next day her father came and said that she could not marry me, and she cried very much. So I said to her, 'Well, there is no use now to wait any longer. Now we will run away into the bush.'" It is conceivable that the girl would often trade the temporary prestige for an escape from the public ordeal, but in proportion as his ambitions were honourable, the boy would frustrate her efforts.

Just as the clandestine and casual "love under the palm trees" is the pattern irregularity for those of humble birth, so the elopement has its archetype in the love affairs of the *taupo,* and the other chiefs' daughters. These girls of noble birth are carefully guarded; not for them are secret trysts at night or stolen meetings in the day time. Where parents of lower rank complacently ignore their daughters' experiments, the high chief guards his daughter's virginity as he guards the honour of his name, his precedence in the kava ceremony or any other prerogative of his high degree. Some old woman of the household is told off to be the girl's constant companion and duenna. The *taupo* may not visit in other houses in the village or leave the house alone at night. When she sleeps, an older woman sleeps by her side. Never may she go to another village unchaperoned. In her own village she goes soberly about her tasks, bathing in the sea, working in the plantation, safe under the jealous guardianship of the women of her own village. She runs little risk from the *moetotolo,* for one who outraged the *taupo* of his village would formerly have been beaten to death, and now would have to flee from the village. The prestige of the village is inextricably bound up with the high repute of the *taupo* and few young men in the village would dare to be her lovers. Marriage to them is out of the question, and their companions would revile them as traitors rather than envy them such doubtful distinction. Occasionally a youth of very high rank in the same village will risk an elopement, but even this is a rare occurrence. For tradition says that the *taupo* must marry outside her village, marry a high chief or a *manaia* of another village. Such a marriage is an occasion for great festivities and solemn ceremony. The chief and all of his talking chiefs must come to propose for her hand, come in person bringing gifts for her talking chiefs. If the talking chiefs of the girl are satisfied that this is a lucrative and desirable match, and the family are satisfied with the rank and appearance of the suitor, the marriage is agreed upon. Little attention is paid to the opinion of the girl. So fixed is the idea that the marriage of the *taupo* is the affair of the talking chiefs that Europeanised natives on the main island refuse to make their daughters *taupos* because the missionaries say a girl should make her own choice, and once she is a *taupo,* they regard the matter as inevitably taken out of their hands. After the betrothal is agreed upon the bridegroom returns to his village to collect food and property for the wedding. His village sets aside a piece of land which is called the "Place of the Lady" and is her property and the property of her children forever, and on this land they build a house for the bride. Meanwhile, the bridegroom has left behind him in the house of the bride a talking chief, the counterpart of the humbler *soa*. This is one of the talking chief's best opportunities to acquire wealth. He stays as the emissary of his chief, to watch over his future bride. He works for the bride's family and each week the *matai* of the bride must reward him with a handsome present. As an affianced wife of a chief, more and more circumspect conduct is enjoined upon the girl. Did she formerly joke with the boys of the village, she must joke no longer, or the talking chief, on the watch for any lapse from high decorum, will go home to his chief and report that his bride is unworthy of such honour. This custom is particularly susceptible to second thought on the part of either side. Does the bridegroom repent of the bargain, he bribes his talking chief (who is usually a young man, not one of the important talking chiefs who will benefit greatly by the marriage itself) to be oversensitive to the behaviour of the bride or the treatment he receives in the bride's family. And this is the time in which the bride will elope, if her affianced husband is too unacceptable. For while no boy of her own village will risk her dangerous favours, a boy from another village will enormously enhance his prestige if he elopes with the *taupo* of a rival community. Once she has eloped, the projected alliance is of course broken off, although her angry parents may refuse to sanction her marriage with her lover and marry her for punishment to some old man.

So great is the prestige won by the village, one of whose young men succeeds in eloping with a *taupo,* that often the whole effort of a *malaga* is concentrated upon abducting the *taupo,* whose virginity will be respected in direct ratio to the chances of her family and village consenting to ratify the marriage. As the abductor is often of high rank, the village often ruefully accepts the compromise.

This elopement pattern, given meaning by the restrictions under which the *taupo* lives and this inter-village rivalry, is carried down to the lower ranks where indeed it is practically meaningless. Seldom is the chaperonage exercised over the girl of average family severe enough to make elopement the only way of consummating a love affair. But the elopement is spectacular; the boy wishes to increase his reputation as a successful Don Juan, and the girl wishes to proclaim her conquest and also often hopes that the elopement will end in marriage. The eloping pair run away to the parents of the boy or to some of his relatives and wait for the girl's relatives to pursue her. As one boy related the tale of such an adventure: "We ran away in the rain, nine miles to Leone, in the pouring rain, to my father's house. The next day her family came to get her, and my father said to me, 'How is it, do you wish to marry this girl, shall I ask her father to leave her here?' And I said, 'Oh, no. I just eloped with her for public information.' " Elopements are much less frequent than the clandestine love affairs because the girl takes far more risk. She publicly renounces her often nominal claims to virginity; she embroils herself with her family, who in former times, and occasionally even to-day, would beat her soundly and shave off her hair. Nine times out of ten, her lover's only motive is vanity and display, for the boys say, "The girls hate a *moetotolo,* but they love an *avaga* (eloping) man."

The elopement also occurs as a practical measure when one family is opposed to a marriage upon which a pair of young people have determined. The young people take refuge with the friendly side of the family. But unless the recalcitrant family softens and consents to legalise the marriage by a formal exchange of property, the principals can do nothing to establish their status. A young couple may have had several children and still be classed as "elopers," and if the marriage is finally legalised after long delay, this stigma will always cling to them. It is far more serious a one than a mere accusation of sexual irregularity, for there is a definite feeling that the whole community procedure has been outraged by a pair of young upstarts.

Reciprocal gift-giving relations are maintained between the two families as long as the marriage lasts, and even afterwards if there are children. The birth of each child, the death of a member of either household, a visit of the wife to her family, or if he lives with her people, of the husband to his, is marked by the presentation of gifts.

In premarital relationships, a convention of love making is strictly adhered to. True, this is a convention of speech, rather than of action.

A boy declares that he will die if a girl refuses him her favours, but the Samoans laugh at stories of romantic love, scoff at fidelity to a long absent wife or mistress, believe explicitly that one love will quickly cure another. The fidelity which is followed by pregnancy is taken as proof positive of a real attachment, although having many mistresses is never out of harmony with a declaration of affection for each. The composition of ardent love songs, the fashioning of long and flowery love letters, the invocation of the moon, the stars and the sea in verbal courtship, all serve to give Samoan love-making a close superficial resemblance to our own, yet the attitude is far closer to that of Schnitzler's hero in *The Affairs of Anatol*. Romantic love as it occurs in our civilisation, inextricably bound up with ideas of monogamy, exclusiveness, jealousy and undeviating fidelity does not occur in Samoa. Our attitude is a compound, the final result of many converging lines of development in Western civilisation, of the institution of monogamy, of the ideas of the age of chivalry, of the ethics of Christianity. Even a passionate attachment to one person which lasts for a long period and persists in the face of discouragement but does not bar out other relationships, is rare among the Samoans. Marriage, on the other hand, is regarded as a social and economic arrangement, in which relative wealth, rank, and skill of husband and wife, all must be taken into consideration. There are many marriages in which both individuals, especially if they are over thirty, are completely faithful. But this must be attributed to the ease of sexual adjustment on the one hand, and to the ascendency of other interests, social organisation for the men, children for the women, over sex interests, rather than to a passionate fixation upon the partner in the marriage. As the Samoans lack the inhibitions and the intricate specialisation of sex feeling which make marriages of convenience unsatisfactory, it is possible to bulwark marital happiness with other props than temporary passionate devotion. Suitability and expediency become the deciding factors.

Adultery does not necessarily mean a broken marriage. A chief's wife who commits adultery is deemed to have dishonoured her high position, and is usually discarded, although the chief will openly resent her remarriage to any one of lower rank. If the lover is considered the more culpable, the village will take public vengeance upon him. In less conspicuous cases the amount of fuss which is made over adultery is dependent upon the relative rank of the offender and offended, or the personal jealousy which is only occasionally aroused. If either the injured husband or the injured wife is sufficiently incensed to threaten physical violence, the trespasser may have to resort to a public *ifoga*, the ceremonial humiliation before some one whose pardon is asked. He goes to the house of the man he has injured, accompanied by all the men of his household, each one wrapped in a fine mat, the currency of the country; the suppliants seat themselves outside the house, fine mats spread over their heads, hands folded on their breasts, heads bent in attitudes of the deepest dejection and humiliation. "And if the man is very angry he will say no word. All day he will go about his business; he will braid cinet with a quick hand, he will talk loudly to his wife, and call out greetings to those who pass in the roadway, but will take no notice of those who sit on his own terrace, who dare not raise their eyes or make any movement to go away. In olden days, if his heart was not softened, he might take a club and together with his relatives go out and kill those who sit without. But now he only keeps them waiting, waiting all day long. The sun will beat down upon them; the rain will come and beat on their heads and still he will say no word. Then towards evening he will say at last: 'Come, it is enough. Enter the house and drink the kava. Eat the food which I will set before you and we will cast our trouble into the sea.' " Then the fine mats are accepted as payment for the injury, the *ifoga* becomes a matter of village history and old gossips will say, "Oh, yes, Lua! no, she's not Iona's child. Her father is that chief over in the next village. He *ifod* to Iona before she was born." If the offender is of much lower rank than the injured husband, his chief, or his father (if he is only a young boy) will have to humiliate himself in his place. Where the offender is a woman, she and her female relatives will make similar amends. But they will run far greater danger of being roundly beaten and berated; the peaceful teachings of Christianity— perhaps because they were directed against actual killing, rather than the slightly less fatal encounters of women—have made far less change in the belligerent activities of the women than in those of the men.

If, on the other hand, a wife really tires of her husband, or a husband of his wife, divorce is a simple and informal matter, the nonresident simply going home to his or her family, and the relationship is said to have "passed away." It is a very brittle monogamy, often trespassed and more often broken entirely. But many adulteries occur— between a young marriage-shy bachelor and a married woman, or a temporary widower and some young girl—which hardly threaten the continuity of established relationships. The claim that a woman has on her family's land renders her as independent as her husband, and so there are no marriages of any duration in which either person is actively unhappy. A tiny flare-up and a woman goes home to her own people; if her husband does not care to conciliate her, each seeks another mate.

Within the family, the wife obeys and serves her husband, in theory, though, of course, the hen-pecked husband is a frequent phenomenon. In families of high rank, her personal service to her husband is taken over by the *taupo* and the talking chief but the wife always retains the right to render a high chief sacred personal services, such as cutting his hair. A wife's rank can never exceed her husband's because it is always directly dependent upon it. Her family may be richer and more illustrious than his, and she may actually exercise more influence over the village affairs through her blood relatives than he, but within the life of the household and the village, she is a *tausi*, wife of talking chief, or a *faletua*, wife of a chief. This sometimes results in conflict, as in the case of Pusa who was the sister of the last holder of the highest title on the island. This title was temporarily extinct. She was also the wife of the highest chief in the village. Should her brother, the heir, resume the higher title, her husband's rank and her rank as his wife would suffer. Helping her brother meant lowering the prestige of her husband. As she was the type of woman who cared a great deal more for wire pulling than for public recognition, she threw her influence in for her brother. Such conflicts are not uncommon, but they present a clear-cut choice, usually reinforced by considerations of residence. If a woman lives in her husband's household, and if, furthermore, that household is in another village, her interest is mainly enlisted in her husband's cause; but if she lives with her own family, in her own village, her allegiance is likely to cling to blood relatives from whom she receives reflected glory and informal privilege, although no status.

3

Living Within Society

In this section we examine major sociological orientations to understanding human behavior, especially that of symbolic interaction. Basic to this perspective is the idea that people live in a world of symbols. These symbols are not forced on people from without, that is, from objective reality, but are human creations. Human beings fill the objects and events in their lives with meaning. This meaning is arbitrary, that is, the meaning any particular symbol has is something which has been arbitrarily agreed upon by people. Once symbols are developed, they are routinely used by people as part of their everyday lives. No interaction of people can be adequately understood without understanding its symbolic aspects, that is, without understanding how the people involved view the situation. The meaning the situation has for them largely determines what they will and will not do. Consequently, much of the sociological task is aimed at analyzing the symbolic nature of human life.

In the first selection, Meltzer summarizes major aspects of the theory of George Herbert Mead. He analyzes the role of symbols in interaction, especially focusing on how perceived intentions underlie the ways people react to one another. He also details the significance of role-playing, gestures, and meaning, as well as the social origins of the self.

In the second selection, we move to a specific case or a particular application of symbolic interaction. This perspective is called dramaturgy because it is modelled after the theater. The basic assumption in this perspective is that in their everyday lives people manipulate symbols in order to lead others to certain definitions. They especially want others to hold certain opinions about themselves, and to this end they employ symbols designed to bring about desired impressions. In this selection, Goffman presents some of the major ideas underlying dramaturgical analysis.

In the next two selections we turn to games analysis. Games analysis is also primarily a specific application of symbolic interaction. In games analysis people are viewed as rational beings who are working towards goals. As they pursue their goals, they operate within a framework of rules and boundaries, strategies and tactics. They make moves as their own responses to the moves of others, always in pursuit of whatever goals they are seeking. As they make their moves and pursue their goals, others are doing the same. In order to succeed in the game of interaction, it is essential that one be able to take the role of the other, that is, one must be able to symbolically place oneself in the shoes of someone else. This is essential because one must be able to anticipate the other's responses in order to develop one's own strategies and tactics.

In the third selection, McCall and Simmons analyze the defensive strategies individuals use when things fail to go properly in their self-presentations. Through various devices people attempt to repair scenes, to extricate the self, to disclaim involvement or intent, and so on, thereby allowing them to continue interaction under conditions more in line with their own expectations. In the fourth selection, Leggett and Cervinka analyze a game played between social groups. In this particular game, the resources are stacked on one side. One group has almost sole access to significant information, and it is they who call the shots. In this case it is the powerful who are following a strategy of manipulating symbols in order to bring about a definition of reality which will further their position of power in the status quo.

In the following three selections we turn to three substantive areas of sociological research, those of homosexuality, mental illness, and juvenile delinquency. In each case sociological theory is applied to the particular behavior. These three areas of behavior, which appear so disparate, all represent learned behavior. They are all social roles. According to sociological theory, there is nothing pathological within an individual which makes him homosexual, mentally ill, or delinquent. Rather, one *learns* to prefer members of one's own sex, one *learns* to violate the assumptions that others take for granted, and one *learns* to engage in lawbreaking activities. Few people any longer think that some people are born lawbreakers. But belief in inherent deviance still persists when it comes to mental illness and homosexuality. The tendency is to look inside the person for causation, to find something pathological within the individual to account for his behavior. The sociological approach stands in marked contrast to this view. The sociologist examines the social milieu to determine what factors are involved in the social learning process. The sociologist analyzes the social situation in which the individual finds himself to see how these external factors operate on the personal level.

In this part's final article we turn to a contrasting perspective on human behavior, that of social exchange theory. The view of human nature basic to social exchange theory corresponds to that of games analysis and dramaturgy: People are assumed to be rational beings who carefully evaluate potential and actual courses of action in order to maximize their pay-offs. They choose those with the greatest pay-offs and reject those with the lesser. As with the other perspectives in this section, to understand any particular choice a person makes one must attain the definition of the situation held by the individual. One must understand how people view reality in order to understand their behavior.

6

Bernard N. Meltzer

The Social Origins of the Self

A symbol is any object, event, relationship, situation, or any other thing to which people attach meaning and by which they communicate meaning to one another. Symbols always represent something beyond the immediate situation. Symbols do not automatically convey meaning, nor is there anything "natural" about them. Rather, a symbol is an arbitrary way of representing agreed-upon meaning.

In this symbolic world in which we live, people symbolically separate themselves from others. By means of symbols we claim a unique identity in this life. We wear clothing and otherwise surround ourselves with various accoutrements which give cues to others regarding such statuses as our sex, age, marriageability, occupation, relative wealth, and class position. We involve ourselves in ritual activities which carry meaning. ("They went to Lauderdale over spring break," or "She took her first communion on Palm Sunday.") We speak in a particular way, use certain gestures, exhibit mannerisms, and by various other aspects of our behavior symbolize our claimed identity to others.

Some symbols that we utilize have been a part of us for so long that they become sort of "second nature." We often think of them as naturally belonging to us, not as learned ways of communicating meaning to others. Our way of walking is one such routine symbol of which we are seldom conscious. We learned to walk in a particular way at such an early age and our walk has been so consistently reinforced that we do not ordinarily think of it as a symbol. Yet

From Bernard N. Meltzer, "Mead's Social Psychology," in Jerome G. Manis and Bernard N. Meltzer, *Symbolic Interaction* (Boston: Allyn and Bacon, Inc.), pp. 5–10, 11, 17–18. Copyright © 1972 by Bernard N. Meltzer. Reprinted by permission.

people certainly take our way of walking as representing something about who we are, about our claimed identity in life. We certainly do not want others to *misinterpret* our walk, and we will, if pressed, take pains to make certain there is no mistake about the identity our walk symbolizes.

In earlier selections we saw the importance of symbols for social life: rulers symbolically separating themselves from the ruled, the "cool" from the "non-cool," linguistic symbols used to develop and maintain relationships with others, and the meanings that different sexual patternings have for people. Sociologists who focus on the symbolic nature of human life also emphasize the role of symbols in the development of the self. It is these *social* origins of the self to which we turn in the following selection.

Society

According to [George Herbert] Mead, all group life is essentially a matter of cooperative behavior. Mead makes a distinction, however, between infrahuman society and human society. Insects—whose society most closely approximates the complexity of human social life—act together in certain ways because of their biological make-up. Thus, their cooperative behavior is physiologically determined. This is shown by many facts, among which is the fact of the fixity, the stability, of the relationships of insect-society members to one another. Insects, according to the evidence, go on for countless generations without any difference in their patterns of association. This picture of infrahuman society remains essentially valid as one ascends the scale of animal life, until we arrive at the human level.

In the case of human association, the situation is fundamentally different. Human cooperation is not brought about by mere physiological factors. The very diversity of the patterns of human group life makes it quite clear that human cooperative life cannot be explained in the same terms as the cooperative life of insects and the lower animals. The fact that human patterns are not stabilized and cannot be explained in biological terms led Mead to seek another basis of explanation of human association. Such cooperation can only be brought about by some process wherein: (a) each acting individual ascertains the *intention* of the acts of others, and then (b) makes his own response on the basis of that intention. What this means is that, in order for human beings to cooperate, there must be present some sort of mechanism whereby each acting individual: (a) can come to understand the lines of action of others, and (b) can guide his own behavior to fit in with those lines of action. Human behavior is not a matter of responding directly to the activities of others. Rather, it involves responding to the *intentions* of others, *i.e.,* to the future, intended behavior of others—not merely to their present actions.

We can better understand the character of this distinctively human mode of interaction between individuals by contrasting it with the infrahuman "conversation of gestures." For example when a mother hen clucks, her chicks will respond by running to her. This does not imply however, that the hen clucks *in order* to guide the chicks, *i.e.*, with the *intention* of guiding them. Clucking is a natural sign or signal—rather than a significant (meaningful) symbol—as it is not meaningful to the hen. That is, the hen (according to Mead) does not take the role, or viewpoint, of the chicks toward its own gesture and respond to it, in imagination, as they do. The hen does not envision the response of the chicks to her clucking. Thus, hens and chicks do not share the same experience.

Let us take another illustration by Mead: Two hostile dogs, in the prefight stage, may go through an elaborate conversation of gestures (snarling, growling, baring fangs, walking stiff-leggedly around one another, etc.). The dogs are adjusting themselves to one another by responding to one another's gestures. (A gesture is that portion of an act which represents the entire act; it is the initial, overt phase of the act, which epitomizes it, *e.g.*, shaking one's fist at someone.) Now, in the case of the dogs the response to a gesture is dictated by pre-established tendencies to respond in certain ways. Each gesture leads to a direct, immediate, automatic, and unreflecting response by the recipient of the gesture (the other dog). Neither dog responds to the *intention* of the gestures. Further, each dog does not make his gestures with the intent of eliciting certain responses in the other dog. Thus, animal interaction is devoid of conscious, deliberate meaning.

To summarize: Gestures, at the non-human or non-linguistic level, do not carry the connotation of conscious meaning or intent, but serve merely as cues for the appropriate responses of others. Gestural communication takes place immediately, without any interruption of the act, without the mediation of a definition or meaning. Each organism adjusts "instinctively" to the other; it does not stop and figure out which response it will give. Its behavior is, largely, a series of direct automatic responses to stimuli.

Human beings, on the other hand, respond to one another on the basis of the intentions or meanings of gestures. This renders the gesture *symbolic, i.e.,* the gesture becomes a symbol to be interpreted; it becomes something which, in the imaginations of the participants, stands for the entire act.

Thus, individual A begins to act, *i.e.*, makes a gesture: for example, he draws back an arm. Individual B (who perceives the gesture) completes, or fills in, the act in his imagination; *i.e.*, B imaginatively projects the gesture into the future: "He will strike me." In other words, B perceives what the gesture stands for, thus getting its meaning. In contrast to the direct responses of the chicks and the dogs, the human being inserts an interpretation between the gesture of another and his response to it. Human behavior involves responses to *interpreted* stimuli.[1]

We see, then, that people respond to one another on the basis of imaginative activity. In order to engage in concerted behavior, however, each participating individual must be able to attach the same meaning to the same gesture. Unless interacting individuals interpret gestures similarly, unless they fill out the imagined portion in the same way, there can be no cooperative action. This is another way of saying what has by now become a truism in sociology and social psychology: Human society rests upon a basis of *consensus*, *i.e.*, the sharing of meanings in the form of common understandings and expectations.

In the case of the human being, each person has the ability to respond to his own gestures; and thus, it is possible to have the same meaning for the gestures as other persons. (For example: As I say "chair," I present to myself the same image as to my hearer; moreover, the same image as when someone else says "chair.") This ability to stimulate oneself as one stimulates another, and to respond to oneself as another does, Mead ascribes largely to man's vocal-auditory mechanism. (The ability to hear oneself implies at least the potentiality for responding to oneself.) When a gesture has a shared, common meaning, when it is—in other words—a *linguistic* element, we can designate it as a "significant symbol." (Take the words, "Open the window": the pattern of action symbolized by these words must be in the mind of the speaker as well as the listener. Each must respond, in imagination, to the words in the same way. The speaker must have an image of the listener responding to his words by opening the window, and the listener must have an image of his opening the window.)

The imaginative completion of an act—which Mead calls "meaning" and which represents mental activity—necessarily takes place through *role-taking*. To complete imaginatively the total act which a gesture stands for, the individual must put himself in the position of the other person, must identify with him. The earliest beginnings of role-taking occur when an already established act of another individual is stopped short of completion, thereby requiring the observing individual to fill in, or complete, the activity imaginatively. (For example, a crying infant may have an image of its mother coming to stop its crying.)

As Mead points out, then, the relation of human beings to one another arises from the developed ability of the human being to respond to his own gestures. This ability enables different human beings to respond in the same way to the same gesture, thereby sharing one another's experience.

This latter point is of great importance. Behavior is viewed as "social" not simply when it is a response to others, but rather when it has incorporated in it the behavior of others. The human being responds to himself as other persons respond to him, and in so doing he imaginatively shares the conduct of others. That is, in imagining their response he shares that response.[2]

Self

To state that the human being can respond to his own gestures necessarily implies that he possesses a *self*. In referring to the human being as having a self, Mead simply means that such an individual may act socially toward himself, just as toward others. He may praise, blame, or encourage himself; he may become disgusted with himself, may seek to punish himself, and so forth. Thus, the human being may become the object of his own actions. The self is formed in the same way as other objects—through the "definitions" made by others.

The mechanism whereby the individual becomes able to view himself as an object is that of role-taking, involving the process of communication, especially by vocal gestures or speech. (Such communication necessarily involves role-taking.) It is only by taking the role of others that the individual can come to see himself as an object. The standpoint of others provides a platform for getting outside oneself and thus viewing oneself. The development of the self is concurrent with the development of the ability to take roles.

The crucial importance of language in this process must be underscored. It is through language (significant symbols) that the child acquires the meanings and definitions of those around him. By learning the symbols of his groups, he comes to internalize their definitions of events or things, including their definitions of his own conduct.

It is quite evident that, rather than assuming the existence of selves and explaining society thereby, Mead starts out from the prior existence of society as the context within which selves arise. This view contrasts with the nominalistic position of the Social Contract theorists and of various individualistic psychologies.

Genesis of the Self

The relationship between role-playing and various stages in the development of the self is described below:

1. *Preparatory Stage* (not explicitly named by Mead, but inferable from various fragmentary essays). This stage is one of meaningless imitation by the infant (for example, "reading" the newspaper). The child does certain things that others near it do without any understanding of what he is doing. Such imitation, however, implies that the child is incipiently taking the roles of those around it, *i.e.,* is on the verge of putting itself in the position of others and acting like them.

2. *Play Stage.* In this stage the actual playing of roles occurs. The child plays mother, teacher, storekeeper, postman, streetcar conductor, Mr. Jones, etc. What is of central importance in such play-acting is that it places the child in the position where it is able to act back toward itself in such roles as "mother" or "teacher." In this stage, then, the child first begins to form a self, that is, to direct activity toward itself—and it does so by taking the roles of others. This is clearly indicated by use of the third person in referring to oneself instead of the first person: "John wants . . . ," "John is a bad boy."

   However, in this stage the young child's configuration of roles is unstable; the child passes from one role to another in unorganized, inconsistent fashion. He has, as yet, no unitary standpoint from which to view himself, and hence, he has no unified conception of himself. In other words, the child forms a number of separate and discrete objects of itself, depending on the roles in which it acts toward itself.

3. *Game Stage.* This is the "completing" stage of the self. In time, the child finds himself in situations wherein he must take a number of roles simultaneously. That is, he must respond to the expectations of several people at the same time. This sort of situation is exemplified by the game of baseball—to use Mead's own illustration. Each player must visualize the intentions and expectations of several other players. In such situations the child must take the roles of groups of individuals as over against particular roles. The child becomes enabled to do this by abstracting a "composite" role out of the concrete roles of particular persons. In the course of his association with others, then, he builds up a *generalized other,* a generalized role or standpoint from which he views himself and his behavior. This generalized other represents, then, the set of standpoints which are common to the group.

   Having achieved this generalized standpoint, the individual can conduct himself in an organized, consistent manner. He can view himself from a consistent standpoint. This means, then, that the individual can transcend the local and present expectations and definitions with which he comes in contact. An illustration of this point would be the Englishman who "dresses for dinner" in the wilds of Africa. Thus, through having a generalized other, the individual becomes emancipated from the pressures of the peculiarities of the immediate situation. He can act with a certain amount of consistency in a variety of situations because he acts in accordance with a generalized set of expectations and definitions that he has internalized. . . .

Implications of Selfhood

Some of the major implications of selfhood in human behavior are as follows:

1. The possession of a self makes of the individual a society in miniature. That is, he may engage in interaction with himself just as two or more different individuals might. In the course of this interaction, he can come to view himself in a new way, thereby bringing about changes in himself.
2. The ability to act toward oneself makes possible an inner experience which need not reach overt expression. That is, the individual, by virtue of having a self, is thereby endowed with the possibility of having a mental life: He can make indications to himself—which constitutes *mind*.
3. The individual with a self is thereby enabled to direct and control his behavior. Instead of being subject to all impulses and stimuli directly playing upon him, the individual can check, guide, and organize his behavior. He is, then, *not* a mere passive agent.

All three of these implications of selfhood may be summarized by the statement that the self and the mind (mental activity) are twin emergents in the social process.

Summary

. . . The human individual is born into a society characterized by *symbolic interaction*. The use of *significant symbols* by those around him enables him to pass from the conversation of gestures—which involves direct, unmeaningful response to the overt acts of others—to the occasional *taking of the roles* of others. This role-taking enables him to share the perspectives of others. Concurrent with role-taking, the *self* develops, *i.e.*, the capacity to act toward oneself. Action toward oneself comes to take the form of viewing oneself from the standpoint, or perspective, of the *generalized other* (the composite representative of others, of society, within the individual), which implies defining one's behavior in terms of the expectations of others. In the process of such viewing of oneself, the individual must carry on symbolic interaction with himself, involving an internal conversation between his impulsive aspect (the "I") and the incorporated perspectives of others (the "Me"). The *mind*, or mental activity, is present in behavior whenever such symbolic interaction goes on—whether the individual is merely "thinking" (in the everyday sense of the word) or is also interacting with another individual. (In both cases the individual must indicate things to himself.) Mental activity necessarily involves *meanings*, which usually attach to, and define, *objects*. The meaning of an object or event is simply an image of the pattern of action which defines the object or event. That is, the completion in one's imagination of an act, or the mental picture of the actions and experiences symbolized by an object, defines the act or the object. In the unit of study that Mead calls "the *act*," all of the foregoing processes are usually entailed. The concluding point to be made in this summary is the same as the point with which I began: Mead's concepts intertwine and mutually imply one another. To drive home this important point, I must emphasize that human society (characterized by symbolic interaction) both precedes the rise of individual selves and minds, and is maintained by the rise of individual selves and minds. This means, then, that symbolic interaction is both the medium for the development of human beings and the process by which human beings associate as human beings. . . .

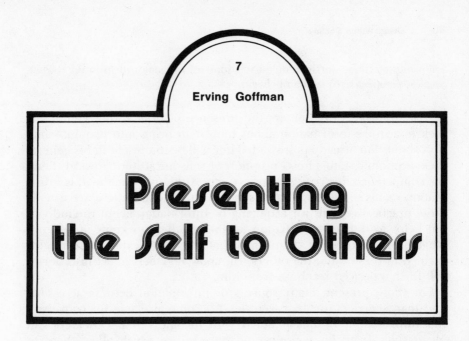

7

Erving Goffman

Presenting the Self to Others

The self originates in interaction with others. Not only is the self socially bestowed, however, but it is also socially maintained. That is, just as the self depends on interaction for its origin, so it depends on interaction for its continuity. By their reactions to us, others either validate or refuse to validate the claims we make for ourselves.

As we interact with others, we attempt to control the information others receive of us. We try to manage the impressions we give others by exerting control over the *settings* in which we interact, that is, by decorating our homes in particular styles or being seen in certain places and not others; by carefully designing our *appearance,* that is, by wearing certain clothing and surrounding ourselves with other objects which we think reflect favorably on ourselves; and by exhibiting a certain *manner,* that is, by acting toward others in ways we feel will develop the impressions or images we desire others to have of us.

This dramaturgical perspective on human behavior, based on an extended analogy of the theater, sensitizes us to view the social world as consisting of actors and audiences, plays and scenes, parts and performers, costuming and make-up, directors and stars, stagehands and understudies, and presentations of roles and deliveries of lines on various stages. The dramaturgical approach to understanding human behavior is solidly rooted in the symbolic interaction discussed in the preceding selection. Its basic idea is that in all situations in life people use symbols to communicate to others ideas about themselves. In the

following selection, Goffman delineates some of the major ideas in the dramaturgical perspective of human behavior.

□ When an individual enters the presence of others, they commonly
seek to acquire information about him or to bring into play information about him already possessed. They will be interested in his general
socio-economic status, his conception of self, his attitude toward them,
his competence, his trustworthiness, etc. Although some of this information seems to be sought almost as an end in itself, there are usually
quite practical reasons for acquiring it. Information about the individual helps to define the situation, enabling others to know in advance
what he will expect of them and what they may expect of him. Informed in these ways, the others will know how best to act in order to
call forth a desired response from him.

For those present, many sources of information become accessible
and many carriers (or "sign-vehicles") become available for conveying
this information. If unacquainted with the individual, observers can
glean clues from his conduct and appearance which allow them to
apply their previous experience with individuals roughly similar to the
one before them or, more important, to apply untested stereotypes to
him. They can also assume from past experience that only individuals
of a particular kind are likely to be found in a given social setting. They
can rely on what the individual says about himself or on documentary
evidence he provides as to who and what he is. If they know, or know
of, the individual by virtue of experience prior to the interaction, they
can rely on assumptions as to the persistence and generality of psychological traits as a means of predicting his present and future behavior.

However, during the period in which the individual is in the immediate presence of the others, few events may occur which directly provide
the others with the conclusive information they will need if they are to
direct wisely their own activity. Many crucial facts lie beyond the time
and place of interaction or lie concealed within it. For example, the
"true" or "real" attitudes, beliefs, and emotions of the individual can be
ascertained only indirectly, through his avowals or through what appears to be involuntary expressive behavior. Similarly, if the individual
offers the others a product or service, they will often find that during
the interaction there will be no time and place immediately available
for eating the pudding that the proof can be found in. They will be
forced to accept some events as conventional or natural signs of something not directly available to the senses. In Ichheiser's terms,[1] the individual will have to act so that he intentionally or unintentionally *expresses* himself, and the others will in turn have to be *impressed* in some
way by him.

The expressiveness of the individual (and therefore his capacity to give impressions) appears to involve two radically different kinds of sign activity: the expression that he *gives,* and the expression that he *gives off.* The first involves verbal symbols or their substitutes which he uses admittedly and solely to convey the information that he and the others are known to attach to these symbols. This is communication in the traditional and narrow sense. The second involves a wide range of action that others can treat as symptomatic of the actor, the expectation being that the action was performed for reasons other than the information conveyed in this way. As we shall have to see, this distinction has an only initial validity. The individual does of course intentionally convey misinformation by means of both of these types of communication, the first involving deceit, the second feigning.

Taking communication in both its narrow and broad sense, one finds that when the individual is in the immediate presence of others, his activity will have a promissory character. The others are likely to find that they must accept the individual on faith, offering him a just return while he is present before them in exchange for something whose true value will not be established until after he has left their presence. (Of course, the others also live by inference in their dealings with the physical world, but it is only in the world of social interaction that the objects about which they make inferences will purposely facilitate and hinder this inferential process.) The security that they justifiably feel in making inferences about the individual will vary, of course, depending on such factors as the amount of information they already possess about him, but no amount of such past evidence can entirely obviate the necessity of acting on the basis of inferences. As William I. Thomas suggested:

> It is also highly important for us to realize that we do not as a matter of fact lead our lives, make our decisions, and reach our goals in everyday life either statistically or scientifically. We live by inference. I am, let us say, your guest. You do not know, you cannot determine scientifically, that I will not steal your money or your spoons. But inferentially I will not, and inferentially you have me as a guest.[2]

Let us now turn from the others to the point of view of the individual who presents himself before them. He may wish them to think highly of him, or to think that he thinks highly of them, or to perceive how in fact he feels toward them, or to obtain no clear-cut impression; he may wish to ensure sufficient harmony so that the interaction can be sustained, or to defraud, get rid of, confuse, mislead, antagonize, or insult them. Regardless of the particular objective which the individual has in mind and of his motive for having this objective, it will be in his interests to control the conduct of the others, especially their responsive treatment of him.[3] This control is achieved largely by influencing the definition of the situation which the others come to formulate, and he can influence this definition by expressing himself in such a way as to give them the kind of impression that will lead them to act voluntarily in accordance with his own plan. Thus, when an individual appears in the presence of others, there will usually be some reason for him to mobilize his activity so that it will convey an impression to others which it is in his interests to convey. Since a girl's dormitory mates will glean evidence of her popularity from the calls she receives on the phone, we can suspect that some girls will arrange for calls to be made, and Willard Waller's finding can be anticipated:

> It has been reported by many observers that a girl who is called to the telephone in the dormitories will often allow herself to be called several times, in order to give all the other girls ample opportunity to hear her paged.[4]

Of the two kinds of communication—expressions given and expressions given off—this report will be primarily concerned with the latter, with the more theatrical and contextual kind, the non-verbal, presumably unintentional kind, whether this communication be purposely engineered or not. As an example of what we must try to examine, I would like to cite at length a novelistic incident in which Preedy, a vacationing Englishman, makes his first appearance on the beach of his summer hotel in Spain:

> But in any case he took care to avoid catching anyone's eye. First of all, he had to make it clear to those potential companions of his holiday that they were of no concern to him whatsoever. He stared through them, round them, over them—eyes lost in space. The beach might have been empty. If by chance a ball was thrown his way, he looked surprised; then let a smile of amusement lighten his face (Kindly Preedy), looked round dazed to see that there *were* people on the beach, tossed it back with a smile to himself and not a smile *at* the people, and then resumed carelessly his nonchalant survey of space.
>
> But it was time to institute a little parade, the parade of the Ideal Preedy. By devious handlings he gave any who wanted to look a chance to see the title of his book—a Spanish translation of Homer, classic thus, but not daring, cosmopolitan too—and then gathered together his beachwrap and bag into a neat sand-resistant pile (Methodical and Sensible Preedy), rose slowly to stretch at ease his huge frame (Big-Cat Preedy), and tossed aside his sandals (Carefree Preedy, after all).

The marriage of Preedy and the sea! There were alternative rituals. The first involved the stroll that turns into a run and a dive
straight into the water, thereafter smoothing into a strong splashless
crawl towards the horizon. But of course not really to the horizon.
Quite suddenly he would turn on to his back and thrash great white
splashes with his legs, somehow thus showing that he could have
swum further had he wanted to, and then would stand up a quarter
out of water for all to see who it was.

The alternative course was simpler, it avoided the cold-water shock
and it avoided the risk of appearing too high-spirited. The point was
to appear to be so used to the sea, the Mediterranean, and this particular beach, that one might as well be in the sea as out of it. It involved a slow stroll down and into the edge of the water—not even
noticing his toes were wet, land and water all the same to *him!*—with
his eyes up at the sky gravely surveying portents, invisible to others,
of the weather (Local Fisherman Preedy).[5]

The novelist means us to see that Preedy is improperly concerned with
the extensive impressions he feels his sheer bodily action is giving off to
those around him. We can malign Preedy further by assuming that he
has acted merely in order to give a particular impression, that this is a
false impression, and that the others present receive either no impression at all, or, worse still, the impression that Preedy is affectedly trying
to cause them to receive this particular impression. But the important
point for us here is that the kind of impression Preedy thinks he is
making is in fact the kind of impression that others correctly and incorrectly glean from someone in their midst.

I have said that when an individual appears before others his actions
will influence the definition of the situation which they come to have.
Sometimes the individual will act in a thoroughly calculating manner,
expressing himself in a given way solely in order to give the kind of impression to others that is likely to evoke from them a specific response
he is concerned to obtain. Sometimes the individual will be calculating
in his activity but be relatively unaware that this is the case. Sometimes
he will intentionally and consciously express himself in a particular
way, but chiefly because the tradition of his group or social status
require this kind of expression and not because of any particular response (other than vague acceptance or approval) that is likely to be
evoked from those impressed by the expression. Sometimes the traditions of an individual's role will lead him to give a well-designed impression of a particular kind and yet he may be neither consciously nor
unconsciously disposed to create such an impression. The others, in
their turn, may be suitably impressed by the individual's efforts to convey something, or may misunderstand the situation and come to con-

clusions that are warranted neither by the individual's intent nor by the facts. In any case, in so far as the others act *as if* the individual had conveyed a particular impression, we may take a functional or pragmatic view and say that the individual has "effectively" projected a given definition of the situation and "effectively" fostered the understanding that a given state of affairs obtains.

There is one aspect of the others' response that bears special comment here. Knowing that the individual is likely to present himself in a light that is favorable to him, the others may divide what they witness into two parts: a part that is relatively easy for the individual to manipulate at will, being chiefly his verbal assertions, and a part in regard to which he seems to have little concern or control, being chiefly derived from the expressions he gives off. The others may then use what are considered to be the ungovernable aspects of his expressive behavior as a check upon the validity of what is conveyed by the governable aspects. In this a fundamental asymmetry is demonstrated in the communication process, the individual presumably being aware of only one stream of his communication, the witnesses of this stream and one other. For example, in Shetland Isle one crofter's wife, in serving native dishes to a visitor from the mainland of Britain, would listen with a polite smile to his polite claims of liking what he was eating; at the same time she would take note of the rapidity with which the visitor lifted his fork or spoon to his mouth, the eagerness with which he passed food into his mouth, and the gusto expressed in chewing the food, using these signs as a check on the stated feelings of the eater. The same woman, in order to discover what one acquaintance (A) "actually" thought of another acquaintance (B), would wait until B was in the presence of A but engaged in conversation with still another person (C). She would then covertly examine the facial expressions of A as he regarded B in conversation with C. Not being in conversation with B, and not being directly observed by him, A would sometimes relax usual constraints and tactful deceptions, and freely express what he was "actually" feeling about B. This Shetlander, in short, would observe the unobserved observer.

Now given the fact that others are likely to check up on the more controllable aspects of behavior by means of the less controllable, one can expect that sometimes the individual will try to exploit this very possibility, guiding the impression he makes through behavior felt to be reliably informing.[6] For example, in gaining admission to a tight social circle, the participant observer may not only wear an accepting look while listening to an informant, but may also be careful to wear the same look when observing the informant talking to others; observers of the observer will then not as easily discover where he actually stands. A specific illustration may be cited from Shetland Isle. When a neighbor dropped in to have a cup of tea, he would ordinarily wear at least a hint of an expectant warm smile as he passed through the door into the cottage. Since lack of physical obstructions outside the cottage and lack of light within it usually made it possible to observe the visitor unobserved as he approached the house, islanders sometimes took pleasure in watching the visitor drop whatever expression he was manifesting and replace it with a sociable one just before reaching the door. However, some visitors, in appreciating that this examination was occurring, would blindly adopt a social face a long distance from the house, thus ensuring the projection of a constant image.

This kind of control upon the part of the individual reinstates the symmetry of the communication process, and sets the stage for a kind of information game—a potentially infinite cycle of concealment, discovery, false revelation, and rediscovery. It should be added that since the others are likely to be relatively unsuspicious of the presumably unguided aspect of the individual's conduct, he can gain much by controlling it. The others of course may sense that the individual is manipulating the presumably spontaneous aspects of his behavior, and seek in this very act of manipulation some shading of conduct that the individual has not managed to control. This again provides a check upon the individual's behavior, this time his presumably uncalculated behavior, thus re-establishing the asymmetry of the communication process. Here I would like only to add the suggestion that the arts of piercing an individual's effort at calculated unintentionality seem better developed than our capacity to manipulate our own behavior, so that regardless of how many steps have occurred in the information game, the witness is likely to have the advantage over the actor, and the initial asymmetry of the communication process is likely to be retained.

When we allow that the individual projects a definition of the situation when he appears before others, we must also see that the others, however passive their role may seem to be, will themselves effectively project a definition of the situation by virtue of their response to the individual and by virtue of any lines of action they initiate to him. Ordinarily the definitions of the situation projected by the several different participants are sufficiently attuned to one another so that open contradiction will not occur. I do not mean that there will be the kind of consensus that arises when each individual present candidly expresses what he really feels and honestly agrees with the expressed feelings of the others present. This kind of harmony is an optimistic ideal and in any case not necessary for the smooth working of society. Rather, each participant is expected to suppress his immediate heartfelt feelings, conveying a view of the situation which he feels the others will be able to find at least temporarily acceptable. The maintenance of this surface of agreement, this veneer of consensus, is facilitated by each participant concealing his own wants behind statements which assert values to which everyone present feels obliged to give lip service. Further, there is usually a kind of division of definitional labor. Each participant is allowed to establish the tentative official ruling regarding matters which are vital to him but not immediately important to others, e.g., the rationalizations and justifications by which he accounts for his past activity. In exchange for this courtesy he remains silent or non-committal on matters important to others but not immediately important to him. We have then a kind of interactional *modus vivendi*. Together the participants contribute to a single over-all definition of the situation which involves not so much a real agreement as to what exists but rather a real agreement as to whose claims concerning what issues will be temporarily honored. Real agreement will also exist concerning the desirability of avoiding an open conflict of definitions of the situation.[7] I will refer to this level of agreement as a "working consensus." It is to be understood that the working consensus established in one interaction setting will be quite different in content from the working consensus established in a different type of setting. Thus, between two friends at lunch, a reciprocal show of affection, respect, and concern for the other is maintained. In service occupations, on the other hand, the specialist often maintains an image of disinterested involvement in the problem of the client, while the client responds with a show of respect for the competence and integrity of the specialist. Regardless of such differences in content, however, the general form of these working arrangements is the same.

In noting the tendency for a participant to accept the definitional claims made by the others present, we can appreciate the crucial importance of the information that the individual *initially* possesses or acquires concerning his fellow participants, for it is on the basis of this initial information that the individual starts to define the situation and starts to build up lines of responsive action. The individual's initial projection commits him to what he is proposing to be and requires him to drop all pretenses of being other things. As the interaction among the participants progresses, additions and modifications in this initial informational state will of course occur, but it is essential that these later developments be related without contradiction to, and even built up from, the initial positions taken by the several participants. It would seem that an individual can more easily make a choice as to what line of treatment to demand from and extend to the others present at the beginning of an encounter than he can alter the line of treatment that is being pursued once the interaction is underway.

In everyday life, of course, there is a clear understanding that first impressions are important. Thus, the work adjustment of those in service occupations will often hinge upon a capacity to seize and hold the initiative in the service relation, a capacity that will require subtle aggressiveness on the part of the server when he is of lower socioeconomic status than his client. W. F. Whyte suggests the waitress as an example:

> The first point that stands out is that the waitress who bears up under pressure does not simply respond to her customers. She acts with some skill to control their behavior. The first question to ask when we look at the customer relationship is, "Does the waitress get the jump on the customer, or does the customer get the jump on the waitress?" The skilled waitress realizes the crucial nature of this question. . . .
>
> The skilled waitress tackles the customer with confidence and without hesitation. For example, she may find that a new customer has seated himself before she could clear off the dirty dishes and change the cloth. He is now leaning on the table studying the menu. She greets him, says, "May I change the cover, please?" and, without waiting for an answer, takes his menu away from him so that he moves back from the table, and she goes about her work. The relationship is handled politely but firmly, and there is never any question as to who is in charge.[8]

When the interaction that is initiated by "first impressions" is itself merely the initial interaction in an extended series of interactions involving the same participants, we speak of "getting off on the right foot" and feel that it is crucial that we do so. Thus, one learns that some teachers take the following view:

> You can't ever let them get the upper hand on you or you're through. So I start out tough. The first day I get a new class in, I let them know who's boss . . . You've got to start off tough, then you can ease up as you go along. If you start out easy-going, when you try to be tough, they'll just look at you and laugh.[9]

Similarly, attendants in mental institutions may feel that if the new patient is sharply put in his place the first day on the ward and made to see who is boss, much future difficulty will be prevented.[10]

Given the fact that the individual effectively projects a definition of the situation when he enters the presence of others, we can assume that events may occur within the interaction which contradict, discredit, or otherwise throw doubt upon this projection. When these disruptive events occur, the interaction itself may come to a confused and embarrassed halt. Some of the assumptions upon which the responses of the participants had been predicated become untenable, and the participants find themselves lodged in an interaction for which the situation has been wrongly defined and is now no longer defined. At such moments the individual whose presentation has been discredited may feel ashamed while the others present may feel hostile, and all the participants may come to feel ill at ease, nonplussed, out of countenance, embarrassed, experiencing the kind of anomy that is generated when the minute social system of face-to-face interaction breaks down.

In stressing the fact that the initial definition of the situation projected by an individual tends to provide a plan for the co-operative activity that follows—in stressing this action point of view—we must not overlook the crucial fact that any projected definition of the situation also has a distinctive moral character. It is this moral character of projections that will chiefly concern us in this report. Society is organized on the principle that any individual who possesses certain social characteristics has a moral right to expect that others will value and treat him in an appropriate way. Connected with this principle is a second, namely that an individual who implicitly or explicitly signifies that he has certain social characteristics ought in fact to be what he claims he is. In consequence, when an individual projects a definition of the situation and thereby makes an implicit or explicit claim to be a person of a particular kind, he automatically exerts a moral demand upon the others, obliging them to value and treat him in the manner that persons of his kind have a right to expect. He also implicitly forgoes all claims to be things he does not appear to be [11] and hence forgoes the treatment that would be appropriate for such individuals. The others find, then, that the individual has informed them as to what is and as to what they *ought* to see as the "is."

One cannot judge the importance of definitional disruptions by the frequency with which they occur, for apparently they would occur more frequently were not constant precautions taken. We find that preventive practices are constantly employed to avoid these embarrassments and that corrective practices are constantly employed to compensate for discrediting occurrences that have not been successfully avoided. When the individual employs these strategies and tactics to protect his own projections, we may refer to them as "defensive practices"; when a participant employs them to save the definition of the situation projected by another, we speak of "protective practices" or "tact." Together, defensive and protective practices comprise the techniques employed to safeguard the impression fostered by an individual during his presence before others. It should be added that while we may be ready to see that no fostered impression would survive if defensive practices were not employed, we are less ready perhaps to see that few impressions could survive if those who received the impression did not exert tact in their reception of it.

In addition to the fact that precautions are taken to prevent disruption of projected definitions, we may also note that an intense interest in these disruptions comes to play a significant role in the social life of the group. Practical jokes and social games are played in which embarrassments which are to be taken unseriously are purposely engineered.[12] Fantasies are created in which devastating exposures occur. Anecdotes from the past—real, embroidered, or fictitious—are told and retold, detailing disruptions which occurred, almost occurred, or occurred and were admirably resolved. There seems to be no grouping which does not have a ready supply of these games, reveries, and cautionary tales, to be used as a source of humor, a catharsis for anxieties, and a sanction for inducing individuals to be modest in their claims and reasonable in their projected expectations. The individual may tell himself through dreams of getting into impossible positions. Families tell of the time a guest got his dates mixed and arrived when neither the house nor anyone in it was ready for him. Journalists tell of times when an all-too-meaningful misprint occurred, and the paper's assumption of objectivity or decorum was humorously discredited. Public servants tell of times a client ridiculously misunderstood form instructions, giving answers which implied an unanticipated and bizarre definition of the situation.[13] Seamen, whose home away from home is rigorously he-man, tell stories of coming back home and inadvertently asking mother to "pass the fucking butter." [14] Diplomats tell of the time a near-sighted queen asked a republican ambassador about the health of his king.[15]

To summarize, then, I assume that when an individual appears before others he will have many motives for trying to control the impression they receive of the situation.

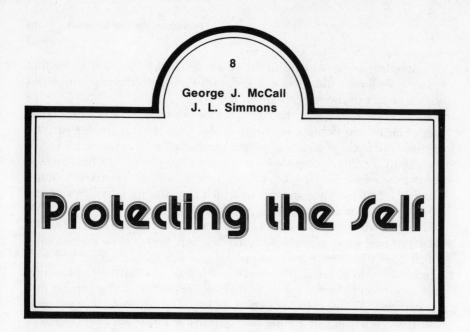

8

George J. McCall
J. L. Simmons

Protecting the Self

The analyses of interaction presented in this and the preceding article make human interaction seem like a game. This impression is not accidental, for these articles represent a gaming approach to understanding social life. In games analysis people are viewed as pursuing various goals. As they pursue their goals, they interact within a framework of boundaries, expectations (or rules), strategies, tactics, moves, and countermoves. In order to bring themselves closer to their desired goals, as a regular part of their lives people utilize both their own and others' expectations. They develop their strategies, follow their tactics, and make their moves, all the while keeping a close watch on others to adjust their performances as the need arises.

Much of everyday life can be profitably analyzed within such a games framework. The gaming approach can be applied to what happens when people are at school, on the bus, on dates, with their families, in restaurants, in the military, relaxing over coffee, telling jokes, out drinking, and even making love. In all such cases strategies are developed, tactics followed, and moves made—all within an imposed boundary of expectations. This framework for understanding human life can be applied to almost every situation in which people come face to face with one another.

Some of the devices people use in order to manage the impressions they desire others to receive were analyzed by Goffman in the preceding selection. As people make their various presentations of self, however, they sometimes fail in their endeavors. That is, they sometimes do not present the self in a way which matches the impressions that they want others to have of themselves. When this occurs, they then bring into play various legitimating devices. It is those mechanisms of legitimation which McCall and Simmons analyze in the following selection.

□ . . . Our empirical performances almost always depart in some degree from the idealized images we have of ourselves in particular social positions. The central question of this section is: How do we deal with this discrepancy? How do we "make things right"? [1]

Many of our daily role-performances are, of course, so routine, even habitual, that we are scarcely conscious of them. Their crucial importance for some of our major identities may be brought home to us only when they are impeded, interrupted, or called into question. Only then do they pose real problems of legitimation. The smoothly executed habits that make up a fair proportion of our daily activities are therefore not considered in the following discussion, unless and until they have gone awry for some reason.

The first "mechanism" of legitimation, of coping with the discrepancy, is simply the fact that identities and support need not correspond completely or on each and every occasion. Serious legitimation problems usually arise only if the discrepancy is dangerously large during a single encounter or if it remains fairly large during each of a series of encounters. Most of us are realistic enough to be fairly satisfied with role-support that approaches rather than entirely meets the self-expectations engendered by our identities. We build up short-term credit, so to speak, both with ourselves and with others by occasional exceptional performances that leave a certain margin of social capital to gamble with or live off for a time. The successful poet is thus allowed an occasional cliché, the good cook is free to experiment and to fail occasionally, and the brave man can indulge himself in an occasional flinch.

But habitual performances and the existence of a certain fleeting amount of interpersonal credit and tolerance form only the background for our more active strivings—albeit sometimes a quite pleasant background. They are, as it were, the open ground that lies before the person's first perimeters of self-defense.

At the level at which the individual must strive more actively for legitimation, we find, first of all, that people employ a good deal of *selective perception* of their own actions.[2] The individual knows in a general, though not necessarily consciously thought-out, sense what identities he is laying claim to and attempting to fulfill through his actions, and he can therefore ignore and disattend those features of his conduct that

are not relevant parts of the performances of these roles. Unfortunately, the person's other audiences typically lack this knowledge, and
consequently they can never be sure what is message and what is noise
in the person's actions—at least until they are quite familiar with his
particular dramaturgical idiom. In general, the person is able to pay
most attention to a selected fraction of his own actions and the complementary actions of others, that fraction that is most favorable to his
self-conceptions. . . .

There is a not too infrequent curious inversion of this first mechanism, in which the insecure or self-effacing person selectively perceives
and exaggerates cues that are unfavorable to him. The psychological
nuances of this strategy are very complex, but it seems usually to involve the handling of a threat to one's identities by "withdrawing from
the race." That is, it seems to involve a subtle plea to be released from
the standards of performance normally implied by others.

Second, there is a related mechanism of *selective interpretation* of the
audience's response to our actions.[3] There are two characteristics of interpersonal encounters that facilitate this selective interpretation. In
the first place, audiences often respond in an equivocal manner that is
open to a number of interpretations. In fact, the audience must sometimes reiterate its evaluations several times before they are brought
home in a straightforward meaning to the individual. In the second
place, the norms of propriety and polite discourse (which, in fact, is
what much of our daily interactions are) dictate that we "nicify" our
responses to the person. An example of this process is the common
practice of prefacing a criticism with a complimentary or ingratiating
remark; another is the etiquette of flattering hosts and guests. Such
polite conduct on the part of others—whether or not they are really
persuaded—may be interpreted by the performer as supportive of his
performance.

These two mechanisms of selective perception and selective interpretation stand as the performer's first line of active defense. Not infrequently, however, the discrepancy between performance and role-
identity is so great that it overwhelms these primary mechanisms, and
the person must employ other measures to maintain a going concern,
psychologically speaking.

If these mechanisms fail, the person may employ any one of a
number of alternative strategies. Just which one or which combination
of these strategies he uses depends upon his psychological predilections
and interpersonal habits, as well as upon the situation and the audience. This group of mechanisms cannot be ranked, given our present
state of knowledge about human beings, nor can firm generalizations
be made about them. As their nature is still so poorly understood and

as they are so difficult to define unambiguously, we shall only describe and briefly illustrate them in this book.

The individual may respond to the discrepancy by withdrawing from the interaction (what Lewin termed "leaving the field," *aus dem felde gehen*).[4] This response is a likely strategy, particularly in the early phases of the interaction, when the first hints of the outcome may be sensed but while the person has not yet staked his identities in it very deeply. The tentative nature of the early phases of most interactions facilitates the employment of this strategy. If later phases of the interaction have already been reached, the individual may still partially withdraw from the obligation to make good his claims by lapsing into a more passive performance and perhaps ceding the spotlight to another actor.

The person may also handle the hinted threat of a discrepancy by switching to the enactment of another role-identity that he judges more likely to be successful in that situation. This strategy, rather than withdrawal, is likely to be adopted in interaction situations in which the person is under some formal or informal obligation not to leave, for example, when he is interacting with superiors, with guests, or with intimates.

The person may also employ what is termed *rationalization*, explaining away the discrepancy as having arisen from extenuating and unanticipated circumstances in the encounter that upset the performance. We may think of ourselves as fairly expert ping-pong players, for example, but have a bad evening "because of the bad background you have to hit against at Jason's house," or, thinking of ourselves as witty conversationalists, we may explain away our verbal ineptness during a particular exchange as having been due to the fact that we were too preoccupied with more pressing matters to devote ourselves to such repartee.

The individual may also resort to what is termed *scapegoating*, blaming someone else for his having failed to come through with a really impressive performance himself: The performance did not come off because others were too inept at performing the necessary counterroles or because those he was competing with used unfair practices. Who could be a good lover with such an unresponsive partner? How can you win against collusion? How can even a good parent bring up a boy who is bad by nature?

Sometimes, however, the fault does indeed lie with others, so we must be careful to distinguish between instances of scapegoating and examples of realistic perception by the individual. Often, of course, the individual's perception is neither clearly one nor the other but some admixture of the two. Students of subcultures and social classes tell us that these admixtures are frequently major aspects of group ideology. Unprivileged groups in particular tend to employ such beliefs in a sweeping, universalistic manner to account for their failures and tribulations. These beliefs usually contain some truth, of course, and often a good deal of it, but when they are employed to absolve group members automatically from striving to perform well, they appear to be scapegoating. (In a curious sense, scapegoating is thus a two-way street, with the majority group castigating the minority and the minority using the privileged majority as a means of excusing what are sometimes its own shortcomings.)

The individual threatened with a gross discrepancy between identity and support may also employ what is termed *disavowal* of the performance's serious relevance to the identity. In this strategy, he makes the claim that a seemingly relevant performance should not be taken seriously because he was only joking or caricaturing or because he was not really trying. Use of this strategy is facilitated by the fact that the person has some freedom to designate when he is frivolous and when his performances should be taken seriously.

A further mechanism one may employ when an audience other than himself is not sufficiently persuaded or is even unequivocally negative in its response to the performance is simply to *reject* or *deprecate* any audience that withholds role-support from him on the basis of that performance.[5] If the individual himself judges his performance to have been satisfactory and if he feels fairly self-confident about his judgment, it then follows that an unimpressed audience must be incompetent to evaluate him. The person may not put this appraisal to empirical test but may shun those audiences that he anticipates might not furnish him support if he were to go before them. And, simultaneously, he tends to underline his continuing allegiance to those alternative audiences that do confer full role-support or would, he thinks, if they were present. In general, this mechanism is employed perhaps more often in selecting audiences *before* the performance is staged than after the fact. But, as long as the person has alternative audiences to whom he can, in imagination, appeal, it is an available strategy when the audience present does not confer the required support.

Not only does this mechanism (that of rejecting the evaluations of the present audience and imaginatively referring a performance to other audiences not physically present) help one to deal with a gap between identity and support, but it also frees him to some extent from control by the social pressures of the immediate situation.

He may have no personal acquaintance with the hypothetical other audience; it may be only some group he wishes to emulate and aspires to join. The other audience may even exist only as a myth. But, real or not, the imagined reactions of other audiences provide him with a means of shifting perspective on his own performances. In a provocative discussion of this aspect of the relationship between reference groups and social control, Shibutani quotes Thoreau's famous lines: "If a man does not keep pace with his companions, perhaps it is because he hears a different drummer." [6]

But, in the course of every human life, there are times when all these mechanisms fail us and we cannot escape the awareness that an important audience judges us to have failed in a serious role-performance. One of the ironies of our human existence is that some of our most important role-identities—like those involving the opposite sex, our careers, our parents, and our children—are, at the same time, the most vulnerable because we cannot take lightly these identities or the intimate audiences that judge the performance of them. The more involved we are, the more we have to gain, but the corollary of this assertion is that we also have more to lose.

If an important role-identity has been unequivocally threatened by loss of role-support from an important audience, one is likely to experience misery and anguish. He may attempt partially to alleviate this reaction by shifting his identity hierarchy, by giving higher salience to his more successful role-identities. He deprecates the threatened identity—chiding himself for being so obsessed with it and derogating the audience that holds it to be so important. That is, he tries to maintain a going concern psychologically by reducing his investment in the threatened role-identity. In a sense, he thus sacrifices a role-identity in an attempt to save the standing of the self as a whole. [7]

For most people, however, the salience hierarchy is not that fluid, and therefore this defense is usually only partly successful. It is likely to be a temporary "wild-eyed" reaction that fades within a few days as the intensity of the anguish fades, and the salience hierachy tends to return to something like its precrisis form. In an important sense, then, the individual often handles such a failure by simply learning to live with it. Time does not exactly heal such wounds; it tends rather to form scar tissue. "Once burned—well learned."

Through such painful experiences, most of us learn to be more cautious in committing ourselves so fully to given role performances with particular audiences; we hedge our bets; we adopt a strategy of minimizing losses rather than of maximizing gains. This change also involves an irony, because the very fact that we commit ourselves less wholly means that we cannot succeed so completely in realizing our ideal images through interactions.

If all these mechanisms fail, and on occasion they do, the individual may experience a generalized sense of self-derogation and unworthiness if the threatened identity is a prominent one. This feeling may be so painful that he believes he can resolve it only by self-destruction. At the least, contemplation of suicide may be the only background against which the self seems worthy to continue to live; it may be the only reference point from which life seems worth living. As Durkheim and other students have pointed out, the likelihood of this extreme outcome increases if the individual lacks supportive interpersonal ties. Suicides resulting from loss of face, as documented by Durkheim and Malinowski, are the prototypical cases of this process.[8]

The frequency and intensity of such threats to one's role-identities are, however, fortunately diminished by *overvaluation* of performance, both on his own part and on the part of those closest to him, as Claude Bowman has so beautifully demonstrated.[9] A teen-age girl considers a poem, written for her by her swain, to be of real literary quality, whereas the very same poem, word for word, if written by a stranger, would be judged more realistically. As a further example, our friends are "spontaneous, fun-loving, and firm in their convictions"; our enemies are "irresponsible, self-indulgent, and pig-headed." We "discuss"; others "gossip." One of the major functions of "in-groups" seems to be the mutual maintenance and reinforcement of the members' self-conceptions. As Merton has so nicely pointed out, the very "virtues" of the in-group become vices when practiced by out-groups.[10]

This mutual overvaluation may occur by default, in a sense, out of sheer delight in finding another person who shares even the vocabulary associated with a given identity. This result is particularly likely when the opportunity structure is exceedingly limited or when the content of the identity is more idiosyncratic. In either of these cases it is far more difficult for the person to find satisfactory role partners, and anyone who is minimally adequate is likely to be treasured. The lonelier a girl is, the greater proportion of men who will be acceptable to her. Sometimes the person's choice of colleagues and acquaintances, or even of friends and spouse, is determined in part by this "default" process. Sometimes people become so starved for audiences who will help to confer role-support upon some of their more esoteric but treasured identities that they set up what amount to reciprocal trade agreements in overvaluation. The sensitive young man thus has a charming admirer who has the intuition to recognize the merits of his poetry; a lonely girl has found a man whose phrases touch upon her daydreams. Each is richer for his overvaluation of the other. . . .

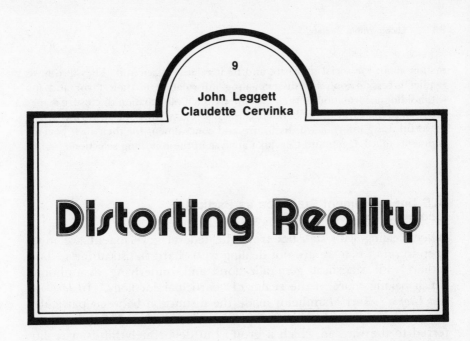

9

John Leggett
Claudette Cervinka

Distorting Reality

Analyzing human behavior within a games framework especially lends itself to understanding power relations. Power is commonly defined as the ability to get what you want in spite of the objections of others who have some interest in the matter. The games people play with one another in their everyday lives are frequently a means of obtaining or maintaining control over others. When others stand in the way of the goals one is pursuing, control often can be gained and power maximized by means of gaming strategies.

Not only do individuals use gaming strategies in both their routine and their esoteric interactions with one another, but, similarly, so do groups of people when they are dealing with other groups. Our society is a pluralistic society, that is, it is made up of many different groups. Many of these groups are engaged in active competition with one another in an intense effort to obtain for themselves a larger share of scarce resources. Some resources are material, such as money and property, while others are non-material, such as power and prestige. Groups having few of these resources jockey for a position which affords them better access to those things they highly desire. Groups which already have access to them are seldom inclined easily to give up their advantage. They consequently manipulate symbols both to reveal and to conceal relevant information in order to maintain and consolidate their favored positions in the social structure.

Groups already in the more powerful position have readier access to infor-

Reprinted from "Countdown: How to Lie with Statistics" [pp. 235–244, 251–252, 254] in *Social Problems in American Society* by James Henslin and Larry Reynolds. Copyright © 1973 by Holbrook Press, Inc. Used by permission.

mation about the social structure and their relative place in it. They also have readier access to tools for disseminating information in their favor and for withholding information to their detriment. Such information disclosure sometimes takes the form of deliberately falsifying reality. It is one such case of the powerful using information disclosure and concealment for their own goal-attainments that Leggett and Cervinka analyze in the following selection.

BLS Unemployment Statistics as Particular Ideology: The Assertion

When dealing with statistics from the federal government, we must keep in mind that we are not dealing with "hard statistical facts," but, rather, with statistical generalizations and underlying assumptions which belong more in the realm of "particular ideology." In *Ideology and Utopia* [1] Karl Mannheim made the distinction between particular and total ideology. In the case of *particular* ideology, Mannheim referred to the ways in which a group can deliberately falsify a reality through the conscious application of formulas, half-truths, innuendos, and plain lies. For example, one group can use distorted or warped statements to paint a damning or glowing picture at the expense of certain groups in the community. By contrast, in the case of *total* ideology, Mannheim has referred to the way in which objectively false portraits of reality pervade human relations so as to mar the perspectives of people, none of whom have consciously or maliciously forged this distortion of reality. In this sense, total ideology most clearly resembles many definitions of culture. [2]

BLS Statistics as Particular Ideology: An Instance

A most crass instance of statistical obfuscation occurred in January 1971, when the U.S. Department of Labor changed some of its counting procedures. Harry Brill, a sociologist at the University of Massachusetts and a skilled interpreter of labor statistics, noticed the change and sensitized a number of us to what was going on when he editorialized on the pages of *The Nation* as follows: [3]

> President Nixon recently told the press and the public that the actual unemployment rate averaged lower in 1970 than during the recession years of the 1960's. He is, unfortunately, mistaken. Actually, the current estimate of unemployment would read higher had the De-

partment of Labor not changed its counting procedures. Until 1967, the Department in its monthly survey counted as unemployed all those who volunteered that they were too discouraged to look for work. According to its own study, the rate then would have been fifty percent higher if it had solicited the reasons for not actively seeking work. Despite these findings, the Department of Labor decided to assume that anyone not actively looking for work must therefore not be interested in working. So now even those who volunteer their despair—and more are despairing—are no longer regarded as unemployed.

The Department counted as unemployed until recently * those who were actively seeking a job within the last sixty days. This too was drastically changed—to four weeks. Altogether dropped from the calculations of the unemployment rate are the youngest members of the labor force, ages fourteen and fifteen.† Since their chances of being out of work are extremely high, excluding them from the labor force count further reduces the official rate of unemployment. Formerly ‡ tallied as unemployed were workers who had jobs, but for various reasons were not working and were looking for work. For example, workers laid off because of weather conditions, such as those in the construction trades, fall into this category. Those belonging to this group are now counted as employed even though they are not receiving pay and are actively in pursuit of work.

Deleted, then, from the officially unemployed are people who failed to seek work in the last month even after they had earlier sought work in vain and later given up. Dropped from the unemployed are the fourteen and fifteen-year-olds who seek employment. Gone from the roles of the unemployed are job holders who may be seeking another job because inclement weather and like hazards have moved them into the category of the temporarily laid-off. But in effect they are unemployed during the winter months, or whatever the time span might be. Still, according to these changed rules, they are counted as being employed.

Most curious is the deletion of the fourteen-fifteen-year-olds. Officially, they are no longer in the labor force. In fact, however, they are still counted by the Bureau of Labor Statistics. (See Table 1.) One's curiosity on this matter is whetted by what the findings indicate:

---

* Recently refers to 1967.
† The fourteen and fifteen-year-olds were dropped in 1967.
‡ Prior to 1967.

Table 1 Employment Status of Fourteen–Fifteen-Year-Olds by Sex and Color, September 1971 (in thousands)

	Total			White			Negro and Other Races		
	Both Sexes	Male	Female	Both Sexes	Male	Female	Both Sexes	Male	Female
Non-Institution Population	8,147	4,127	4,019	6,987	3,552	3,436	1,159	576	384
Civilian labor force	1,338	782	555	1,249	731	518	88	51	37
Employed	1,223	717	505	1,168	682	486	54	35	19
Agriculture	159	136	23	150	131	19	10	5	5
Nonagricultural industries	1,063	581	482	1,019	551	468	45	30	14
Unemployed	115	65	50	81	49	32	34	16	18
Not in labor force	6,809	3,345	3,464	5,738	2,821	2,917	1,071	524	547
Keeping house	28	6	21	15	4	11	13	2	11
Going to school	6,675	3,288	3,387	5,627	2,778	2,848	1,048	510	538
Unable to work	8	3	5	7	3	4	2	—	2
All other reasons	98	48	51	90	35	55	9	(¹)	(¹)

¹ Detail not shown due to inconsistencies resulting from the small number of sample cases.
Source: Taken from *Employment and Earnings*, Vol. 18, No. 4, October 1971, p. 43.

1. There are proportionately more blacks than whites unemployed (especially among women). Indeed, the ratio is 6-1 rather than the generally accepted figure of 2-1 for blacks and white (for all of the black and white labor force participants).

2. Less obvious, however, is the extremely *low* incidence of official unemployment among fourteen–fifteen-year-old whites. So low is this figure for whites that it compares favorably with data on all whites during the same period, i.e., September, 1971. Among white fourteen–fifteen-year-olds, there are fewer than seven percent unemployed. In the case of the entire white labor force, the unemployment figure is approximately two-thirds this percentage.

What the data suggest is that dropping out of school to go to work has quite different consequences for blacks than whites. In the case of blacks, dropping out of school quite often means becoming either unemployed or a non-participant in the labor force. In the case of whites, dropping out of school seldom means dropping out of the labor force, or becoming an employed seeker of work, although the acquisition of a job may mean employment in a low paying occupation. By contrast, blacks frequently fail to obtain even these low status positions. What Table 1 suggests is that racial discrimination is severely operative among young dropouts. In a broad sense, dropping out of school is not the problem. Race apparently is. It would appear that we lose a great deal of insight regarding the operation of our economy when we delete the fourteen- and fifteen-year-olds.

The dropping of these kinds of persons accompanied an adjusted comparison. As you will recall, the Bureau of Labor Statistics did draw a comparison between the unemployed of the early 1970's and those of the early 1960's without telling us how, if at all, the BLS had removed the recently deleted categories from the earlier estimates so as to allow for a fair comparison. No such statistical control was applied; unadjusted comparisons were made. The BLS is comparing oranges without peelings (1971) against oranges with peelings (1961) while forgetting to inform the general public how the comparison has been made. Rather than comparing adjusted figures, the BLS supplies figures on dropped groups which are added but separate so that if the researcher wishes, he can compute an adjusted figure.[4] Needless to say, the BLS does not add to our general knowledge of working-class unemployment by suggesting such techniques.

There is no professional excuse for:

1. the juggled criteria on unemployed
2. the unqualified statements on the trend comparisons, and finally
3. the elementary error of comparing two noncomparable quantities.

Being a Member of the Labor Force: The Unemployed and the Employed

Before we can go any further in our analysis we must acquaint ourselves with the way in which the BLS does in fact gauge three things:

1. being a member of the labor force
2. being unemployed, and finally
3. being employed.

First, who is in and who is out of the labor force? [5]

Persons under sixteen years of age are excluded from our count of the labor force, as are all inmates of institutions, regardless of age. All other members of the civilian non-institutional population are eligible for the labor force by our definitions. Therefore, persons age sixteen and over who have no job and are not looking for one are counted as "not in the labor force." For many who do not participate in the labor force, going to school is the reason. Family responsibilities keep others out of the labor force. Still others suffer a physical or mental disability which makes them unable to participate in normal labor force activities.

Most of these situations are quite clear: Bob Jones reports that he is attending college; Barbara Green feels that her two young children need her care; or Stephen Smith would like to work, but his doctor told him that he must not because he recently suffered a heart attack. All three of these people are not in the labor force and are classified accordingly, in their respective categories: "in school," "keeping house," and "unable to work."

There is a fourth group of persons who are not in the labor force. They are classified "other," which includes everyone who did not give any of the above reasons for nonparticipation in the labor force. Such persons may be retired and feel that they have made their contribution to the economy throughout the course of their lives, they may want to work only at certain times of the year, or they may believe that no employment is available for workers with their experience or training.

The illustrations are less than wholly inclusive. The category of labor force excludes, for example, hundreds of thousands of prison inmates who labor in our prisons and asylums. The Attica events have brought their labor and their conditions to our attention, but not into our statistical columns where they belong. In addition, the labor force category also excludes the many who have tired of looking for work and have subsequently disappeared from the ranks of the unemployed. They are shoved into the limbo of "beyond the labor force."

Let us now turn to those whom the BLS has in fact counted (in its monthly survey of 50,000 Americans) as *unemployed*. By 1967, the definition of unemployed had become what it is today: [6]

Persons are unemployed if they have looked for work in the past 4 weeks, are currently available for work, and of course, do not have a job at the same time. Looking for work may consist of any of the following specific activities:

Registering at a public or private employment office
Meeting with prospective employers
Checking with friends or relatives
Placing or answering advertisements
Writing letters of application or
Being on a union or professional register

There are two groups of people who do not have to meet the test of having engaged in a specific jobseeking activity to be counted as unemployed. They are: a. persons waiting to start a new job within thirty days, and b. workers waiting to be recalled from layoff. In all cases, the individual must be currently available for work.

Finally, who are the employed? [7]

There is a wide range of job arrangements possible in the American economy, and not all of them fit neatly into a given category. For example, people are considered employed if they did any work at all for pay or profit during the survey week. This includes all part-time and temporary work as well as regular full-time year-round employment. *Persons are also counted as employed if they have a job at which they did not work during the survey week because they were:*

On vacation
Ill
Involved in an industrial dispute
Prevented from working by bad weather or
Taking time off for various personal reasons

These persons are counted among the employed and tabulated separately as "with a job but not at work," because they have a specific job to which they will return. (Italics added.)

Let us contemplate this specification. Missing from the unemployed, but counted among the employed, are people who work ten, twenty, or thirty hours a week. In fact, all forms of part-time help count as employed. But that ain't all. Finding their way into the employed category are short and long-term strikers,[8] the short and long-term ill (non-institutionalized), plus the two week as well as two month vacationers. To be employed, then, is not the same as to be engaged at work. Stop and think about that one. The distinction between (1) non-work-employment and (2) work-employment is a subtle one that many of us miss even though these millions of the non-working employed fail to earn incomes, as is often the case during a strike, an illness, or a vacation.

What is frequently overlooked is how both (1) the narrow base for computing who is unemployed and (2) the extraordinarily broad criteria for determining who is beyond the labor force—serve to inflate the relative importance of the *employed* in the computation of statistics on unemployment. How does this triangular relationship among numerator, denominator and outcome work? Since many of the objectively unemployed have been secreted by the BLS into the limbo of "not in labor force," where they cannot serve as a sizable portion of what would otherwise be a fairly large numerator in the overall statistical figure on percentage unemployed, and since the not-in-labor-force category fails to include the strikers, the ill, and the vacationers, and furthermore, since these three categories count as employed, the officially unemployed stand as whittled gnats in statistical ratio to the padded employed. In effect, we have an unduly puny numerator peering down at a bloated denominator. What we have is a Kafkaesque situation where a sudden and numerous increase in strikers,[9] (hospital patients and/or vacationers) would inadvertently contribute to the immediate minimization of the official figure on unemployment, even under circumstances of slight increase in the number of those officially counted as unemployed. Think about that one, especially in communities such as Detroit.

The Aggregate Unemployed Rate

Perhaps more puzzling than the "mistaken ratio" of the employed to the unemployed is the periodicity of the count. Even if we were to assume that monthly reports, corrected for their underestimation, would be useful, we could nonetheless use what would appear to be a more demonstrative measure of unemployment, one in fact computed by the BLS but which they inadequately publicize. From the point of view of at least some unemployed, far more important than a monthly rate is the *aggregate unemployment rate*. This BLS rate refers to the number of people who are *unemployed over a period of one year*. Harry Brill makes clear why he thinks this yearly rate is more important: [10]

If on the average, four million people are jobless each month, that does not necessarily mean that the individuals who are counted as unemployed in one month are the same who are counted as unemployed a month later. Turnover among the unemployed occurs, and thus the total percentage, or number, of those who have been unemployed during each year must exceed the average monthly count.

This is not news to the Department of Labor. According to the testimony delivered by Secretary of Labor Wirtz before the Senate Committee on Employment and Man Power, "approximately fourteen million men and women were unemployed at some time during the year of 1962." Fourteen million individuals are roughly twenty percent of the total "labor force"! Therefore, the total annual rate (twenty percent) is 3.77 times the average monthly rate (5.3 percent) of that year. To that must be added millions of unemployed persons who are not counted by the Department of Labor; and the figure soars to represent eighteen or twenty million individuals.

In other words, average monthly gross figures of four million would contrast with a yearly number of approximately fourteen million persons unemployed for an average duration of time that is rather considerable.[11] The figure of fourteen million unemployed does strongly suggest that something may well be organically wrong with our economy.

The BLS has experimented with measures which have in fact more clearly indicated the true number of people without work but with the desire to work should a job become available. In 1964 the Department of Labor published figures which indicated that total monthly unemployment might be considerably higher than the 4.5 million specified in the official figures. The experimental-statistical measure on unemployment did in fact include those not in the official labor force. Specifically, the "unemployed" for the first time included:

1. those who had worked part-time but wanted full-time jobs as well as
2. those who had given up the search for work, plus
3. all of the others found beyond the pale of labor force participation (e.g., those who had never searched for work).

The BLS appeared to be on its way to evolving a measure of work force, one with a more realistic and humane definition than "labor force." The impact of the additional categories was clear: [12]

The figures show that among white men aged 45 to 54 with four years of education or less, 221 of every 1000 are not working. Of these, 84 are listed as unemployed and 137 as "not in the labor force."

Among those with college degrees, the corresponding figure shrinks to 39 who are not working, including ten unemployed and 29 not in the labor force.

Curiously enough, this more representative measure was dropped by the BLS soon after its innovation. In this sense, the BLS erased its justifiable innovation on work force measurement and opted for continuation of the traditional labor force categorization. . . .

Conclusions

For trained economists and statisticians, many with doctorates, to continue to impose invalid statistics on the people of the U.S. constitutes not fraud, not outrage, but predictable service on the part of professionals who owe their jobs and their careers to the politicians found in the executive branches of the federal government. In turn, most politicians of this calibre have developed a reciprocal set of ties with upper-class persons on the assumption that what is good for private corporations on matters of statistics must be good for the state on matters of its longevity. We do not agree.

. . . In fact, the BLS figures now do the working-class people a disservice by understating the overall unemployment condition of the working class. What we need are valid measures of unemployment, the kinds of scientific statistics which will allow us to build a sound case for those millions of Americans who would work were jobs available. . . .

10

Mary McIntosh

The Homosexual Role

In sociological theory, homosexuality is not a condition of abnormality. It is, rather, a sexual orientation which results from a certain type of social learning. People are not born homosexual, but they may learn to prefer members of their own sex for their sexual and emotional satisfactions.

Unlike the dominant orientation of American culture, in some cultures homosexual behaviors are tolerated, in some they are approved, and in others they are even required. The ancient Greeks viewed homosexuality between males as on a higher plane than heterosexual relations. The Siwans of North Africa and the Kerski of New Guinea expect all their males to become involved in homosexual relations. Among the Kerski, men do not have sexual relations with women until they first involve themselves during pre-puberty in passive sexual relations with older males and following puberty engage in sexual relations with younger males. As should be apparent from the earlier selection by Margaret Mead on the Samoans, sexual morality is not a matter of dictates unfolding from within people but is formed through interaction with others. If homosexuality is viewed as wrong within a particular culture, it will tend to be viewed as wrong by persons growing up in that culture. If homosexuality is viewed as right in another culture, so it will tend to be viewed by persons growing up in that culture. There is nothing about homosexual behavior, or the various forms of heterosexuality for that matter, which is in and of itself right or wrong. What is considered right or wrong is the outcome of social learning, whether we are speaking of heterosexuality, homosexuality, or any other form of human behavior.

In the following article, McIntosh explains how a social concept or category affects both perception and behavior. Because we have the category of exclusive heterosexuality and exclusive homosexuality, we tend to see and react to others in different ways than if we did not have this orientation of sexual exclusivity. McIntosh documents the rise of this category in Western culture.

□ Recent advances in the sociology of deviant behavior have not yet affected the study of homosexuality, which is still commonly seen as a condition characterizing certain persons in the way that birthplace or deformity might characterize them. The limitations of this view can best be understood if we examine some of its implications. In the first place, if homosexuality is a condition, then people either have it or do not have it. Many scientists and ordinary people assume that there are two kinds of people in the world: homosexuals and heterosexuals. Some of them recognize that homosexual feelings and behavior are not confined to the persons they would like to call "homosexuals" and that some of these persons do not actually engage in homosexual behavior. This should pose a crucial problem; but they evade the crux by retaining their assumption and puzzling over the question of how to tell whether someone is "really" homosexual or not. Lay people too will discuss whether a certain person is "queer" in much the same way as they might question whether a certain pain indicated cancer. And in much the same way they will often turn to scientists or to medical men for a surer diagnosis. The scientists, for their part, feel it incumbent on them to seek criteria for diagnosis.

Thus one psychiatrist, discussing the definition of homosexuality, has written:

. . . I do not diagnose patients as homosexual unless they have engaged in overt homosexual behavior. Those who also engage in heterosexual activity are diagnosed as bisexual. An isolated experience may not warrant the diagnosis, but repetetive (sic) homosexual behavior in adulthood, whether sporadic or continuous, designates a homosexual.[1]

Along with many other writers, he introduces the notion of a third type of person, the "bisexual," to handle the fact that behavior patterns cannot be conveniently dichotomized into heterosexual and homosexual. But this does not solve the conceptual problem, since bisexuality too is seen as a condition (unless as a passing response to unusual situations such as confinement in a one-sex prison). In any case there is no extended discussion of bisexuality; the topic is usually given a brief mention in order to clear the ground for the consideration of "true homosexuality."

To cover the cases where the symptoms of behavior or of felt attractions do not match the diagnosis, other writers have referred to an adolescent homosexual phase or have used such terms as "latent homosexual" or "pseudo homosexual." Indeed one of the earliest studies of the subject, by Krafft-Ebing, was concerned with making a distinction between the "invert" who is congenitally homosexual and others who, although they behave in the same way, are not true inverts.[2]

A second result of the conceptualization of homosexuality as a condition is that the major research task has been seen as the study of its etiology. There has been much debate as to whether the condition is innate or acquired. The first step in such research has commonly been to find a sample of "homosexuals" in the same way that a medical researcher might find a sample of diabetics if he wanted to study that disease. Yet, after a long history of such studies, the results are sadly inconclusive and the answer is still as much a matter of opinion as it was when Havelock Ellis published *Sexual Inversion* [3] seventy years ago. The failure of research to answer the question has not been due to lack of scientific rigor or to any inadequacy of the available evidence; it results rather from the fact that the wrong question has been asked. One might as well try to trace the etiology of "committee-chairmanship" or "Seventh-Day Adventism" as of "homosexuality."

The vantage-point of comparative sociology enables us to see that the conception of homosexuality as a condition is, in itself, a possible object of study. This conception and the behavior it supports operate as a form of social control in a society in which homosexuality is condemned. Furthermore, the uncritical acceptance of the conception by social scientists can be traced to their concern with homosexuality as a social problem. They have tended to accept the popular definition of what the problem is and they have been implicated in the process of social control.

The practice of the social labeling of persons as deviant operates in two ways as a mechanism of social control.[4] In the first place it helps to provide a clear-cut, publicized, and recognizable threshold between permissible and impermissible behavior. This means that people cannot so easily drift into deviant behavior. Their first moves in a deviant direction immediately raise the question of a total move into a deviant role with all the sanctions that this is likely to elicit. Secondly, the labeling serves to segregate the deviants from others and this means that their deviant practices and their self-justifications for these practices are contained within a relatively narrow group. The creation of a specialized, despised, and punished role of homosexual keeps the bulk of society pure in rather the same way that the similar treatment of some kinds of criminals helps keep the rest of society law-abiding.

However, the disadvantage of this practice as a technique of social control is that there may be a tendency for people to become fixed in their deviance once they have become labeled. This, too, is a process that has become well-recognized in discussions of other forms of deviant behavior such as juvenile delinquency and drug taking and, indeed, of other kinds of social labeling such as streaming in schools and racial distinctions. One might expect social categorizations of this sort to be to some extent self-fulfilling prophecies: if the culture defines people as falling into distinct types—black and white, criminal and noncriminal, homosexual and normal—then these types will tend to become polarized, highly differentiated from each other. Later in this paper I shall discuss whether this is so in the case of homosexuals and "normals" in the United States today.

It is interesting to notice that homosexuals themselves welcome and support the notion that homosexuality is a condition. For just as the rigid categorization deters people from drifting into deviancy, so it appears to foreclose on the possibility of drifting back into normality and thus removes the element of anxious choice. It appears to justify the deviant behavior of the homosexual as being appropriate for him as a member of the homosexual category. The deviancy can thus be seen as legitimate for him and he can continue in it without rejecting the norms of the society.[5]

The way in which people become labeled as homosexual can now be seen as an important social process connected with mechanisms of social control. It is important, therefore, that sociologists should examine this process objectively and not lend themselves to participation in it, particularly since, as we have seen, psychologists and psychiatrists on the whole have not retained their objectivity but become involved as diagnostic agents in the process of social labeling.[6]

It is proposed that the homosexual should be seen as playing a social role rather than as having a condition. The role of "homosexual," however, does not simply describe a sexual behavior pattern. If it did, the idea of a role would be no more useful than that of a condition. For the purpose of introducing the term "role" is to enable us to handle the fact that behavior in this sphere does not match popular beliefs: that sexual behavior patterns cannot be dichotomized in the way that the social roles of homosexual and heterosexual can.

It may seem rather odd to distinguish in this way between role and behavior, but if we accept a definition of role in terms of expectations (which may or may not be fulfilled), then the distinction is both legitimate and useful. In modern societies where a separate homosexual role is recognized, the expectation, on behalf of those who play the role and of others, is that a homosexual will be exclusively or very predominantly homosexual in his feelings and behavior. In addition, there are other expectations that frequently exist, especially on the part of non-homosexuals, but affecting the self-conception of anyone who sees himself as homosexual. These are: the expectation that he will be effeminate in manner, personality, or preferred sexual activity; the expectation that sexuality will play a part of some kind in all his relations with other men; and the expectation that he will be attracted to boys and very young men and probably willing to seduce them. The existence of a social expectation, of course, commonly helps to produce its own fulfillment. But the question of how far it is fulfilled is a matter for empirical investigation rather than a priori pronouncement. Some of the empirical evidence about the chief expectation—that homosexuality precludes heterosexuality—in relation to the homosexual role in America is examined in the final section of this paper.[7]

In order to clarify the nature of the role and demonstrate that it exists only in certain societies, we shall present the cross-cultural and historical evidence available. This raises awkward problems of method because the material has hitherto usually been collected and analyzed in terms of culturally specific modern western conceptions.

The Homosexual Role in Various Societies

To study homosexuality in the past or in other societies we usually have to rely on secondary evidence rather than on direct observation. The reliability and the validity of such evidence is open to question because what the original observers reported may have been distorted by their disapproval of homosexuality and by their definition of it, which may be different from the one we wish to adopt.

For example, Marc Daniel tries to refute accusations of homosexuality against Pope Julian II by producing four arguments: the Pope had many enemies who might wish to blacken his name; he and his supposed lover, Alidosi, both had mistresses; neither of them was at all effeminate; and the Pope had other men friends about whom no similar accusations were made.[8] In other words Daniel is trying to fit an early sixteenth century Pope to the modern conception of the homosexual as effeminate, exclusively homosexual, and sexual in relation to all men. The fact that he does not fit is, of course, no evidence, as Daniel would have it, that his relationship with Alidosi was not a sexual one.

Anthropologists too can fall into this trap. Marvin Opler, summarizing anthropological evidence on the subject, says:

Actually, no society, save perhaps Ancient Greece, pre-Meiji Japan, certain top echelons in Nazi Germany, and the scattered examples of such special status groups as the berdaches, Nata slaves, and one category of Chuckchee shamans, has lent sanction in any real sense to homosexuality.[9]

Yet he goes on to discuss societies in which there are reports of sanctioned adolescent and other occasional "experimentation." Of the Cubeo of the North West Amazon, for instance, he says, "*true* homosexuality among the Cubeo is rare if not absent," giving as evidence the fact that no males with persistent homosexual patterns are reported.[10]

Allowing for such weaknesses, the Human Relations Area Files are the best single source of comparative information. Their evidence on homosexuality has been summarized by Ford and Beach,[11] who identify two broad types of accepted patterns: the institutionalized homosexual role and the liaison between men or boys who are otherwise heterosexual.

The recognition of a distinct role of *berdache* or transvestite is, they say, "the commonest form of institutionalized homosexuality." This form shows a marked similarity to that in our own society, though in some ways it is even more extreme. The Mohave Indians of California and Arizona, for example,[12] recognized both an *alyhā,* a male transvestite who took the role of the woman in sexual intercourse, and a *hwamē,* a female homosexual who took the role of the male. People were believed to be born as *alyhā* or *hwamē,* hints of their future proclivities occuring in their mothers' dreams during pregnancy. If a young boy began to behave like a girl and take an interest in women's things instead of men's, there was an initiation ceremony in which he would become an *alyhā.* After that he would dress and act like a woman, would be referred to as "she" and could take "husbands."

But the Mohave pattern differs from ours in that although the *alyhā* was considered regrettable and amusing, he was not condemned and was given public recognition. The attitude was that "he was an *alyhā,* he could not help it." But the "husband" of an *alyhā* was an ordinary man who happened to have chosen an *alyhā,* perhaps because they were good housekeepers or because they were believed to be "lucky in love," and he would be the butt of endless teasing and joking.

This radical distinction between the feminine passive homosexual and his masculine active partner is one which is not made very much in our own society,[13] but which is very important in the Middle East. There, however, neither is thought of as being a "born" homosexual, although the passive partner, who demeans himself by his feminine submission, is despised and ridiculed, while the active one is not. In most of the ancient Middle East, including among the Jews until the return from the Babylonian exile, there were male temple prostitutes.[14] Thus even cultures that recognize a separate homosexual role may not define it in the same way as our culture does.

Many other societies accept or approve of homosexual liaisons as part of a variegated sexual pattern. Usually these are confined to a particular stage in the individual's life. Among the Aranda of Central Australia, for instance, there are long-standing relationships of several years' duration, between unmarried men and young boys, starting at the age of ten to twelve.[15] This is rather similar to the well-known situation in classical Greece, but there, of course, the older man could have a wife as well. Sometimes, however, as among the Siwans of North Africa,[16] all men and boys can and are expected to engage in homosexual activities, apparently at every stage of life. In all of these societies there may be much homosexual behavior, but there are no "homosexuals."

The Development of the Homosexual Role in England

The problem of method is even more acute in dealing with historical material than with anthropological, for history is usually concerned with "great events" rather than with recurrent patterns. There are some records of attempts to curb sodomy among minor churchmen during the medieval period,[17] which seem to indicate that it was common. At least they suggest that laymen feared on behalf of their sons that it was common. The term "catamite" meaning "boy kept for immoral purposes," was first used in 1593, again suggesting that this practice was common then. But most of the historical references to homosexuality relate either to great men or to great scandals. However, over the last seventy years or so various scholars have tried to trace the history of sex,[18] and it is possible to glean a good deal from what they have found and also from what they have failed to establish.

Their studies of English history before the seventeenth century consist usually of inconclusive speculation as to whether certain men, such as Edward II, Christopher Marlowe, William Shakespeare, were or were not homosexual. Yet the disputes are inconclusive not because of lack of evidence but because none of these men fits the modern stereotype of the homosexual.

It is not until the end of the seventeenth century that other kinds of

information become available and it is possible to move from speculations about individuals to descriptions of homosexual life. At this
period references to homosexuals as a type and to a rudimentary homosexual subculture, mainly in London, begin to appear. But the earliest descriptions of homosexuals do not coincide exactly with the modern conception. There is much more stress on effeminacy and in
particular in transvestism, to such an extent that there seems to be no
distinction at first between transvestism and homosexuality.[19] The
terms emerging at this period to describe homosexuals—Molly, Nancy-
boy, Madge-cull—emphasize effeminacy. In contrast the modern
terms—like fag, queer, gay, bent—do not have this implication.[20]

By the end of the seventeenth century, homosexual transvestites
were a distinct enough group to be able to form their own clubs in London.[21] Edward Ward's *History of the London Clubs*, published in 1709,
describes one called "The Mollies' Club" which met "in a certain tavern
in the City" for "parties and regular gatherings." The members
"adopt(ed) all the small vanities natural to the feminine sex to such an
extent that they try to speak, walk, chatter, shriek and scold as women
do, aping them as well in other respects." The other respects apparently included the enactment of marriages and child-birth. The club
was discovered and broken up by agents of the Reform Society.[22]
There were a number of similar scandals during the course of the
eighteenth century as various homosexual coteries were exposed.

A writer in 1729 describes the widespread homosexual life of the
period:

> They also have their Walks and Appointments, to meet and pick
> up one another, and their particular Houses of Resort to go to,
> because they dare not trust themselves in an open Tavern. About
> twenty of these sort of Houses have been discovered, besides the
> Nocturnal Assemblies of great numbers of the like vile Persons, what
> they call the *Markets,* which are the Royal Exchange, Lincoln's Inn,
> Bog Houses, the south side of St. James's Park, the Piazzas in Covent
> Garden, St. Clement's Churchyard, etc.
>
> It would be a pretty scene to behold them in their clubs and cabals,
> how they assume the air and affect the name of Madam or Miss,
> Betty or Molly, with a chuck under the chin, and "Oh, you bold
> pullet, I'll break your eggs," and then frisk and walk away.[23]

The notion of exclusive homosexuality became well-established during this period. When "two Englishmen, Leith and Drew, were accused
of paederasty. . . . The evidence given by the plaintiffs was, as was
generally the case in these trials, very imperfect. On the other hand the

defendants denied the accusation, and produced witnesses to prove their predeliction for women. They were in consequence acquitted." [24] This could only have been an effective argument in a society that perceived homosexual behavior as incompatible with heterosexual tastes.

During the nineteenth century there are further reports of raided clubs and homosexual brothels. However, by this time the element of transvestism had diminished in importance. Even the male prostitutes are described as being of masculine build and there is more stress upon sexual license and less upon dressing up and play-acting.

The Homosexual Role and Homosexual Behavior

Thus, a distinct, separate, specialized role of "homosexual" emerged in England at the end of the seventeenth century and the conception of homosexuality as a condition which characterizes certain individuals and not others is now firmly established in our society. The term role is, of course, a form of shorthand. It refers not only to a cultural conception or set of ideas but also to a complex of institutional arrangements which depend upon and reinforce these ideas. These arrangements include all the forms of heterosexual activity, courtship, and marriage as well as the labeling processes—gossip, ridicule, psychiatric diagnosis, criminal conviction—and the groups and networks of the homosexual subculture. For simplicity we shall simply say that a specialized role exists.

How does the existence of this social role affect actual behavior? And, in particular, does the behavior of individuals conform to the cultural conception in the sense that most people are either exclusively heterosexual or exclusively homosexual? It is difficult to answer these questions on the basis of available evidence because so many researchers have worked with the preconception that homosexuality is a condition, so that in order to study the behavior they have first found a group of people who could be identified as "homosexuals." Homosexual behavior should be studied independently of social roles, if the connection between the two is to be revealed.

This may not sound like a particularly novel program to those who are familiar with Kinsey's contribution to the field.[25] He, after all, set out to study "sexual behavior;" he rejected the assumptions of scientists and laymen:

. . . that there are persons who are "heterosexual" and persons who are "homosexual," that these two types represent antitheses in the sexual world and that there is only an insignificant class of "bisexuals" who occupy an intermediate position between the other groups

. . . that every individual is innately—inherently—either heterosexual or homosexual . . . (and) that from the time of birth one is fated to be one thing or the other. . . .[26]

But, although some of Kinsey's ideas are often referred to, particularly in polemical writings, surprisingly little use has been made of his actual data.

Most of Kinsey's chapter on the "Homosexual Outlet" [27] centers on his "heterosexual-homosexual rating scale." His subjects were rated on this scale according to the proportion of their "psychologic reactions and overt experience" that was homosexual in any given period of their lives. It is interesting, and unfortunate for our purposes, that this is one of the few places in the book where Kinsey abandons his behavioristic approach to some extent. However, "psychologic reactions" may well be expected to be affected by the existence of a social role in the same way as overt behavior. Another problem with using Kinsey's material is that although he gives very full information about sexual behavior, the other characteristics of the people he interviewed are only given in a very bald form.[28] But Kinsey's study is undoubtedly the fullest description there is of sexual behavior in any society and as such it is the safest basis for generalizations to other Western societies.

The ideal way to trace the effects on behavior of the existence of a homosexual role would be to compare societies in which the role exists with societies in which it does not. But as there are no adequate descriptions of homosexual behavior in societies where there is no homosexual role, we shall have to substitute comparisons within American society.

Polarization

If the existence of a social role were reflected in people's behavior, we should expect to find that relatively few people would engage in bisexual behavior. The problem about investigating this empirically is to know what is meant by "relatively few." The categories of Kinsey's rating scale are, of course, completely arbitrary. He has five bisexual categories, but he might just as well have had more or less, in which case the number falling into each would have been smaller or larger. The fact that the distribution of his scale is U-shaped, then, is in itself meaningless. (See Table 1).

It is impossible to get direct evidence of a polarization between the homosexual and the heterosexual pattern, though we may note the suggestive evidence to the contrary that at every age far more men have bisexual than exclusively homosexual patterns. However, by mak-

Table 1   Heterosexual–Homosexual Rating: Active Incidence by Age

	Percent of each age group of male population having each rating								
	[1]	[2]	[3]	[4]	[5]	[6]	[7]	[8]	[9]
Age	X	0	1	2	3	4	5	6	1–6
15	23.6	48.4	3.6	6.0	4.7	3.7	2.6	7.4	28.0
20	3.3	69.3	4.4	7.4	4.4	2.9	3.4	4.9	27.4
25	1.0	79.2	3.9	5.1	3.2	2.4	2.3	2.9	19.8
30	0.5	83.1	4.0	3.4	2.1	3.0	1.3	2.6	16.4
35	0.4	86.7	2.4	3.4	1.9	1.7	0.9	2.6	12.9
40	1.3	86.8	3.0	3.6	2.0	0.7	0.3	2.3	11.9
45	2.7	88.8	2.3	2.0	1.3	0.9	0.2	1.8	8.5

Source: Based on Kinsey (1948) p. 652, Table 148.

X = unresponsive to either sex; 0 = entirely heterosexual; 1 = largely heterosexual, but with incidental homosexual history; 2 = largely heterosexual but with a distinct homosexual history; 3 = equally heterosexual and homosexual; 4 = largely homosexual but with distinct heterosexual history; 5 = largely homosexual but with incidental heterosexual history; 6 = entirely homosexual.

ing comparisons between one age group and another and between men and women, it should be possible to see some of the effects of the role.

Age Comparison

As they grow older, more and more men take up exclusively heterosexual patterns, as Table 1, Column 2 shows. The table also shows that *each* of the bisexual and homosexual categories, columns 3–8, contains fewer men as time goes by after the age of 20. The greatest losses are from the fifth bisexual category, column 7, with responses that are "almost entirely homosexual." It is a fairly small group to begin with, but by the age of 45 it has almost entirely disappeared. On the other hand the first bisexual category, column 3, with only "incidental homosexual histories" has its numbers not even halved by the age of 45. Yet at all ages the first bisexual category represents a much smaller proportion of those who are almost entirely homosexual (columns 2 and 3) than the fifth category represents of those who are almost entirely homosexual (columns 7 and 8). In everyday language, it seems that proportionately more "homosexuals" dabble in heterosexual activity than "heterosexuals" dabble in homosexual activity and such dabbling is particularly common in the younger age groups of 20 to 30. This indicates that the existence of the despised role operates at all ages to inhibit people from engaging in occasional homosexual behavior, but does not have the effect of making the behavior of many "homosexuals" exclusively homosexual.

On the other hand, the overall reduction in the amount of homosex-

ual behavior with age can be attributed in part to the fact that more
and more men become married. While the active incidence of homosexual behavior is high and increases with age among single men,
among married men it is low and decreases only slightly with age. Unfortunately the Kinsey figures do not enable us to compare the incidence of homosexuality among single men who later marry and those
who do not.

Comparison of Men and Women

The notion of a separate homosexual role is much less well-developed
for women than it is for men and so too are the attendant techniques of
social control and the deviant subculture and organization. So a comparison with women's sexual behavior should tell us something about
the effects of the social role on men's behavior.

Fewer women than men engage in homosexual behavior. By the time
they are 45, 26 percent of women have had *some* homosexual experience, whereas about 50 percent of men have. But this is probably a
cause rather than an effect of the difference in the extent to which the
homosexual role is crystallized, for women engaged in less nonmarital
sexual activity of any kind than men. For instance, by the time they
marry 50 percent of women have had some pre-marital heterosexual
experience to orgasm, whereas as many as 90 percent of men have.

The most revealing contrast is between the male and female distributions on the Kinsey rating scale, shown in Table 2. The distributions
for women follow a smooth J-shaped pattern, while those for men are
uneven with an increase in numbers at the exclusively homosexual end.
The distributions for women are the shape that one would expect on

Table 2 Comparison of Male and Female Heterosexual-Homosexual Ratings:
Active Incidence at Selected Ages

		Percent of each age group having each rating								
	Age	[1] X	[2] 0	[3] 1	[4] 2	[5] 3	[6] 4	[7] 5	[8] 6	[9] 1–6
Male	20	3.3	69.3	4.4	7.4	4.4	2.9	3.4	4.9	27.4
Female		15	74	5	2	1	1	1	1	11
Male	35	0.4	86.7	2.4	3.4	1.9	1.7	0.9	2.6	12.9
Female		7	80	7	2	1	1	1	1	13

Source: Based on Kinsey (1948) p. 652, Table 148 and Kinsey (1953) p. 499, Table 142. For explanation of the ratings, see Table 1.

the assumption that homosexual and heterosexual acts are randomly distributed in a ratio of 1 to 18.[29] The men are relatively more concentrated in the exclusively homosexual category. This appears to confirm the hypothesis that the existence of the role is reflected in behavior.

Finally, it is interesting to notice that although at the age of 20 far more men than women have homosexual and bisexual patterns (27 percent as against 11 percent), by the age of 35 the figures are both the same (13 percent). Women seem to broaden their sexual experience as they get older whereas more men become narrower and more specialized.

None of this, however, should obscure the fact that, in terms of behavior, the polarization between the heterosexual man and the homosexual man is far from complete in our society. Some polarization does seem to have occurred, but many men manage to follow patterns of sexual behavior that are between the two, in spite of our cultural preconceptions and institutional arrangements.

Conclusion

This paper has dealt with only one small aspect of the sociology of homosexuality. It is, nevertheless, a fundamental one. For it is not until he sees homosexuals as a social category, rather than a medical or psychiatric one, that the sociologist can begin to ask the right questions about the specific content of the homosexual role and about the organization and functions of homosexual groups.[30] All that has been done here is to indicate that the role does not exist in many societies, that it only emerged in England towards the end of the seventeenth century, and that, although the existence of the role in modern America appears to have some effect on the distribution of homosexual behavior, such behavior is far from being monopolized by persons who play the role of homosexual.

11

Thomas S. Szasz

The Myth of Mental Illness

In the symbolic interaction framework, including dramaturgy and games analysis, expectations are significant determinants of what people do. The expectations held by others, as well as ourselves, come into play in helping us decide whether or not to follow a particular course of action, to use certain symbols instead of others, to play one role instead of another, or to choose or reject a particular strategy or tactic. Some expectations are *explicit*. They may even take written form, such as rules prohibiting stealing, murder, electronic eavesdropping, or forms of sexual relations deemed undesirable by the influential members of society. When explicit rules are broken, explicit sanctions are brought into play: Members of the law enforcement system go to work apprehending violators; workers are fired; spouses are divorced. Explicit labels are also attached to the violator: In the above cases, he or she might be called a thief, killer, spy, or sexual deviant.

Our behavior also comes under the influence of *implicit* expectations. These expectations, present in every encounter and governing much of what we do with one another, are what we learn "normal" members of society are like. Though they are so influential on our behavior, we are seldom aware of these background expectancies. Rather, they form part of the taken-for-granted assumptions with which we regularly engage in interaction. They involve such things as posture, spatial distance when speaking to others, eye contact, the "correct" way of gesturing, wearing clothing, withholding and showing anger and other emotions, and the various other ways that people in our culture assume are the "correct" ways of dealing with one another.

When someone persistently or bizarrely violates these implicit or background expectancies, and others find this violation disturbing to interaction, sanctions are brought into play. As with the violation of explicit rules, an offender might also be arrested, fired, divorced, or in some explicit fashion be subjected to the harsh wrath of others. The label likely to be attached to the violator, however, rather than being explicit, will probably take one of our many terms referring to mental illness, such as, "loony," "unhinged," "cracked," "nuts," or "touched."

According to sociological theory, mental illness is also a social role. One learns to act in ways which violate the assumptions others make of what normal people in society are like. Not included in the behaviors covered by this sociological theory are organically based failures to meet background expectancies. Brain damage and brain disease, for example, are *physical* abnormalities and come under the heading of physical illnesses, injuries, or disease.

The following article has been highly influential in shaping professional attitudes toward those whose behavior differs from majority expectations. Szasz analyzes ways people cope with problems in living which frequently result in the label of mental illness. This article changes the focus in the study of mental illness from searching the individual for causes of his problems to examining social sources for factors leading to the strain experienced by the individual. As such, though dealing with highly individualistic phenomena, Szasz is following the sociological imagination advocated by Mills.

□ My aim in this essay is to raise the question "Is there such a thing as mental illness?" and to argue that there is not. Since the notion of mental illness is extremely widely used nowadays, inquiry into the ways in which this term is employed would seem to be especially indicated. Mental illness, of course, is not literally a "thing"—or physical object—and hence it can "exist" only in the same sort of way in which other theoretical concepts exist. Yet, familiar theories are in the habit of posing, sooner or later—at least to those who come to believe in them—as "objective truths" (or "facts"). During certain historical periods, explanatory conceptions such as deities, witches, and microorganisms appeared not only as theories but as self-evident *causes* of a vast number of events. I submit that today mental illness is widely regarded in a somewhat similar fashion, that is, as the cause of innumerable diverse happenings. As an antidote to the complacent use of the notion of mental illness—whether as a self-evident phenomenon, theory, or cause—let us ask this question: What is meant when it is asserted that someone is mentally ill?

In what follows I shall describe briefly the main uses to which the concept of mental illness has been put. I shall argue that this notion has outlived whatever usefulness it might have had and that it now functions merely as a convenient myth.

Mental Illness as a Sign of Brain Disease

The notion of mental illness derives its main support from such phenomena as syphilis of the brain or delirious conditions—intoxications, for instance—in which persons are known to manifest various peculiarities or disorders of thinking and behavior. Correctly speaking, however, these are diseases of the brain, not of the mind. According to one school of thought, *all* so-called mental illness is of this type. The assumption is made that some neurological defect, perhaps a very subtle one, will ultimately be found for all the disorders of thinking and behavior. Many contemporary psychiatrists, physicians, and other scientists hold this view. This position implies that people *cannot* have troubles—expressed in what are *now called* "mental illnesses"—because of differences in personal needs, opinions, social aspirations, values, and so on. *All problems in living* are attributed to physiochemical processes which in due time will be discovered by medical research.

"Mental illnesses" are thus regarded as basically no different than all other diseases (that is, of the body). The only difference, in this view, between mental and bodily diseases is that the former, affecting the brain, manifest themselves by means of mental symptoms; whereas the latter, affecting other organ systems (for example, the skin, liver, etc.), manifest themselves by means of symptoms referable to those parts of the body. This view rests on and expresses what are, in my opinion, two fundamental errors.

In the first place, what central nervous system symptoms would correspond to a skin eruption or a fracture? It would *not* be some emotion or complex bit of behavior. Rather, it would be blindness or a paralysis of some part of the body. The crux of the matter is that a disease of the brain, analogous to a disease of the skin or bone, is a neurological defect, and not a problem in living. For example, a *defect* in a person's visual field may be satisfactorily explained by correlating it with certain definite lesions in the nervous system. On the other hand, a person's *belief*—whether this be a belief in Christianity, in Communism, or in the idea that his internal organs are "rotting" and that his body is, in fact, already "dead"—cannot be explained by a defect or disease of the nervous system. Explanations of this sort of occurrence—assuming that one is interested in the belief itself and does not regard it simply as a "symptom" or expression of something else that is *more interesting*—must be sought along different lines.

The second error in regarding complex psychosocial behavior, consisting of communications about ourselves and the world about us, as mere symptoms of neurological functioning is *epistemological*. In other words, it is an error pertaining not to any mistakes in observation or reasoning, as such, but rather to the way in which we organize and express our knowledge. In the present case, the error lies in making a symmetrical dualism between mental and physical (or bodily) symptoms, a dualism which is merely a habit of speech and to which no known observations can be found to correspond. Let us see if this is so. In medical practice, when we speak of physical disturbances, we mean either signs (for example, a fever) or symptoms (for example, pain). We speak of mental symptoms, on the other hand, when we refer to a patient's *communications about himself, others, and the world about him.* He might state that he is Napoleon or that he is being persecuted by the Communists. These would be considered mental symptoms *only* if the observer believed that the patient was *not* Napoleon or that he was *not* being persecuted by the Communists. This makes it apparent that the statement that "X is a mental symptom" involves rendering a judgment. The judgment entails, moreover, a covert comparison or matching of the patient's ideas, concepts, or beliefs with those of the observer and the society in which they live. The notion of mental symptom is therefore inextricably tied to the *social* (including *ethical*) *context* in which it is made in much the same way as the notion of bodily symptom is tied to an *anatomical* and *genetic context* (Szasz, 1957a, 1957b).

To sum up what has been said thus far: I have tried to show that for those who regard mental symptoms as signs of brain disease, the concept of mental illness is unnecessary and misleading. For what they mean is that people so labeled suffer from diseases of the brain; and, if that is what they mean, it would seem better for the sake of clarity to say that and not something else.

Mental Illness as a Name for Problems in Living

The term "mental illness" is widely used to describe something which is very different than a disease of the brain. Many people today take it for granted that living is an arduous process. Its hardship for modern man, moreover, derives not so much from a struggle for biological survival as from the stresses and strains inherent in the social intercourse of complex human personalities. In this context, the notion of mental illness is used to identify or describe some feature of an individual's so-called personality. Mental illness—as a deformity of the personality, so to speak—is then regarded as the *cause* of the human disharmony. It is implicit in this view that social intercourse between people is regarded as something *inherently harmonious,* its disturbance being due solely to the presence of "mental illness" in many people. This is obviously fallacious reasoning, for it makes the abstraction "mental illness" into a *cause*, even though this abstraction was created in the first place to serve only as a shorthand expression for certain types of human behavior. It now becomes necessary to ask: "What kinds of behavior are regarded as indicative of mental illness, and by whom?"

The concept of illness, whether bodily or mental, implies *deviation from some clearly defined norm*. In the case of physical illness, the norm is the structural and functional integrity of the human body. Thus, although the desirability of physical health, as such, is an ethical value, what health *is* can be stated in anatomical and physiological terms. What is the norm deviation from which is regarded as mental illness? This question cannot be easily answered. But whatever this norm might be, we can be certain of only one thing: namely, that it is a norm that must be stated in terms of *psychosocial, ethical,* and *legal* concepts. For example, notions such as "excessive repression" or "acting out an unconscious impulse" illustrate the use of psychological concepts for judging (so-called) mental health and illness. The idea that chronic hostility, vengefulness, or divorce are indicative of mental illness would be illustrations of the use of ethical norms (that is, the desirability of love, kindness, and a stable marriage relationship). Finally, the widespread psychiatric opinion that only a mentally ill person would commit homicide illustrates the use of a legal concept as a norm of mental health. The norm from which deviation is measured whenever one speaks of a mental illness is a *psychosocial and ethical one*. Yet, the remedy is sought in terms of *medical* measures which—it is hoped and assumed—are free from wide differences of ethical value. The definition of the disorder and the terms in which its remedy are sought are therefore at serious odds with one another. The practical significance of this covert conflict between the alleged nature of the defect and the remedy can hardly be exaggerated.

Having identified the norms used to measure deviations in cases of mental illness, we will now turn to the question: "Who defines the norms and hence the deviation?" Two basic answers may be offered: a. It may be the person himself (that is, the patient) who decides that he deviates from a norm. For example, an artist may believe that he suffers from a work inhibition; and he may implement this conclusion by seeking help *for* himself from a psychotherapist. b. It may be someone other than the patient who decides that the latter is deviant (for example, relatives, physicians, legal authorities, society generally, etc.). In such a case a psychiatrist may be hired by others to do something *to* the patient in order to correct the deviation.

These considerations underscore the importance of asking the question "Whose agent is the psychiatrist?" and of giving a candid answer to it (Szasz, 1956, 1958). The psychiatrist (psychologist or nonmedical psychotherapist), it now develops, may be the agent of the patient, of the relatives, of the school, of the military services, of a business organization, of a court of law, and so forth. In speaking of the psychiatrist as the agent of these persons or organizations, it is not implied that his values concerning norms, or his ideas and aims concerning the proper nature of remedial action, need to coincide exactly with those of his employer. For example, a patient in individual psychotherapy may believe that his salvation lies in a new marriage; his psychotherapist need not share this hypothesis. As the patient's agent, however, he must abstain from bringing social or legal force to bear on the patient which would prevent him from putting his beliefs into action. If his *contract* is with the patient, the psychiatrist (psychotherapist) may disagree with him or stop his treatment; but he cannot engage others to obstruct the patient's aspirations. Similarly, if a psychiatrist is engaged by a court to determine the sanity of a criminal, he need not fully share the legal authorities' values and intentions in regard to the criminal and the means available for dealing with him. But the psychiatrist is expressly barred from stating, for example, that it is not the criminal who is "insane" but the men who wrote the law on the basis of which the very actions that are being judged are regarded as "criminal." Such an opinion could be voiced, of course, but not in a courtroom, and not by a psychiatrist who makes it his practice to assist the court in performing its daily work.

To recapitulate: In actual contemporary social usage, the finding of a mental illness is made by establishing a deviance in behavior from certain psychosocial, ethical, or legal norms. The judgment may be made, as in medicine, by the patient, the physician (psychiatrist), or others. Remedial action, finally, tends to be sought in a therapeutic—or covertly medical—framework, thus creating a situation in which *psychosocial, ethical* and/or *legal deviations* are claimed to be correctible by (so-called) *medical action*. Since medical action is designed to correct only medical deviations, it seems logically absurd to expect that it will help solve problems whose very existence had been defined and established on nonmedical grounds. I think that these considerations may be fruitfully applied to the present use of tranquilizers and, more generally, to what might be expected of drugs of whatever type in regard to the amelioration or solution of problems in human living.

The Role of Ethics in Psychiatry

Anything that people *do*—in contrast to things that *happen* to them (Peters, 1958)—takes place in a context of value. In this broad sense, no human activity is devoid of ethical implications. When the values underlying certain activities are widely shared, those who participate in their pursuit may lose sight of them altogether. The discipline of medicine, both as a pure science (for example, research) and as a technology (for example, therapy), contains many ethical considerations and judgments. Unfortunately, these are often denied, minimized, or merely kept out of focus; for the ideal of the medical profession as well as of the people whom it serves seems to be having a system of medicine (allegedly) free of ethical value. This sentimental notion is expressed by such things as the doctor's willingness to treat and help patients irrespective of their religious or political beliefs, whether they are rich or poor, etc. While there may be some grounds for this belief—albeit it is a view that is not impressively true even in these regards—the fact remains that ethical considerations encompass a vast range of human affairs. By making the practice of medicine neutral in regard to some specific issues of value need not, and cannot, mean that it can be kept free from all such values. The practice of medicine is intimately tied to ethics; and the first thing that we must do, it seems to me, is to try to make this clear and explicit. I shall let this matter rest here, for it does not concern us specifically in this essay. Lest there be any vagueness, however, about how or where ethics and medicine meet, let me remind the reader of such issues as birth control, abortion, suicide, and euthanasia as only a few of the major areas of current ethicomedical controversy.

Psychiatry, I submit, is very much more intimately tied to problems of ethics than is medicine. I use the word "psychiatry" here to refer to that contemporary discipline which is concerned with *problems in living* (and not with diseases of the brain, which are problems for neurology). Problems in human relations can be analyzed, interpreted, and given meaning only within given social and ethical contexts. Accordingly, it *does* make a difference—arguments to the contrary notwithstanding— what the psychiatrist's socioethical orientations happen to be; for these will influence his ideas on what is wrong with the patient, what deserves comment or interpretation, in what possible directions change might be desirable, and so forth. Even in medicine proper, these factors play a role, as for instance, in the divergent orientations which physicians, depending on their religious affiliations, have toward such things as birth control and thereapeutic abortion. Can anyone really believe that a psychotherapist's ideas concerning religious belief, slavery, or other similar issues play no role in his practical work? If they do make a difference, what are we to infer from it? Does it not seem reasonable that we ought to have different psychiatric therapies—each expressly recognized for the ethical positions which they embody—for, say, Catholics and Jews, religious persons and agnostics, democrats and communists, white supremacists and Negroes, and so on? Indeed, if we look at how psychiatry is actually practiced today (especially in the United States), we find that people do seek psychiatric help in accordance with their social status and ethical beliefs (Hollingshead and Redlich, 1958). This should really not surprise us more than being told that practicing Catholics rarely frequent birth control clinics.

The foregoing position which holds that contemporary psychotherapists deal with problems in living, rather than with mental illnesses and their cures, stands in opposition to a currently prevalent claim, according to which mental illness is just as "real" and "objective" as bodily illness. This is a confusing claim since it is never known exactly what is meant by such words as "real" and "objective." I suspect, however, that what is intended by the proponents of this view is to create the idea in the popular mind that mental illness is some sort of disease entity, like an infection or a malignancy. If this were true, one could *catch* or *get* a "mental illness," one might *have* or *harbor* it, one might *transmit* it to others, and finally one could get *rid* of it. In my opinion, there is not a shred of evidence to support this idea. To the contrary, all the evidence is the other way and supports the view that what people now call mental illnesses are for the most part *communications* expressing unacceptable ideas, often framed, moreover, in an unusual idiom. The scope of this essay allows me to do no more than mention this alternative theoretical approach to this problem (Szasz, 1957c).

This is not the place to consider in detail the similarities and differences between bodily and mental illnesses. It shall suffice for us here to emphasize only one important difference between them: namely, that whereas bodily disease refers to public, physicochemical occurrences, the notion of mental illness is used to codify relatively more private, sociopsychological happenings of which the observer (diagnostician) forms a part. In other words, the psychiatrist does not stand *apart* from what he observes, but is, in Harry Stack Sullivan's apt words, a "participant observer." This means that he is *committed* to some picture of what he considers reality—and to what he thinks society considers reality—and he observes and judges the patient's behavior in the light of these considerations. This touches on our earlier observation that the notion of mental symptom itself implies a comparison between observer and observed, psychiatrist and patient. This is so obvious that I may be charged with belaboring trivialities. Let me therefore say once more that my aim in presenting this argument was expressly to criticize and counter a prevailing contemporary tendency to deny the moral aspects of psychiatry (and psychotherapy) and to substitute for them allegedly value-free medical considerations. Psychotherapy, for example, is being widely practiced as though it entailed nothing other than restoring the patient from a state of mental sickness to one of mental health. While it is generally accepted that mental illness has something to do with man's social (or interpersonal) relations, it is paradoxically maintained that problems of values (that is, of ethics) do not arise in this process.[1] Yet, in one sense, much of psychotherapy may revolve around nothing other than the elucidation and weighing of goals and values—many of which may be mutually contradictory—and the means whereby they might best be harmonized, realized, or relinquished.

The diversity of human values and the methods by means of which they may be realized is so vast, and many of them remain so unacknowledged, that they cannot fail but lead to conflicts in human relations. Indeed, to say that human relations at all levels—from mother to child, through husband and wife, to nation and nation—are fraught with stress, strain, and disharmony is, once again, making the obvious explicit. Yet, what may be obvious may be also poorly understood. This I think is the case here. For it seems to me that—at least in our scientific theories of behavior—we have failed to *accept* the simple fact that human relations are inherently fraught with difficulties and that to make them even relatively harmonious requires much patience and hard work. I submit that the idea of mental illness is now being put to work to obscure certain difficulties which at present may be inherent—not that they need be unmodifiable—in the social intercourse of persons. If this is true, the concept functions as a disguise; for instead of calling attention to conflicting human needs, aspirations, and values, the notion of mental illness provides an amoral and impersonal "thing" (an "illness") as an explanation for *problems in living* (Szasz, 1959). We may recall in this connection that not so long ago it was devils and witches who were held responsible for men's problems in social living. The belief in mental illness, as something other than man's trouble in getting along with his fellow man, is the proper heir to the belief in demonology and witchcraft. Mental illness exists or is "real" in exactly the same sense in which witches existed or were "real."

Choice, Responsibility, and Psychiatry

While I have argued that mental illnesses do not exist, I obviously did not imply that the social and psychological occurrences to which this label is currently being attached also do not exist. Like the personal and social troubles which people had in the Middle Ages, they are real enough. It is the labels we give them that concerns us and, having labelled them, what we do about them. While I cannot go into the ramified implications of this problem here, it is worth noting that a demonologic conception of problems in living gave rise to therapy along theological lines. Today, a belief in mental illness implies—nay, requires—therapy along medical or psychotherapeutic lines.

What is implied in the line of thought set forth here is something quite different. I do not intend to offer a new conception of "psychiatric illness" nor a new form of "therapy." My aim is more modest and yet also more ambitious. It is to suggest that the phenomena now called mental illnesses be looked at afresh and more simply, that they be removed from the category of illnesses, and that they be regarded as the expressions of man's struggle with the problem of *how* he should live. The last mentioned problem is obviously a vast one, its enormity reflecting not only man's inability to cope with his environment, but even more his increasing self-reflectiveness.

By problems in living, then, I refer to that truly explosive chain reaction which began with man's fall from divine grace by partaking of the fruit of the tree of knowledge. Man's awareness of himself and of the world about him seems to be a steadily expanding one, bringing in its wake an ever larger *burden of understanding* (an expression borrowed from Susanne Langer, 1953). *This burden, then, is to be expected and must not be misinterpreted.* Our only *rational* means for lightening it is *more understanding,* and appropriate *action* based on such understanding. The main alternative lies in acting as though the burden were not what in fact we perceive it to be and taking refuge in an outmoded theological view of man. In the latter view, man does not fashion his life and much of his world about him, but merely lives out his fate in a world created by superior beings. This may logically lead to pleading nonresponsibility in the face of seemingly unfathomable problems and difficulties. Yet, if man fails to take increasing responsibility for his actions, individually as well as collectively, it seems unlikely that some higher power or being would assume this task and carry this burden for him. Moreover, this seems hardly the proper time in human history for obscuring the issue of man's responsibility for his actions by hiding it behind the skirt of an all-explaining conception of mental illness.

Conclusions

I have tried to show that the notion of mental illness has outlived whatever usefulness it might have had and that it now functions merely as a convenient myth. As such, it is a true heir to religious myths in general, and to the belief in witchcraft in particular; the role of all these belief-systems was to act as *social tranquilizers,* thus encouraging the hope that mastery of certain specific problems may be achieved by means of sub-stitutive (symbolic-magical) operations. The notion of mental illness thus serves mainly to obscure the everyday fact that life for most peo-ple is a continuous struggle, not for biological survival, but for a "place in the sun," "peace of mind," or some other human value. For man aware of himself and of the world about him, once the needs for pre-serving the body (and perhaps the race) are more or less satisfied, the problem arises as to what he should do with himself. Sustained adher-ence to the myth of mental illness allows people to avoid facing this problem, believing that mental health, conceived as the absence of mental illness, automatically insures the making of right and safe choices in one's conduct of life. But the facts are all the other way. It is the making of good choices in life that others regard, retrospectively, as good mental health!

The myth of mental illness encourages us, moreover, to believe in its logical corollary: that social intercourse would be harmonious, satisfy-ing, and the secure basis of a "good life" were it not for the disrupting influences of mental illness or "psychopathology." The potentiality for universal human happiness, in this form at least, seems to me but another example of the I-wish-it-were-true type of fantasy. I do believe that human happiness or well-being on a hitherto unimaginably large scale, and not just for a select few, is possible. This goal could be achieved, however, only at the cost of many men, and not just a few being willing and able to tackle their personal, social, and ethical con-flicts. This means having the courage and integrity to forego waging battles on false fronts, finding solutions for substitute problems—for instance, fighting the battle of stomach acid and chronic fatigue instead of facing up to a marital conflict.

Our adversaries are not demons, witches, fate, or mental illness. We have no enemy whom we can fight, exorcise, or dispel by "cure." What we do have are *problems in living*—whether these be biologic, economic, political, or sociopsychological. In this essay I was concerned only with problems belonging in the last mentioned category, and within this group mainly with those pertaining to moral values. The field to which modern psychiatry addresses itself is vast, and I made no effort to en-compass it all. My argument was limited to the proposition that mental illness is a myth, whose function it is to disguise and thus render more palatable the bitter pill of moral conflicts in human relations.

References

HOLLINGSHEAD, A. B., AND REDLICH, F. C. *Social Class and Mental Illness*. New York: John Wiley & Sons, Inc., 1958.

JONES, E. *The Life and Work of Sigmund Freud*. Vol. III. New York: Basic Books, 1957.

LANGER, S. K. *Philosophy in a New Key*. New York: Mentor Books, 1953.

PETERS, R. S. *The Concept of Motivation*. London: Routledge & Kegan Paul, 1958.

SZASZ, T. S. Malingering: "Diagnosis" or Social Condemnation? *AMA Archives of Neurology and Psychiatry*, 1956, 76, 432–443.

SZASZ, T. S. *Pain and Pleasure: A Study of Bodily Feelings*. New York: Basic Books, 1957. (a)

SZASZ, T. S. The Problem of Psychiatric Nosology: A Contribution to a Situational Analysis of Psychiatric Operations. *American Journal of Psychiatry*, 1957, 114, 405–413. (b)

SZASZ, T. S. On the Theory of Psychoanalytic Treatment. *International Journal of Psycho-Analysis*, 1957, 38, 166–182. (c)

SZASZ, T. S. Psychiatry, Ethics and the Criminal Law. *Columbia Law Review*, 1958, 58, 193–198.

SZASZ, T. S. Moral Conflict and Psychiatry. *Yale Review*, 1959.

12

Albert K. Cohen
James F. Short Jr.

Delinquent Subcultures

When sociologists attempt to understand the "why" of human behavior, they do not search for a single cause. Human behavior is extremely complex, and seldom, if ever, is behavior due to just one "cause." Certain factors may be more important than others in influencing some specific behavior, but always many factors are involved.

As we saw in the preceding article, some people violate background expectancies, or residual rules, which most of us meet as a matter of course. This frequently leads to the label of mental illness being applied to the violator. Possible reasons for violations of implicit assumptions of interaction include organic bases, subcultural learning, individuated or idiosyncratic learning experiences, stress, anger, pain, and accident, as well as attempts at humor and the desire to hurt, embarrass, or ridicule others. Any of these factors could be the major underlying reason for the violation of residual rules.

So it also is with adequately accounting for violations of explicit rules, such as acts of juvenile delinquency. No single factor suffices. Many factors are involved, and they work in combination. To explain involvement in juvenile delinquency, one would include such variables as where juveniles in a particular culture find themselves relative to other age groups, the values in the culture whose violation results in the label of juvenile delinquent, problems of access to material goods, norms and values of the peer group, policing activities by the various agents of formal social control, involvements in alternative activi-

From Albert K. Cohen and James F. Short, Jr., "Research in Delinquent Subcultures," in *Journal of Social Issues*, vol. 14, no. 3, pp. 20–37. Copyright 1958 by the Society for the Psychological Study of Social Issues. Reprinted by permission.

ties, and ways in which delinquent involvement meets the perceived needs of the individual. So complex is human behavior that even answering all these problematic areas would not produce a complete account of delinquent involvement.

In the following article, Cohen and Short focus on the subcultures of delinquency. They especially analyze how values and expectations lead to law-breaking behavior. Note that as with the behaviors described in the earlier articles by Horton and Mead, one can understand human behavior only by seeing how people view their own situations. The behavior of others, indeed, frequently does not even make sense if we look at it only in terms of our own experiences in life. A major sociological lesson is to "take the role of the other," that is, to put oneself in someone else's shoes in order to see how the world looks from that vantage point. Taking the role of others yields a different understanding of human behavior, one essential to a sociological imagination.

Delinquent Subcultures: Male
The Parent Male Subculture

This is what the book, *Delinquent Boys,* calls "the" delinquent subculture. It has been described as non-utilitarian, malicious, negativistic, versatile, and characterized by short-run hedonism and group autonomy. We refer to it as the parent subculture because it is probably the most common variety in this country—indeed, it might be called the "garden variety" of delinquent subculture—and because the characteristics listed above seem to constitute a common core shared by other important variants. However, in addition, these variants possess distinctive attributes or emphases which are not fully accounted for by the argument of *Delinquent Boys.* We believe the parent subculture is a working-class subculture. This position, however, is open to question and we shall consider the matter further in our discussion of the middle-class subculture.

The Conflict-Oriented Subculture

This is the subculture most prominent in the news today and is probably regarded by many laymen as the typical form which delinquency takes. In its highly developed forms it has the following characteristics. It is a culture of large gangs, whose membership numbers ordinarily in the scores and may run into the hundreds; in this respect contrasting to the parent subculture, whose members consist of small gangs or cliques. These gangs have a relatively elaborate organization, including such differentiated roles as president, vice-president, war-chief, and armorer. The gang may be subdivided into sub-gangs on an age or territorial basis and may have alliances with other gangs. These gangs have names, a strong sense of corporate identity, a public personality or "rep" in the gang world. The gang is identified with a territory or "turf" which it tries to defend or to extend. The status of the gang is largely determined by its toughness, that is, its readiness to engage in physical conflict with other gangs and its prowess in intergang "rumbles." Although fighting occupies but a small portion of the gang's time, "heart" or courage in fighting is the most highly prized virtue and the most important determinant of the position of gang members within the gang as well as that of the gang among other gangs. Fighting within the gang is regulated by a code of fairness; gang members, however, are relatively unconstrained by any concepts of chivalry or fairness in warfare with other gangs. To demonstrate "heart" it is not necessary to give the other fellow a decent chance or to show forbearance toward an outnumbered or defeated enemy. There is evident ambivalence about fighting; it is not a simple outpouring of accumulated aggression. Members are afraid of rumbles, and are frequently relieved when police intervention prevents a scheduled rumble, but the ethic of the gang requires the suppression of squeamishness, an outward demeanor of toughness, and a readiness to defend turf and rep with violence and even brutality. In their other activities, these gangs exhibit the general characteristics of the delinquent subculture. Drinking, sex, gambling, stealing, and vandalism are prominent. Such gangs include a wide age range. They are concentrated in sections of the city that are highly mobile, working-class, impoverished, and characterized by a wide variety of indices of disorganization.

This is the full-blown conflict gang. Although large conflict gangs may be found in many cities, it is doubtful that the degree of organization, including the officers and functionaries, found in the New York gangs is to be found elsewhere. Probably more common than the type of gang described here is a form intermediate between the conflict gang and the parent subculture: a loosely organized and amorphous coalition of cliques with only a vague sense of corporate identity, coalescing sporadically and frequently for displays of open violence. But the reality of gangs in New York and in other cities, similar to those we have described, cannot be doubted.

The Drug Addict Subculture

What we know of this subculture is derived primarily from two large-scale research projects conducted in New York and Chicago respectively. Although these studies do not agree in all respects, especially with reference to etiological questions, it is clear that the subculture which centers around the use of narcotic drugs provides a markedly distinct way of life. Both studies are agreed that drug addiction and criminality go hand-in-hand, that addiction arises in communities where delinquency is already endemic, that most juvenile addicts— although not all—were delinquent prior to their addiction. They are agreed that the addict eschews the more violent forms of delinquency—rape, assault, gang warfare, "general hellraising"—and prefers income-producing forms of delinquency, which are essential to the support of a drug habit in a society in which drugs are obtainable only in an illegal market and at great cost. The addict subculture, therefore, in contrast to the parent and the conflict gang cultures, has a marked utilitarian quality, but this utilitarianism is in support of and a precondition of the addict way of life.

The kinship of the addict and other delinquent subcultures is brought out in the finding of the New York study that addicts are usually members of organized gangs and share the general philosophy of those gangs. After the onset of addiction, however, their participation in the more violent and disorderly activities of the gangs is reduced and they tend to cluster in cliques on the periphery of the gangs. There is little moral disapproval of drug use on the part of gang members, but it is usually discouraged and the status of the addict within the larger gang is lowered on the practical grounds that addiction lowers the value of the addict to the group. The reports of the Chicago investigators, however, suggest that they were studying a more "mature" addict subculture, one that is not peripheral to more "conventional" subcultures and in a merely tolerated status, but one that has achieved a higher degree of autonomy, with a loose and informal but independent organization, enjoying a relatively high status in the communities within which it flourishes. The Chicago addict, as described, is not a hanger-on of a conflict gang but moves proudly in the world of the "cats." The characteristics of the cat culture are suggested in the reports of the New York study, but are elaborately and richly described in the Chicago reports. Central to the cat culture is the "kick," defined by Finestone as "any act tabooed by 'squares' that heightens and intensifies the present moment of experience and differentiates it as much as possible from the humdrum routine of daily life," and the "hustle," defined as "any nonviolent means of making some bread (money) which does not require work." Heroin is "the greatest kick of them all"; pimping, conning, pickpocketing, and such are approved and respectable hustles. Both the kick and the hustle, notes Finestone, are in direct antithesis to the central values of the dominant culture. The cat cultivates an image of himself as "cool," self-possessed, assured, and quietly competent, places great value upon the esthetic amenities of clothes and music, and possesses a discriminating and critical taste.

Both studies locate the addict subculture in those areas of the city which are most deprived, of the lowest socio-economic status, most lacking in effective adult controls—characterized by extensive family disorganization, high mobility, and recently arrived populations. Addiction characteristically occurs after the age of sixteen and is most heavily concentrated among the most-discriminated-against minority groups, especially Negroes.

Semi-Professional Theft

The word "professional" is not intended to connote the "professional thief" of Sutherland's description. The latter represents the elite of the criminal underworld, skilled, sophisticated, nonviolent, specialized. It is intended to suggest, rather, a stage in a life history which has been described by Sutherland and Cressey as proceeding "from trivial to serious, from occasional to frequent, from sport to business, and from crimes committed by isolated individuals or by very loosely organized groups to crime committed by rather tightly organized groups." This sequence appears to characterize especially "persons who in young adult life become robbers and burglars." The earlier stage of this sequence describes what we have called the parent subculture. Most participants in this subculture appear to drop out or to taper off after the age of sixteen or seventeen. A minority, however, begin to differentiate themselves from their fellows, at about this age, and to move in the direction of more utilitarian, systematic, and pecuniary crime—what we are calling "semi-professional theft."

Systematic research on this pattern, as a differentiated variant or offspring of the parent subculture, is scanty. . . . Preliminary analysis strongly suggests that the following characteristics, all presumptive evidence of a strong utilitarian emphasis, tend to go together with the later stages of a long history of frequent stealing which began at an early age:

a. the use of strong-arm methods (robbery) of obtaining money.

b. the *sale* of stolen articles, *versus* using for oneself, giving or throwing away, or returning stolen articles.

c. stating, as a reason for continued stealing, "want things" or "need money" *versus* stealing for excitement, because others do it, because they like to, or for spite.

In the areas studied, this semi-professional stealing appears to be more of a differentiation of emphasis within a more diversified climate of delinquency than an autonomous subculture independently organized. Boys who show the characteristics listed above commonly participate in nonutilitarian delinquency as well; *e.g.*, giving or throwing away stolen articles or indicating that they steal for excitement, because they like to, or for spite. Furthermore, they belong to gangs the majority of whose members may engage in predominantly non-utilitarian delinquency. It seems probable, although it has not been demonstrated, that the semi-professional thieves constitute cliques within the larger gangs and that they are differentiated from other delinquents in the same gangs with respect to other characteristics than patterns of stealing alone. We would surmise that, to the degree to which stealing becomes rational, systematic, deliberate, planned, and pursued as a primary source of income, it becomes incompatible with anarchic, impulsive, mischievous, and malicious characteristics of non-utilitarian delinquent subcultures and that its practitioners tend to segregate themselves into more professionally oriented and "serious-minded" groups. This, however, is speculation and is a subject for further research.

The Middle-Class Delinquent Subculture

Thus far we have distinguished subcultures primarily on empirical grounds; that is, investigators have observed the differences we have described. Middle-class delinquency commonly takes a subcultural form as well, but there is as yet no firm basis in research for ascribing to it a different content from that of the parent male subculture. We distinguish it rather on theoretical grounds; since none of the problems of adjustment to which the working-class subcultures seem to constitute plausible and intelligible responses appear to be linked with sufficient frequency to middle-class status, we assume that middle-class subcultures arise in response to problems of adjustment which are characteristic products of middle-class socialization and middle-class life situations. The notion that different patterns of behavior may be "functionally equivalent" solutions to the same or similar problems is familiar. We are suggesting that the same or similar patterns of behavior may be "functionally versatile" solutions to different problems of adjustment. However, we are persuaded that further research will reveal subtle but important differences between working-class and middle-class patterns of delinquency. It seems probable that the qualities of malice, bellicosity, and violence will be underplayed in the middle-class subcultures and that these subcultures will emphasize more the deliberate courting of danger (suggested by the epithet

"chicken") and a sophisticated, irresponsible, "playboy" approach to activities symbolic, in our culture, of adult roles and centering largely
around sex, liquor, and automobiles.

Determinants of the Male Subcultures

A fully satisfactory theory of delinquent subcultures must specify the
different problems of adjustment to which each of these subcultures is
a response, and the ways in which the social structure generates these
problems of adjustment and determines the forms which the solutions
take.

Definitive theory can grow only out of research specifically concerned with differences among these subcultures. Such research is in its
infancy. For example, it is not possible to determine from the published literature what are the characteristics of the cities in which the
conflict gang appears and of those in which it does not; the specific
characteristics which differentiate urban areas in which delinquency assumes this form and those in which it does not; or the specific characteristics of the children who become involved in this sort of delinquency and of those who do not. There is a literature, most of it
growing out of the work of the New York City Youth Board, which is
valuable and suggestive. Little of this literature, however, employs a
systematic comparative perspective designed to throw light on the *differential* characteristics of this subculture and its social setting. With respect to the conditions which favor the emergence of a semi-professional subculture, the literature is practically silent. On the matter of
middle-class delinquency, there is an enormous emotional to-do and
vocal alarm, but little more. There is a great need of case studies of
middle-class delinquent groups, including detailed descriptions of the
specific quality of their delinquencies and the behavioral context and
community settings of these delinquencies. It is interesting that some of
our most adequate and illuminating research concerns the drug addict
subculture, which is numerically perhaps the least significant delinquent subculture and is restricted to a few sections of our larger cities,
although where it appears it is a grave social problem and is most omi-
nous for the young people who are caught up in it.

To us, the subculture of the conflict gang is the most baffling. Several
years ago Solomon Kobrin suggested, on the basis of his intimate
knowledge of delinquency in Chicago, the differential characteristics of
areas in which delinquency assumes the semi-professional form, and of
those in which it assumes a violent, "hoodlum," conflict form. These

differences he described as differences in the degree of integration between the conventional and criminal value systems. In areas in which adults are engaged in consistently profitable and highly organized illegal enterprises and also participate in such conventional institutions as churches, fraternal and mutual benefit societies, and political parties, criminal adult role models have an interest in helping to contain excesses of violence and destructiveness; in these areas youngsters may perceive delinquency as a means to the acquisition of skills which are useful to the achievement of conventional values and which may, as a matter of fact, lead to a career in the rackets, and to prestige in the community. Here delinquency tends to assume a relatively orderly, systematic, rational form. We suspect that this type of area is relatively rare and that the pattern of semi-professional theft is correspondingly rare, as compared with the occurrence of the parent and hoodlum-type patterns. In a contrasting type of area adults may violate the law, but this violation is not systematic and organized, and the criminal and conventional value systems do not mesh through the participation of criminals in the conventional institutions. "As a consequence, the delinquency in areas of this type tends to be unrestrained by controls originating *at any point* in the adult social structure." Delinquency takes on a wild, untrammeled, violent character. "Here groups of delinquents may be seen as excluded, isolated conflict groups dedicated to an unending battle against all forms of restraint."

This is the kind of provocative formulation of which we stand much in need. However, Kobrin's formulations have not, to our knowledge, led to research to test their validity. Furthermore, although this formulation specifies the kind of breakdown of controls under which a conflict subculture can flourish, it does not account for the positive motivation to large-scale organized gangs, the warlike relationships between gangs, and the idealization of toughness, relatively unregulated by an intergang code of chivalry and fairness. It is a defect of many of our theories of delinquency that they try to account for delinquency by demonstrating the absence of effective restraints. Delinquency, however, and certainly this particular form of delinquency, cannot be assumed to be a potentiality of human nature which automatically erupts when the lid is off. Nor do we believe that the emphasis on conflict can be explained as a way of expressing and channelizing aggression accumulated through a variety of frustrations. We do not deny either the frustrations or the aggression of many of the youngsters in this subculture. But it is apparent from the reports of workers that the violence we see is as much a matter of conformity, sometimes in the face of great fear and reluctance, to a highly compulsive group-enforced ideal of toughness as it is a simple outburst of pent-up hostility. We will not at this point add our own speculations to those of others. It is our purpose here merely to indicate the nature of the problem.

It is a matter for further research to determine the extent to which the patterns we have described, and other patterns, are *variants* of a common subculture or subcultures, with qualitatively distinct etiologies, or *quantitative extremes* of the common subculture with the same variables accounting for their existence and their extremity. In this paper we have chosen to describe these patterns as variants. The description of these variants, and their accounting, in etiological research and theory, is the major task of the larger project of which this paper is a partial report.

With respect to the drug addict subculture, the New York and Chicago investigators present different interpretations, and it is an interesting challenge to theory to account for these differences or to reconcile them. The New York investigators state unequivocally that "All juvenile drug addicts are severely disturbed individuals," and that "adolescents who become addicts have deep-rooted, major personality disorders." Specifically, they suffer from a weak ego, an inadequately functioning superego, and inadequate masculine identification. These defects, in turn, can be traced to family experiences. Up to the age of sixteen or so these boys do not behave very differently from the ordinary gang delinquent. At about this age the emotionally healthy youngsters develop a new conception of themselves consistent with age-graded role definitions and expectations in our culture. The gang activities become kid stuff, the gang begins to break up, the boy begins to organize his life around a job, his girl, his future. "It is at this stage that those members or hangers-on who are too disturbed emotionally to face the future as adults find themselves seemingly abandoned by their old cronies and begin to feel increasingly anxious." They take to the use of drugs because drugs help to reduce anxieties resulting from personal incapacity and because they make it easy to deny and to avoid facing deep-seated personal problems.

The Chicago investigators, on the contrary, question the concept of the addict as a "sick person," whose addiction is a symptom of personality defects. They emphasize, on the one hand, the breakdown of controls which occurs in areas which "are characterized by a high density of a recently arrived and largely unsettled population," and whose residents cannot mobilize effectively to secure law enforcement against even that behavior which offends their own standards. They emphasize, on the other hand, the problems of adjustment which are a function of the social position of the populations within those areas, the problems, that is, of the most depressed sectors of the most disadvantaged minority groups, who are increasingly sensitized to the values, goals, and conceptions of success of the dominant social order but who are categorically excluded from the opportunity for legitimately achieving them. Since they are denied participation, except in a servile and unrewarding capacity, in those activities which are defined by the dominant institutional order as the legitimate, "serious," and really important activities, these groups turn their back on this order and the sober virtues which it enjoins, and make a virtue and an ideal of "play," of irresponsible, autonomous, hedonically oriented activity which seeks its consummation and reward in the extraction of the maximum "kick" from the present moment. The problems of adjustment to which the cat culture is a response are not a function of a pathological character structure; they are socially structured strains endemic in the lower-class urban Negro and other minority group populations.

How are we to account for the contrast between the two interpretations? It is possible that one or the other represents faulty speculation which is not in keeping with the data and which is a product of a sociologistic or psychologistic bias. However, both grow out of responsible, systematic research and neither can be lightly dismissed as an autistic distortion of the plain facts. It is possible that the two populations studied cannot be equated, that we are dealing with two different addict subcultures. It is possible, also, that the cat culture described by the Chicago researchers is a logical extreme of the gradual isolation from the more conventional gangs which is documented by the New York studies. This still does not explain the differences noted in the two studies, however. It is further possible that the two sets of conclusions are not mutually exclusive. With respect to the Chicago study we may make two observations: (1) it is always a minority of young people in any given area who become addicts, and therefore there must be selective processes at work in addition to those stressed by the Chicago investigators; (2) the methods of the Chicago study were not designed to reveal the kinds of data concerning personality structure to which the New York investigators attach such importance. It may well be that, without regard to individual peculiarities and abnormalities, the social setting described in the Chicago reports is one in which the addict subculture is attractive and possible, but that, within this general setting, the attractiveness of this response is further enhanced for those with the character structure described in the New York reports. Furthermore, it is possible that this kind of character structure occurs with exceptionally high frequency in lower-class Negro areas. A family constellation of floating, irresponsible males centering around a hard-working, overburdened mother is common in this segment of the Negro population, and it is the sort of constellation that might be expected to produce the weak ego, inadequately functioning superego, and inadequate masculine identification that are ascribed to the addict's personality. In short, it is possible, although it is still speculative, that the methods of the two studies illuminate different aspects of the same reality.

In *Delinquent Boys,* it was suggested that the middle-class delinquent subculture is a response to ambivalence and anxiety in the area of sex-role identification, aggravated by the prolonged dependence of the boy upon his family, and the indefinite postponement of adult self-sufficiency and self-determination. This interpretation has been questioned by Wilensky and Lebeaux who argue that anxiety about male identity is greater in the *lower class.* The working-class delinquent subculture, therefore, is determined by both status anxiety and sex-role anxiety; the middle-class subculture is determined by anxiety about becoming a man, an adult. Wilensky and Lebeaux conclude that this theory would predict even sharper contrasts between working-class and middle-class delinquency than the official statistics would show.

A recent study based on self-reported behavior of western and midwestern high school students does not support this prediction or suggest that there is any significant difference in middle-class and working-class delinquency rates in the several communities studied. The same findings might not obtain in large urban areas or noncaucasian populations, which were not studied, but at least in this one respect the findings are not consistent with inference from the Wilensky and Lebeaux hypothesis. This argument does not lack plausibility, however, and research is obviously necessary to decide between what are, at this point, rival speculations.

In an effort to account for the apparent increase in middle-class delinquency, Cohen suggested that, as a result of changes in the structure of our economy, labor market, and school system, the traditional deferred gratification pattern of the middle-class boy is breaking down. In an economy of scarcity this pattern of deferred gratification did, as a matter of fact, "pay off." It was a prerequisite to movement through the schools and to the economic opportunities to which the schools were an avenue. Furthermore, middle-class parents could point to the obviously greater economic affluence of themselves in contrast to the unskilled and generally unprotected mass of working class people. Thus, with support from parents, the economy, and the school, the "college boy" way of life, to use Whyte's felicitous phrase, was inculcated in middle-class children and in working-class children who aspired to "better themselves." This pattern was incompatible with commitment to a delinquent way of life. . . .

Sociologists have pointed out that our society provides no well-defined role for adolescence, a period in the child's life when the problem of establishing his personal identity becomes especially crucial. With the weakening of the deferred gratification pattern, the choice among alternatives as the boy seeks to fill this status void is more likely to become a delinquent choice. When he tries to establish his identity as an adult, or as a man, he finds the "conventional," the "respectable," the "responsible" criteria of adult status denied him. Hence, he tends to symbolize his adulthood by irresponsible, hedonically oriented behavior involving the courting of danger, liquor, sex, cars, etc.

Still other changes in society and in child rearing patterns, especially among middle-class parents, may have contributed to an increase in delinquency in this class of youngsters. These changes have to do with the relatively greater independence from each other of family members as a result of the economic changes we have talked about, the democratization of family relations, vacillation in child rearing philosophy as a result of increasing concern with what the "experts" in the field have to say (together with vacillation on the part of the latter), and the "cult of youth" which holds that all pain, especially psychic pain, is injurious to children and that it is the responsibility of parents to minimize pain and frustration for their children. All of these things require documentation in the form of carefully conducted research. All, however, appear to weaken the deferred gratification pattern of socialization and the authority of parental figures, to retard the internalization of authority, to reduce the ability to tolerate frustration, and to contribute to an increase in delinquency among middle-class children.

This is, perhaps, more than enough speculation on the conditions which migh facilitate the formation of middle-class delinquent subcultures. The saddest commentary, however, is that we are faced with a poverty of speculation, without which there can be no meaningful research, without which, in turn, there can be no conclusions that are more than speculation.

Delinquent Subcultures: Female

With a very few exceptions, the professional literature on female delinquency is of little help in determining how, in what ways, and to what extent that delinquency is subculturally patterned. There is little on what this delinquency actually consists of, other than that it usually involves sexual misconduct of some kind; or on the relationships of the girls to the boys and men with whom they are involved, and how these relationships, as well as the girls' relationships to other peers of both sexes, are affected by their sexual behavior; or on the contexts of other activities; or on other characteristics of the social settings within which sexual episodes occur. It is our position that the meaning and function, for the persons concerned, of any form of delinquent behavior can only be inferred from rich and detailed descriptive data about the behavior itself, about its position in a larger context of interaction, and about how it is perceived and reacted to by the actor himself and by other participants in that interactive context. These data are largely lacking for female delinquency.

In *Delinquent Boys* Cohen suggested the socially structured motivations to participation in what might be called a female parent delinquent subculture. He argues that a girl's status depends largely upon the status of the males with whom she is identified; that, in order to achieve respectability, a girl must be able to attract the "honorable" attention of respectable and responsible males; that many girls, especially of lower socioeconomic status, have not been trained in the arts and graces and lack the material means necessary for competing successfully for such attentions; that such girls, despairing of respectable marriage and social mobility, are inclined to seek reassurance of their sense of adequacy *as girls* by abandoning their reputation for chastity, which has proven, for them, an unrewarding virtue, and by making themselves sexually available; that they gain, thereby, the assurance of male attention and male favors, albeit within transitory and unstable relationships which further lower their value on the marriage market. Like its male counterpart, this pattern represents the rejection of conventional and respectable but unattainable status goals and the disciplines which lead to them, and the substitution therefor of the satisfactions to be obtained in the immediate present with the resources presently available. The complete mechanism whereby the social structure generates this subculture is surely much more complex than this, but the argument is intended only to suggest a common core of motivation which goes far to explain the characteristic sexual content of this subculture and, indeed, of female delinquency in general.

Not only is little known about this parent subculture. With perhaps one exception, still less is known about the numerous varieties of female delinquent subcultures, except that they exist. There are gangs of girls organized for and around sexual activities; there are mixed groups of middle- and upper-middle-class boys and girls organized as sex gangs, with an emphasis on refinement, gentility, and sophistication; and there are gangs of girls strongly resembling the male hoodlum gang. At the present time little can be said, even in a descriptive way, about any of these.

It is possible to say a little more about the female drug addict subculture, on the basis of our analysis of interview material gathered in the course of the Chicago drug use study, and of material in preparation for a Master's degree thesis at the University of Chicago. The observations to be set forth here are tentative and will be more fully elaborated in a later publication.

The girls whose interviews we have read are predominantly Negro, of low social status, and located in the same type of area as that from which the male addicts characteristically come. However, some of them come from relatively respectable and well-off Negro families and there are no strikingly obvious common patterns, sequences, or problems of adjustment exhibited by all the cases. However, certain features recur with impressive frequency. Almost all of these girls have had difficulty in establishing satisfactory relationships with the other sex, although for divers reasons. A theme which runs through history after history is isolation from the main stream of normal, relaxed, boy-girl relationships, loneliness, depression, and a pathetic yearning for marriage to a stable, responsible, respectable man. These girls appear to fall prey easily to exploitative and irresponsible men, who exercise extraordinary power over them apparently because of the girls' need for male companionship and love, or a simulacrum thereof. Pregnancy, desertion, and "hustling" occur with monotonous regularity. The girl may be introduced to opiate drugs by other girls, by male companions, or in mixed groups of "fast" company. The nature of these circumstances is such that the girls often find themselves isolated, depressed, and threatened. These conditions heighten their dependence on the drug and upon social contacts which assure the completion of the cycle.

After addiction, hustling on a full time basis in order to support her habit and sometimes her lover's habit is almost invariable. During the period of addiction her range of associates is almost entirely narrowed to other addicts and prostitutes, but her relationships with even these people are likely to be tangential and incidental to the procurement of the drug, and to her profession. A vicious cycle is characteristic of all the histories we have read: addiction and prostitution lead to a further isolation from respectable society and a lowering of status; these, in turn, increase loneliness and depression and the girl's vulnerability to exploitation by men; and these, in turn, encourage continuation in or relapse into the use of drugs.

Although these girls move on the fringes of the cat culture, they do not, we think, participate fully in it. They are not "fast, noisy, aggressive cats," seeking status among other cats through their kicks and their hustle. They are not proud of their habit and their hustle is strictly business, frequently a distasteful one. Without exception, these girls express a desire for respectability, but they find it difficult to escape from the vicious circle in which they have become entrapped.

Summary

It is apparent that we have barely stepped over the threshold of the study of delinquent subcultures. The purpose of this paper has been to enumerate some of the principal varieties of these subcultures, to describe or to suggest some of their important features, to speculate on their origins, to indicate the types of research and theoretical work which are most needed, and to provide some suggestive hypotheses to be tested or revised by later research.

13

Peter M. Blau

The Exchange
of
Social Rewards

As people interact with one another, they follow a course of action designed to bring them the greatest possible pay-offs. This is the basic assumption of social exchange theory. People are viewed as highly rational beings who evaluate alternative courses of action, weigh their potential rewards and costs, and choose those holding the promise of the highest value or net reward (the reward of an activity minus its cost).

All activities involve rewards and costs. Rewards are whatever an individual finds rewarding. Not everyone finds the same things rewarding; even when they do, they seldom find them rewarding to the same degree. Similarly, costs must also be defined from the framework of the individual, as not everyone finds the same things costly to the same degree. Costs center on what an individual dislikes about some activity, but they also include activities foregone; that is, activities which the individual would have liked to do but had to give up for another activity are also costs.

By anticipating net reward, then, an individual chooses and rejects activities. As many of the previous selections have pointed out to us, in social exchange theory one must also gain the perspective of the persons one is studying. It is their perspectives, their definitions of rewards and costs, which will determine their involvement or non-involvement in activities.

In order to understand human behavior, however, it is also vitally necessary to supplement the individual's perspective. The individuals involved in a situation see the world from only highly limited and limiting circumstances. Consequently, they are wearing blinders which open to them certain perceptions and definitions but close others. To understand the structural sources of such limitations requires that the social analyst go beyond the individual. He must also obtain information on social class membership, as well as cultural and subcultural values, expectations, and other orientations which so greatly affect the way people view their situations in life.

To do this, he might supplement social exchange theory with perspectives gained from linguistics, historical and cross-cultural data, studies in social stratification, and from dramaturgy and games analysis. Just as there is no single cause which adequately accounts for what people do, so there is no single theoretical perspective yet developed which adequately accounts for human behavior. The perspectives we currently have must be worked in combination if we are to understand social life.

In the following selection, Blau applies the social exchange perspective to everyday life situations. He demonstrates how seeking rewards in the form of social approval permeates our daily activities, including our intimate relations.

> By Honour, in its proper and genuine Signification, we mean nothing else but the good Opinon of others. . . .
>
> The Reason why there are so few Men of real Virtue, and so many of real Honour, is, because all the Recompence a Man has of a virtuous Action, is the Pleasure of doing it, which most People reckon but poor Pay; but the Self-denial a Man of Honour submits to in one Appetite, is immediately rewarded by the Satisfaction he receives from another, and what he abates of his Avarice, or any other Passion, is doubly repaid to his Pride. . . .
>
> MANDEVILLE, *The Fable of the Bees*

Most human pleasures have their roots in social life. Whether we think of love or power, professional recognition or sociable companionship, the comforts of family life or the challenge of competitive sports, the gratifications experienced by individuals are contingent on actions of others. The same is true for the most selfless and spiritual satisfactions. To work effectively for a good cause requires making converts to it. Even the religious experience is much enriched by communal worship. Physical pleasures that can be experienced in solitude pale in significance by comparison. Enjoyable as a good dinner is, it is the social occasion that gives it its luster. Indeed, there is something pathetic about the person who derives his major gratification from food or drink as such, since it reveals either excessive need or excessive greed; the pauper illustrates the former, the glutton, the latter. To be sure, there are profound solitary enjoyments—reading a good book, creating a piece of art, producing a scholarly work. Yet these, too, derive much of their significance from being later communicated to and shared with others. The lack of such anticipation makes the solitary activity again somewhat pathetic: the recluse who has nobody to talk to about what he reads; the artist or scholar whose works are completely ignored, not only by his contemporaries but also by posterity.

Much of human suffering as well as much of human happiness has its source in the actions of other human beings. One follows from the other, given the facts of group life, where pairs do not exist in complete isolation from other social relations. The same human acts that cause pleasure to some typically cause displeasure to others. For one boy to enjoy the love of a girl who has committed herself to be his steady date, other boys who had gone out with her must suffer the pain of having been rejected. The satisfaction a man derives from exercising power over others requires that they endure the deprivation of being subject to his power. For a professional to command an outstanding reputation in his field, most of his colleagues must get along without such pleasant recognition, since it is the lesser professional esteem of the majority that defines his as outstanding. The joy the victorious team members experience has its counterpart in the disappointment of the losers. In short, the rewards individuals obtain in social associations tend to entail a cost to other individuals. This does not mean that most social associations involve zero-sum games in which the gains of some rest on the losses of others. Quite the contrary, individuals associate with one another because they all profit from their association. But they do not necessarily all profit equally, nor do they share the cost of providing the benefits equally, and even if there are no direct costs to participants there are often indirect costs borne by those excluded from the association, as the case of the rejected suitors illustrates.

Some social associations are intrinsically rewarding. Friends find pleasure in associating with one another, and the enjoyment of whatever they do together—climbing a mountain, watching a football game—is enhanced by the gratification that inheres in the association itself. The mutual affection between lovers or family members has the same result. It is not what lovers do together but their doing it *together* that is the distinctive source of their special satisfaction—not seeing a play but sharing the experience of seeing it. Social interaction in less intimate relations than those of lovers, family members, or friends, however, may also be inherently rewarding. The sociability at a party or among neighbors or in a work group involves experiences that are not especially profound but are intrinsically gratifying. In these cases, all associates benefit simultaneously from their social interaction, and the only cost they incur is the indirect one of giving up alternative opportunities by devoting time to the association.

Social associations may also be rewarding for a different reason. Individuals often derive specific benefits from social relations because their associates deliberately go to some trouble to provide these benefits for them. Most people like helping others and doing favors for them— to assist not only their friends but also their acquaintances and occasionally even strangers, as the motorist who stops to aid another with his stalled car illustrates. Favors make us grateful, and our expressions of gratitude are social rewards that tend to make doing favors enjoyable, particularly if we express our appreciation and indebtedness publicly and thereby help establish a person's reputation as a generous and competent helper. Besides, one good deed deserves another. If we feel grateful and obligated to an associate for favors received, we shall seek to reciprocate his kindness by doing things for him. He in turn is likely to reciprocate, and the resulting mutual exchange of favors strengthens, often without explicit intent, the social bond between us.

A person who fails to reciprocate favors is accused of ingratitude. This very accusation indicates that reciprocation is expected, and it serves as a social sanction that discourages individuals from forgetting their obligations to associates. Generally, people are grateful for favors and repay their social debts, and both their gratitude and their repayment are social rewards for the associate who has done them favors.[1] The fact that furnishing benefits to others tends to produce these social rewards is, of course, a major reason why people often go to great trouble to help their associates and enjoy doing so. We would not be human if these advantageous consequences of our good deeds were not important inducements for our doing them.[2] There are, to be sure, some individuals who selflessly work for others without any thought of reward and even without expecting gratitude, but these are virtually saints, and saints are rare. The rest of us also act unselfishly sometimes, but we require some incentive for doing so, if it is only the social acknowledgment that we are unselfish.

An apparent "altruism" pervades social life; people are anxious to benefit one another and to reciprocate for the benefits they receive. But beneath this seeming selflessness an underlying "egoism" can be discovered; the tendency to help others is frequently motivated by the expectation that doing so will bring social rewards. Beyond this self-interested concern with profiting from social associations, however, there is again an "altruistic" element or, at least, one that removes social transactions from simple egoism or psychological hedonism. A basic reward people seek in their associations is social approval, and selfish disregard for others makes it impossible to obtain this important reward.[3]

The social approval of those whose opinions we value is of great significance to us, but its significance depends on its being genuine. We cannot force others to give us their approval, regardless of how much power we have over them, because coercing them to express their admiration or praise would make these expressions worthless. "Action can be coerced, but a coerced show of feeling is only a show." [4] Simulation robs approval of its significance, but its very importance makes associates reluctant to withhold approval from one another and, in particular, to express disapproval, thus introducing an element of simulation and dissimulation into their communications. As a matter of fact, etiquette prescribes that approval be simulated in disregard of actual opinions under certain circumstances. One does not generally tell a hostess, "Your party was boring," or a neighbor, "What you say is stupid." Since social conventions require complimentary remarks on many occasions, these are habitually discounted as not reflecting genuine approbation, and other evidence that does reflect it is looked for, such as whether guests accept future invitations or whether neighbors draw one into further conversations.

In matters of morality, however, individuals have strong convictions that constrain them to voice their actual judgments more freely. They usually do not hesitate to express disapproval of or, at least, withhold approval from associates who have violated socially accepted standards of conduct. Antisocial disregard for the welfare of the ingroup meets universally with disapprobation regardless of how immoral, in terms of the mores of the wider community, the norms of a particular group may be. The significance of social approval, therefore, discourages conduct that is utterly and crudely selfish. A more profound morality must rest not merely on group pressure and long-run advantage but primarily on internalized normative standards. In the ideal case, an individual unerringly follows the moral commands of his conscience whatever the consequences. While such complete morality is attained only by the saint and the fool, and most men make some compromises,[5] moral standards clearly do guide and restrain human conduct. Within the rather broad limits these norms impose on social relations, however, human beings tend to be governed in their associations with one another by the desire to obtain social rewards of various sorts, and the resulting exchanges of benefits shape the structure of social relations.

The question that arises is whether a rationalistic conception of human behavior underlies this principle that individuals pursue social rewards in their social associations. The only assumption made is that human beings choose between alternative potential associates or courses of action by evaluating the experiences or expected experiences with each in terms of a preference ranking and then selecting the best alternative. Irrational as well as rational behavior is governed by these considerations, as Boulding has pointed out:

> All behavior, in so far as the very concept of behavior implies doing one thing rather than another, falls into the above pattern, even the behavior of the lunatic and the irrational or irresponsible or erratic person. The distinction between rational and irrational behavior lies in the degree of self-consciousness and the stability of the images involved rather than in any distinction of the principle of optimum.[6]

What is explicitly *not* assumed here is that men have complete information, that they have no social commitments restricting their alternatives, that their preferences are entirely consistent or remain constant, or that they pursue one specific ultimate goal to the exclusion of all others. These more restrictive assumptions, which are not made in the present analysis, characterize rationalistic models of human conduct, such as that of game theory.[7] Of particular importance is the fact that men strive to achieve diverse objectives. The statement that men select the most preferred among available alternatives does not imply that they always choose the one that yields them the greatest material profit.[8] They may, and often do, choose the alternative that requires them to make material sacrifices but contributes the most to the attainment of some lofty ideal, for *this* may be their objective. Even in this choice they may err and select an alternative that actually is not the best means to realize their goal. Indeed, the need to anticipate in advance the social rewards with which others will reciprocate for favors in exchange relations inevitably introduces uncertainty and recurrent errors of judgment that make perfectly rational calculations impossible. Granted these qualifications, the assumption that men seek to adjust social conditions to achieve their ends seems to be quite realistic, indeed inescapable. . . .

4
Social Control and Social Change

Some of the farthest-reaching control exerted over others is accomplished not by force but by the manipulation of symbols. If those in power are able to control a people's definitions of reality, they are able to maintain a firm grip on their elite positions. Attempting to control reality through controlling definitions appears to characterize social institutions everywhere. To this end, many governments attempt to monopolize the means of mass communication. If they attain this control, they then possess effective means for directing interpretations of reality singularly favorable to their own continuance in power.

The first article in this section treats a social institution which is extremely powerful in fostering definitions of reality. The legal institution is not only buttressed by force, but through it the codifications under which we live are formulated. These codifications give shape to much of our reality. They dictate in a formal manner what behaviors are right and wrong, determining much of what we can and cannot do. All of us become subject to these dictates. What happens to definitions of reality and to consequent behavior when someone is formally brought before the bar of justice is the topic of Blumberg's analysis.

In the second article we turn to another powerful social institution, that of the political, as manifested through activities of the Pentagon. In some of his writings Mills analyzed the coalescing interests of the top leaders of the major institutions in our society, those of the military, political, and industrial sectors. He said that the top echelons of these social institutions were becoming increasingly interchangeable, that their merged interests had made them highly interdependent. He warned that we are consequently increasingly coming under the control of these top leaders without a balancing of interests and power elsewhere. Melman analyzes some of the strategies Pentagon officials have used in their rapid and escalating consolidation of power.

The social institution in which the greatest physical control was brought to bear was that of slavery. Persons coming under the dominance of this institution were literally captives—not only was reality defined for them, but so was almost every aspect of their lives. Only at the literal risk of life and limb could a slave attempt to become independent of this totally encapsulating institution. The slave system as practiced in the United States, however, was not the only form this institution took. Though still slavery, in some other countries it took a milder form. Elkins compares slavery in the United States with slavery in Brazil and the rest of Latin America, providing us a comparative context for viewing this aspect of our cultural background.

Racism developed out of slavery. Justifications were put forth to legitimate the continued bondage of a people. The characteristics slaves developed in their adaptation to slavery were also put forward as reasons for their continued enslavement. A whole racist ideology became highly developed and was actively taught, ultimately becoming a basic part of the American consciousness. The legacy of slavery is still with us, continuously affecting both the ways different peoples interact with one another and their perceptions of the other. Racist ideology also serves yet today as a major means of justifying dominant and subdominant positions. In the fourth article in this section, Perucci and Pilisuk examine some of the interrelationships between racism and poverty in the contemporary United States.

Discrimination is also regularly experienced by female Americans, regardless of their race. This discrimination on the basis of sexual membership is another major means of social control. It keeps one group in the dominant position, provides low-cost labor for low skilled positions, and makes a large proportion of the population feel that they are uniquely qualified on the basis of their sex to be the servants of the dominant sex. The historical relationship between the sexes is political, that is, it is based on the exercise of power—power wielded by one group to maintain their privileged position at the expense of a second group kept in a subservient position. It is this political relationship between the sexes that Millett examines in her article.

Social change takes place in many ways. Breakthroughs in technology occur, and people adapt their life ways to their changed circumstances. The world shrinks in size with the development of speedy, long-range transportation and almost instantaneous communications. Cultures once separated by aeons now come into regular contact with one another. Adaptations result which modify and in some cases destroy ways of life centuries old. Conflicts between nations force developments in military technology which are later applied to the civilian population. Further change occurs as a result of this application, in this case likely to be in the direction of increased surveillance and population containment capabilities.

Other changes occur over a long period of time. People's ideas of what they have a right legitimately to expect in life, for example, undergo gradual modification. When dissatisfactions become focused and people come to share sentiments regarding the source of their problems and the areas and direction of desired change, a social movement is probably in the offing. It is this type of social change that Blumer analyzes in the last article in this section.

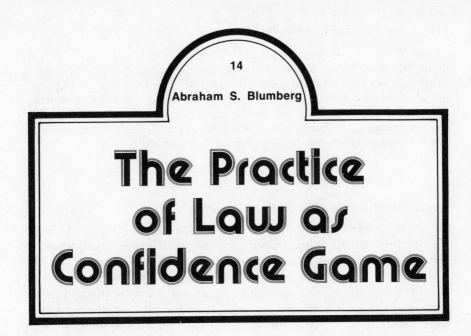

14

Abraham S. Blumberg

The Practice of Law as Confidence Game

Reality has an objective basis, that is, there are indeed things "out there." But the meanings given to the "things out there" are social constructions; it is people who construct meanings. They give whatever meanings they desire to the things, objects, events, and relationships in their worlds of experience. Through the use of symbols, especially linguistic symbols, people both construct and maintain meanings. By using the symbols they construct, they then create and sustain definitions of a situation. This process of the symbolic construction and maintenance of social meanings is characteristic of all peoples throughout the world.

Because meaning is a human construction, symbols lend themselves well to the manipulation of meaning. By bringing various symbols into play, people attempt to control the definitions others hold. In previous selections we have already seen examples of this use of symbols. We have seen how people use symbols to control others through language, to communicate emotions, to express disapproval of sexual practices, and to distort reality.

In this article Blumberg examines the practice of law in terms of a confidence game. In a confidence game, "con men" gain the confidence of a victim or "mark," usually for the purpose of relieving him of property. Conning always involves the fraudulent staging of reality in order to gain the confidence of the victim. Reality can be staged in any number of ways, as what we view as reality does not depend primarily on the "things out there" but on the way

From Abraham S. Blumberg, "The Practice of Law as Confidence Game: Organizational Cooptation of a Profession," in *Law & Society Review*, vol. 1, issue 2 (June, 1967), pp. 18–31. Reprinted by permission of The Law and Society Association and Abraham S. Blumberg.

those "things out there" are defined. Con men manipulate symbols in order to sustain a desired definition of reality. If successful, they then gain control over the situation. As we have seen in preceding selections, manipulating symbols for purposes of control is a common feature of everyday life in which we all routinely engage. But fraudulently manipulating symbols for social or interpersonal control purposes is a confidence game, or "conning."

Court Structure Defines Role of Defense Lawyer

. . . The overwhelming majority of convictions in criminal cases (usually over 90 per cent) are not the product of a combative, trial-by-jury process at all, but instead merely involve the sentencing of the individual after a negotiated, bargained-for plea of guilty has been entered.[1] Although more recently the overzealous role of police and prosecutors in producing pretrial confessions and admissions has achieved a good deal of notoriety, scant attention has been paid to the organizational structure and personnel of the criminal court itself. Indeed, the extremely high conviction rate produced without the features of an adversary trial in our courts would tend to suggest that the "trial" becomes a perfunctory reiteration and validation of the pretrial interrogation and investigation.[2]

The institutional setting of the court defines a role for the defense counsel in a criminal case radically different from the one traditionally depicted.[3] Sociologists and others have focused their attention on the deprivations and social disabilities of such variables as race, ethnicity, and social class as being the source of an accused person's defeat in a criminal court. Largely overlooked is the variable of the court organization itself, which possesses a thrust, purpose, and direction of its own. It is grounded in pragmatic values, bureaucratic priorities, and administrative instruments. These exalt maximum production and the particularistic career designs of organizational incumbents, whose occupational and career commitments tend to generate a set of priorities. These priorities exert a higher claim than the stated ideological goals of "due process of law," and are often inconsistent with them.

Organizational goals and discipline impose a set of demands and conditions of practice on the respective professions in the criminal court, to which they respond by abandoning their ideological and professional commitments to the accused client, in the service of these higher claims of the court organization. All court personnel, including the accused's own lawyer, tend to be coopted to become agent-mediators[4] who help the accused redefine his situation and restructure his perceptions concomitant with a plea of guilty.

Of all the occupational roles in the court the only private individual who is officially recognized as having a special status and concomitant obligations is the lawyer. His legal status is that of "an officer of the court" and he is held to a standard of ethical performance and duty to his client as well as to the court. This obligation is thought to be far higher than that expected of ordinary individuals occupying the various occupational statuses in the court community. However, lawyers, whether privately retained or of the legal-aid, public defender variety, have close and continuing relations with the prosecuting office and the court itself through discreet relations with the judges via their law secretaries or "confidential" assistants. Indeed, lines of communication, influence and contact with those offices, as well as with the Office of the Clerk of the court, Probation Division, and with the press, are essential to present and prospective requirements of criminal law practice. Similarly, the subtle involvement of the press and other mass media in the court's organizational network is not readily discernible to the casual observer. Accused persons come and go in the court system schema, but the structure and its occupational incumbents remain to carry on their respective career, occupational and organizational enterprises. The individual stridencies, tensions, and conflicts a given accused person's case may present to all the participants are overcome, because the formal and informal relations of all the groups in the court setting require it. The probability of continued future relations and interaction must be preserved at all costs.

This is particularly true of the "lawyer regulars" *i.e.*, those defense lawyers, who by virtue of their continuous appearances in behalf of defendants, tend to represent the bulk of a criminal court's non-indigent case workload, and those lawyers who are not "regulars," who appear almost casually in behalf of an occasional client. Some of the "lawyer regulars" are highly visible as one moves about the major urban centers of the nation, their offices line the back streets of the courthouses, at times sharing space with bondsmen. Their political "visibility" in terms of local club house ties, reaching into the judge's chambers and prosecutor's office, are also deemed essential to successful practitioners. Previous research has indicated that the "lawyer regulars" make no effort to conceal their dependence upon police, bondsmen, jail personnel. Nor do they conceal the necessity for maintaining intimate relations with all levels of personnel in the court setting as a means of obtaining, maintaining, and building their practice. These informal relations are the *sine qua non* not only of retaining a practice, but also in the negotiation of pleas and sentences.[5]

The client, then, is a secondary figure in the court system as in certain other bureaucratic settings.[6] He becomes a means to other ends of the organization's incumbents. He may present doubts, contingencies, and pressures which challenge existing informal arrangements or disrupt them; but these tend to be resolved in favor of the continuance of the organization and its relations as before. There is a greater community of interest among all the principal organizational structures and their incumbents than exists elsewhere in other settings. The accused's lawyer has far greater professional, economic, intellectual and other ties to the various elements of the court system than he does to his own client. In short, the court is a closed community.

This is more than just the case of the usual "secrets" of bureaucracy which are fanatically defended from an outside view. Even all elements of the press are zealously determined to report on that which will not offend the board of judges, the prosecutor, probation, legal-aid, or other officials, in return for privileges and courtesies granted in the past and to be granted in the future. Rather than any view of the matter in terms of some variation of a "conspiracy" hypothesis, the simple explanation is one of an ongoing system handling delicate tensions, managing the trauma produced by law enforcement and administration, and requiring almost pathological distrust of "outsiders" bordering on group paranoia.

The hostile attitude toward "outsiders" is in large measure engendered by a defensiveness itself produced by the inherent deficiencies of assembly line justice, so characteristic of our major criminal courts. Intolerably large caseloads of defendants which must be disposed of in an organizational context of limited resources and personnel, potentially subject the participants in the court community to harsh scrutiny from appellate courts, and other public and private sources of condemnation. As a consequence, an almost irreconcilable conflict is posed in terms of intense pressures to process large numbers of cases on the one hand, and the stringent ideological and legal requirements of "due process of law," on the other hand. A rather tenuous resolution of the dilemma has emerged in the shape of a large variety of bureaucratically ordained and controlled "work crimes," short cuts, deviations, and outright rule violations adopted as court practice in order to meet production norms. Fearfully anticipating criticism on ethical as well as legal grounds, all the significant participants in the court's social structure are bound into an organized system of complicity. This consists of a work arrangement in which the patterned, covert, informal breaches, and evasions of "due process" are institutionalized, but are, nevertheless, denied to exist.

These institutionalized evasions will be found to occur to some degree, in all criminal courts. Their nature, scope and complexity are largely determined by the size of the court, and the character of the community in which it is located, *e.g.,* whether it is a large, urban institution, or a relatively small rural county court. In addition, idiosyncratic, local conditions may contribute to a unique flavor in the character and quality of the criminal law's administration in a particular community. However, in most instances a variety of stratagems are employed—some subtle, some crude, in effectively disposing of what are often too large caseloads. A wide variety of coercive devices are employed against an accused-client, couched in a depersonalized, instrumental, bureaucratic version of due process of law, and which are in reality a perfunctory obeisance to the ideology of due process. These include some very explicit pressures which are exerted in some measure by all court personnel, including judges, to plead guilty and avoid trial. In many instances the sanction of a potentially harsh sentence is utilized as the visible alternative to pleading guilty, in the case of recalcitrants. Probation and psychiatric reports are "tailored" to organizational needs, or are at least responsive to the court organization's requirements for the refurbishment of a defendant's social biography, consonant with his new status. A resourceful judge can, through his subtle domination of the proceedings, impose his will on the final outcome of a trial. Stenographers and clerks, in their function as record keepers, are on occasion pressed into service in support of a judicial need to "rewrite" the record of a courtroom event. Bail practices are usually employed for purposes other than simply assuring a defendant's presence on the date of a hearing in connection with his case. Too often, the discretionary power as to bail is part of the arsenal of weapons available to collapse the resistance of an accused person. The foregoing is a most cursory examination of some of the more prominent "short cuts" available to any court organization. There are numerous other procedural strategies constituting due process deviations, which tend to become the work style artifacts of a court's personnel. Thus, only court "regulars" who are "bound in" are really accepted; others are treated routinely and in almost a coldly correct manner.

The defense attorneys, therefore, whether of the legal-aid, public defender variety, or privately retained, although operating in terms of pressures specific to their respective role and organizational obligations, ultimately are concerned with strategies which tend to lead to a plea. It is the rational, impersonal elements involving economies of time, labor, expense and a superior commitment of the defense counsel to these rationalistic values of maximum production [7] of court organization that prevail, in his relationship with a client. The lawyer "regulars" are frequently former staff members of the prosecutor's office and utilize the prestige, know-how and contacts of their former affiliation as part of their stock in trade. Close and continuing relations between the lawyer "regular" and his former colleagues in the prosecutor's office generally overshadow the relationship between the regular and his client. The continuing colleagueship of supposedly adversary counsel rests on real professional and organizational needs of a *quid pro quo,* which goes beyond the limits of an accommodation or *modus vivendi* one might ordinarily expect under the circumstances of an otherwise seemingly adversary relationship. Indeed, the adversary features which are manifest are for the most part muted and exist even in their attenuated form largely for external consumption. The principals, lawyer and assistant district attorney, rely upon one another's cooperation for their continued professional existence, and so the bargaining between them tends usually to be "reasonable" rather than fierce.

Fee Collection and Fixing

The real key to understanding the role of defense counsel in a criminal case is to be found in the area of the fixing of the fee to be charged and its collection. The problem of fixing and collecting the fee tends to influence to a significant degree the criminal court process itself, and not just the relationship of the lawyer and his client. In essence, a lawyer-client "confidence game" is played. A true confidence game is unlike the case of the emperor's new clothes wherein that monarch's nakedness was a result of inordinate gullibility and credulity. In a genuine confidence game, the perpetrator manipulates the basic dishonesty of his partner, the victim or mark, toward his own (the confidence operator's) ends. Thus, "the victim of a con scheme must have some larceny in his heart." [8]

Legal service lends itself particularly well to confidence games. Usually, a plumber will be able to demonstrate empirically that he has performed a service by clearing up the stuffed drain, repairing the leaky faucet or pipe—and therefore merits his fee. He has rendered, when summoned, a visible, tangible boon for his client in return for the requested fee. A physician, who has not performed some visible surgery or otherwise engaged in some readily discernible procedure in connection with a patient, may be deemed by the patient to have "done nothing" for him. As a consequence, medical practitioners may simply prescribe or administer by injection a placebo to overcome a patient's potential reluctance or dissatisfaction in paying a requested fee, "for nothing."

In the practice of law there is a special problem in this regard, no matter what the level of the practitioner or his place in the hierarchy of prestige. Much legal work is intangible either because it is simply a few words of advice, some preventive action, a telephone call, negotiation of some kind, a form filled out and filed, a hurried conference with another attorney or an official of a government agency, a letter or opinion written, or a countless variety of seemingly innocuous, and even prosaic procedures and actions. These are the basic activities, apart from any possible court appearance, of almost all lawyers, at all levels of practice. Much of the activity is not in the nature of the exercise of the traditional, precise professional skills of the attorney such as library resarch and oral argument in connection with appellate briefs, court motions, trial work, drafting of opinions, memoranda, contracts, and other complex documents and agreements. Instead, much legal activity, whether it is at the lowest or highest "white shoe" law firm levels, is of the brokerage, agent, sales representative, lobbyist type of activity, in which the lawyer acts for someone else in pursuing the latter's interests and designs. The service is intangible.[9]

The large scale law firm may not speak as openly of their "contacts," their "fixing" abilities, as does the lower level lawyer. They trade instead upon a facade of thick carpeting, walnut panelling, genteel low pressure, and superficialities of traditional legal professionalism. There are occasions when even the large firm is on the defensive in connection with the fees they charge because the services rendered or results obtained do not appear to merit the fee asked.[10] Therefore, there is a recurrent problem in the legal profession in fixing the amount of fee, and in justifying the basis for the requested fee.

Although the fee at times amounts to what the traffic and the conscience of the lawyer will bear, one further observation must be made with regard to the size of the fee and its collection. The defendant in a criminal case and the material gain he may have acquired during the course of his illicit activities are soon parted. Not infrequently the ill gotten fruits of the various modes of larceny are sequestered by a defense lawyer in payment of his fee. Inexorably, the amount of the fee is a function of the dollar value of the crime committed, and is frequently set with meticulous precision at a sum which bears an uncanny relationship to that of the net proceeds of the particular offense involved. On occasion, defendants have been known to commit additional offenses while at liberty on bail, in order to secure the requisite funds with which to meet their obligations for payment of legal fees. Defense lawyers condition even the most obtuse clients to recognize that there is a firm interconnection between fee payment and the zealous exercise of professional expertise, secret knowledge, and organizational "connections" in their behalf. Lawyers, therefore, seek to keep their clients in a proper state of tension, and to arouse in them the precise edge of anxiety which is calculated to encourage prompt fee payment. Consequently, the client attitude in the relationship between defense counsel and an accused is in many instances a precarious admixture of hostility, mistrust, dependence, and sycophancy. By keeping his client's anxieties aroused to the proper pitch, and establishing a seemingly causal relationship between a requested fee and the accused's ultimate extrication from his onerous difficulties, the lawyer will have established the necessary preliminary groundwork to assure a minimum of haggling over the fee and its eventual payment.

In varying degrees, as a consequence, all law practice involves a manipulation of the client and a stage management of the lawyer-client relationship so that at least an *appearance* of help and service will be forthcoming. This is accomplished in a variety of ways, often exercised in combination with each other. At the outset, the lawyer-professional employs with suitable variation a measure of sales-puff which may range from an air of unbounding selfconfidence, adequacy, and dominion over events, to that of complete arrogance. This will be supplemented by the affectation of a studied, faultless mode of personal attire. In the larger firms, the furnishings and office trappings will serve as the backdrop to help in impression management and client intimidation. In all firms, solo or large scale, an access to secret knowledge, and to the seats of power and influence is inferred, or presumed to a varying degree as the basic vendible commodity of the practitioners.

The lack of visible end product offers a special complication in the course of the professional life of the criminal court lawyer with respect to his fee and in his relations with his client. The plain fact is that an accused in a criminal case always "loses" even when he has been exonerated by an acquittal, discharge, or dismissal of his case. The hostility of an accused which follows as a consequence of his arrest, incarceration, possible loss of job, expense and other traumas connected with his case is directed, by means of displacement, toward his lawyer. It is in this sense that it may be said that a criminal lawyer never really "wins" a case. The really satisfied client is rare, since in the very nature of the situation even an accused's vindication leaves him with some degree of dissatisfaction and hostility. It is this state of affairs that makes for a lawyer-client relationship in the criminal court which tends to be a somewhat exaggerated version of the usual lawyer-client confidence game.

At the outset, because there are great risks of nonpayment of the fee, due to the impecuniousness of his clients, and the fact that a man who is sentenced to jail may be a singularly unappreciative client, the criminal lawyer collects his fee *in advance*. Often, because the lawyer and the accused both have questionable designs of their own upon each other, the confidence game can be played. The criminal lawyer must serve three major functions, or stated another way, he must solve three problems. First, he must arrange for his fee; second, he must prepare and then, if necessary, "cool out" his client in case of defeat [11] (a highly likely contingency); third, he must satisfy the court organization that he has performed adequately in the process of negotiating the plea, so as to preclude the possibility of any sort of embarrassing incident which may serve to invite "outside" scrutiny.

In assuring the attainment of one of his primary objectives, his fee, the criminal lawyer will very often enter into negotiations with the accused's kin, including collateral relatives. In many instances, the accused himself is unable to pay any sort of fee or anything more than a token fee. It then becomes important to involve as many of the accused's kin as possible in the situation. This is especially so if the attorney hopes to collect a significant part of a proposed substantial fee. It is not uncommon for several relatives to contribute toward the fee. The larger the group, the greater the possibility that the lawyer will collect a sizable fee by getting contributions from each.

A fee for a felony case which ultimately results in a plea, rather than a trial, may ordinarily range anywhere from $500 to $1,500. Should the case go to trial, the fee will be proportionately larger, depending upon the length of the trial. But the larger the fee the lawyer wishes to exact, the more impressive his performance must be, in terms of his stage managed image as a personage of great influence and power in the court organization. Court personnel are keenly aware of the extent to which a lawyer's stock in trade involves the precarious stage management of an image which goes beyond the usual professional flamboyance, and for this reason alone the lawyer is "bound in" to the authority system of the court's organizational discipline. Therefore, to some extent, court personnel will aid the lawyer in the creation and maintenance of that impression. There is a tacit commitment to the lawyer by the court organization, apart from formal etiquette, to aid him in this. Such augmentation of the lawyer's stage managed image as this affords, is the partial basis for the *quid pro quo* which exists between the lawyer and the court organization. It tends to serve as the continuing basis for the higher loyalty of the lawyer to the organization; his relationship with his client, in contrast, is transient, ephemeral and often superficial.

Defense Lawyer as Double Agent

The lawyer has often been accused of stirring up unnecessary litigation, especially in the field of negligence. He is said to acquire a vested interest in a cause of action or claim which was initially his client's. The strong incentive of possible fee motivates the lawyer to promote litigation which would otherwise never have developed. However, the criminal lawyer develops a vested interest of an entirely different nature in his client's case: to limit its scope and duration rather than do battle. Only in this way can a case be "profitable." Thus, he enlists the aid of relatives not only to assure payment of his fee, but he will also rely on these persons to help him in his agent-mediator role of convincing the accused to plead guilty, and ultimately to help in "cooling out" the accused if necessary.

It is at this point that an accused-defendant may experience his first sense of "betrayal." While he had perhaps perceived the police and prosecutor to be adversaries, or possibly even the judge, the accused is wholly unprepared for his counsel's role performance as an agent-mediator. In the same vein, it is even less likely to occur to an accused that members of his own family or other kin may become agents, albeit at the behest and urging of other agents or mediators, acting on the principle that they are in reality helping an accused negotiate the best possible plea arrangement under the circumstances. Usually, it will be the lawyer who will activate next of kin in this role, his ostensible motive being to arrange for his fee. But soon latent and unstated motives will assert themselves, with entreaties by counsel to the accused's next of kin, to appeal to the accused to "help himself" by pleading. *Gemeinschaft* sentiments are to this extent exploited by a defense lawyer (or even at times by a district attorney) to achieve specific secular ends, that is, of concluding a particular matter with all possible dispatch.

The fee is often collected in stages, each installment usually payable prior to a necessary court appearance required during the course of an accused's career journey. At each stage, in his interviews and communications with the accused, or in addition, with members of his family, if they are helping with the fee payment, the lawyer employs an air of professional confidence and "inside-dopesterism" in order to assuage anxieties on all sides. He makes the necessary bland assurances, and in effect manipulates his client, who is usually willing to do and say the things, true or not, which will help his attorney extricate him. Since the dimensions of what he is essentially selling, organizational influence and expertise, are not technically and precisely measurable, the lawyer can make extravagant claims of influence and secret knowledge with impunity. Thus, lawyers frequently claim to have inside knowledge in connection with information in the hands of the D. A., police, probation officials or to have access to these functionaries. Factually, they often do, and need only to exaggerate the nature of their relationships with them to obtain the desired effective impression upon the client.

But, as in the genuine confidence game, the victim who has partici-pated is loathe to do anything which will upset the lesser plea which his lawyer has "conned" him into accepting.[12]

In effect, in his role as double agent, the criminal lawyer performs an extremely vital and delicate mission for the court organization and the accused. Both principals are anxious to terminate the litigation with a minimum of expense and damage to each other. There is no other per-sonage or role incumbent in the total court structure more strategically located, who by training and in terms of his own requirements, is more ideally suited to do so than the lawyer. In recognition of this, judges will cooperate with attorneys in many important ways. For example, they will adjourn the case of an accused in jail awaiting plea or sentence if the attorney requests such action. While explicitly this may be done for some innocuous and seemingly valid reason, the tacit purpose is that pressure is being applied by the attorney for the collection of his fee, which he knows will probably not be forthcoming if the case is con-cluded. Judges are aware of this tactic on the part of lawyers, who, by requesting an adjournment, keep an accused incarcerated a while longer as a not too subtle method of dunning a client for payment. However, the judges will go along with this, on the ground that impor-tant ends are being served. Often, the only end served is to protect a lawyer's fee.

The judge will help an accused's lawyer in still another way. He will lend the official aura of his office and courtroom so that a lawyer can stage manage an impression of an "all out" performance for the ac-cused in justification of his fee. The judge and other court personnel will serve as a backdrop for a scene charged with dramatic fire, in which the accused's lawyer makes a stirring appeal in his behalf. With a show of restrained passion, the lawyer will intone the virtues of the ac-cused and recite the social deprivations which have reduced him to his present state. The speech varies somewhat, depending on whether the accused has been convicted after trial or has pleaded guilty. In the main, however, the incongruity, superficiality, and ritualistic character of the total performance is underscored by a visibly impassive, almost bored reaction on the part of the judge and other members of the court retinue.

Afterward, there is a hearty exchange of pleasantries between the lawyer and district attorney, wholly out of context in terms of the sup-posed adversary nature of the preceding events. The fiery passion in defense of his client is gone, and the lawyers for both sides resume their offstage relations, chatting amiably and perhaps including the judge in their restrained banter. No other aspect of their visible con-duct so effectively serves to put even a casual observer on notice, that these individuals have claims upon each other. These seemingly innocuous actions are indicative of continuing organizational and informal relations, which, in their intricacy and depth, range far beyond any priorities or claims a particular defendant may have.[13]

Criminal law practice is a unique form of private law practice since it really only appears to be private practice.[14] Actually it is bureaucratic practice, because of the legal practitioner's enmeshment in the authority, discipline, and perspectives of the court organization. Private practice, supposedly, in a professional sense, involves the maintenance of an organized, disciplined body of knowledge and learning; the individual practitioners are imbued with a spirit of autonomy and service, the earning of a livelihood being incidental. In the sense that the lawyer in the criminal court serves as a double agent, serving higher organizational rather than professional ends, he may be deemed to be engaged in bureaucratic rather than private practice. To some extent the lawyer-client "confidence game," in addition to its other functions, serves to conceal this fact.

15

Seymour Melman

Pentagon Politics

Ideology has been defined in innumerable ways, but central to many definitions is the idea of ideology as a set of interrelated beliefs, forming a particular picture of reality, used for purposes of buttressing the status quo. As we have discussed in preceding introductions, our ideas of reality come neither full-blown from the objects and events external to us nor from some mysterious source deep within us. They are, rather, the result of the social definitions that we learn through interaction with others.

We learn the basic beliefs of our people at a very tender age, at a time when we are uncritical, naive, and almost fully accepting. These beliefs about the world become part of our consciousness, a part of the basic orientation with which we approach the world. Only later do we begin to haltingly question our basic ideologies and that only with difficulty, for it means unsettling basic presuppositions which have become a central part of our outlook towards our world of experiences.

As ideology is not only learned at an early age but also regularly reinforced by the major institutions of society, ideology usually goes unquestioned. We may critically examine a bit of our ideologies from time to time, but few of us overthrow them. Most of us make adjustments in our ideologies in response to changed circumstances, and a few make radical and wholesale switches. All of us, however, become captive to basic ways of constructing our worlds of reality.

Excerpted from *Pentagon Capitalism: The Political Economy of War* [pp. 206–207, 211–214, 215, 218, 222–223, 224–226] by Seymour Melman. Copyright © 1970 by Seymour Melman. Used with permission of McGraw-Hill Book Company.

Consequently, ideology is one of the major sets of symbols that can be manipulated in order to control definitions of situations.

It is especially in the political institution that ideologies are manipulated on a vast scale in order to control reality for large numbers of people. Basic symbols are continually brought into play by political leaders in order to enforce their particular definitions. Ideology is especially used to maintain the established positions of those already in power. By manipulating ideology, the powerful justify the various acts they take to maintain their wealth and power. Examples are legion, from our recent participation in warfare in Southeast Asia to our devaluation of the dollar, from each decision to raise taxes to each decision to raise the ceiling on the national debt. Each is accompanied by ideology to justify the actions taken. If the opposite action had been taken, it, too, would have been accompanied by ideology ceremoniously paraded in its defense before the public.

In the following selection, Melman analyzes various strategies used by the Pentagon politicians in their largely successful efforts at controlling large sectors of the American public and of the world. Note especially how reality is distorted for purposes of power, how it is twisted and bent whenever it suits the purposes of those in power, and how it becomes an outright fraud in a con game in which the American public and publics throughout the world are the victims.

☐ The state-management was formed and enlarged under the direction of President John F. Kennedy. He and his advisors centralized and consolidated control over military industry. Thereby, they gathered into very few hands the top economic, political, and military power in the United States. These men were evidently captured by the prospect of wielding political decision-power by applying America's technical brains and industrial capacity toward forging a super military machine, capable of "flexible response" in diverse situations. This was their first priority. So they escalated the nuclear overkill forces, created the "Green Berets" to fight guerrillas, enlarged the Army to eighteen divisions, and lavished money, manpower, and industrial might on the military without stint.

The armed forces were redesigned and enlarged in accordance with war plans that included required capability for fighting three wars at once: a NATO war; a war in Southeast Asia; and a smaller Western-Hemisphere operation. It was beyond the imagination of the designers and managers of such a military machine that their will might be frustrated by a small, impoverished people, lacking in sophisticated munitions, without armor or an air force or a navy—as in Vietnam. The Kennedy administration, helped into office by a proclaimed "missile gap" (later conceded to be unsubstantiated), never admitted the human irrationality of piling up nuclear overkill. If that were conceded, then it would be hard to prevent the emergence of the idea that the overkill buildup was a rational procedure to a different end—enlarging the state-management's control over research and the nation's industry. It is not likely that such a stated purpose would be well received by many Americans.

The Kennedy establishment, suffused with boundless confidence in its own competence and wisdom, created in the state-management their new instrument of power in American society. How different from the old General-President Eisenhower—who tried to warn his successor and the nation against excesses of power by the "military-industrial complex" of his time. The Kennedy administration swiftly made this warning obsolete by creating a new institution—the state-management in the Pentagon. How all this was carried off to the accompaniment of claims of "cost effectiveness" will surely engage the historians of this period. Apart from the political behavior of the Kennedy administration, however, the meaning of its handiwork is most significant in terms of the underlying relation of the new institution to the structure of American economy and society. . . .

Evidently, the state-management in the United States is the result of a nationally and politically specific set of developments. This does not detract from the importance of the institution, but it does tell us that the operation and formation of this institution is not necessarily intrinsic to industrial capitalism itself. Knowing this is significant for an assessment of possible options within American society concerning the state-management and its operation. Since the future of the state-management is not determined by a built-in economic necessity of industrial capitalism, this leaves the future of the institution as a political issue. The issue is clearly political because the Congress has the key regulatory power by its control over the state-management's capital. Just as the Congress can enlarge the state-management by appropriating more money, the same mechanism could enable the Congress to check or diminsh the state-management's power.

Who needs the state-management, and who opposes it? Here is an enumeration of principal groups within American society that have supported the state-management (by backing its policies), despite the contradictions and depletions that have arisen from its operations:

The administrative staff of the state-management

Career men, military and civilian, in the armed forces

People employed in military industry

People working in the military research-and-development establishment.

Communities and parts of communities dependent on military industry and bases

Many members of Congress representing areas of high military activity

Believers in a world Communist conspiracy against the United States

People of strongly authoritarian personality, who identify with martial leadership

The directorate of the state-management is committed to its professional role not only because it is there, but also because military organization is the purest hierarchical organizational form and therefore its enlargement produces a maximum extension of decision-power over the people directly involved.

The men and women accounted for by these categories are appreciable in number, even discounting the last two categories of political belief. But the 8 million persons directly employed in military work, and those indirectly connected to military work, who may be three to five times as many, are still not a majority of the American population. The importance of these groups, however, is not accounted for simply by numbers. The various "think tanks"—research establishments supported by the military—include about 12,000 employees. Research activity carried on within universities for the Pentagon accounts for the full-time professional work of about 20,000 people. Taken together, this is a relatively small group of people in a society of 200 million. But their influence is considerable, since they are a part of those institutions upon which the whole society depends for the creation of new knowledge and teaching of the young.

The Congress has been a crucial supporter of the state-management, since the Congress must vote the capital funds without which the Pentagon could not function. Beyond that, however, many members of Congress are actively involved in securing industrial contracts for firms located in their districts or states. In some areas, groups of Congressmen have formed regular committees, with designated persons to look after these matters of liaison with the Department of Defense. These relationships are, in part, facilitated by the large staff of liaison officers which the Department of Defense deploys in the halls of Congress. Further, many Congressmen get involved in efforts to locate and continue the operation of military bases in their districts or states. In part, this is viewed as a continuation of a classic sort of "pork-barreling"—efforts by energetic Congressmen to secure government-financed public works for their districts. Finally, many Congressmen belong to the military reserve.

On the other hand, there are definable groups in America that constitute the state-management's potential opposition, whether from interested or disinterested motives:

The more educated part of the population

Education and health professionals

A major part of the clergy

Part of the management and labor force of civilian business and finance

Parts of the racial underclasses

People with strong commitment to values of humanism and personal freedom

Opponents of the Vietnam war and its conduct

. . . Neither of the defined groups of fairly committed Americans comprises a clear majority of American society. Other factors, notably the impact of Pentagon operations on American society, as well as ideology and belief, are significant in determining the balance of political forces in the United States. The Pentagon's military failure in Vietnam shattered the major myth of its military invincibility. The political and moral criticism of the war, including the outcry against U.S. casualties, exposed the Pentagon to opposition that cut through occupational-class lines. The failure of the "guns and butter" promise, plus rapid price inflation produced disillusion with the morality of government, even among those hitherto committed to patriotic acquiescence to government policy. These considerations, cutting across occupational, class, and political lines, could lead to a national majority rejecting the Pentagon, and its parasitism at home and abroad, as the dominant institution of government.

If the state-management institution and its priorities are continued, then the following may be expected: increased international competition in nuclear weapons and delivery systems, with emphasis on shorter response time and, hence, more reliance on mechanisms and greater probability of nuclear war by accident; continuation of the Vietnam wars program elsewhere; acceleration of domestic depletion as a consequence of greatly enlarged Department of Defense budgets; decline in the international value of the dollar as a consequence of unacceptable accumulation of dollars abroad owing to world-wide United States military spending. Even in the absence of society-destroying nuclear war, these effects would, in turn, greatly aggravate the race problems in the United States, for domestic economic development would be foreclosed. The same depletion process would produce increasing rebellion against the authority of government and its allies. Altogether, these would be profoundly destabilizing effects in society, possibly including mass violence and civil war mainly along racial lines.

These consequences from the continued operation of the state-management and its priorities would be forestalled only in the measure that declining support for the state-management is translated into political action that is competent to substantially reduce its decision-power. The critical test of this is either a drastic reduction in money allotted to the Pentagon by the Congress or significant withdrawal of popular readiness to implement Pentagon decisions, or both. . . .

Until now, the most durable source of support for sustaining and enlarging the operation of the state-management has been the pattern of antagonistic cooperation between the U.S. state-management and its Soviet counterpart. On each side, there is an appeal to the respective society to grant resources necessary for attaining superiority in particular weapons systems—qualitatively and numerically. On both sides, the appeal is similar—that the competitor is proceeding along lines that must be matched or exceeded under penalty of being disadvantaged. These appeals continue, successfully thus far, despite the fact that neither state-management is able to break through the limits on "defense" and military "superiority" that were imposed by the application of nuclear weapons to offensive military purposes. Despite this, the mutual appeal to fear—pointing to the hostile behavior of the antagonist—has become the single most powerful ingredient making for sustained build-up of the state-managements and their military organizations on each side.

On the American side this pattern is likely to continue until two things are perceived: first, that military priority imposes an unbearably high cost in the form of a depletion process, while the military cannot deliver on their promises of military advantage or a defensive shield; and second, that a politically vigorous part of the population has to marshal a cross-population coalition to compel the Congress to suppress the Pentagon and its society-destroying programs. . . .

The capital of the state-management is obtained by alleging the existence of external "threats." This word implies both imminent dangers and the promise of future danger. Pentagon spokesmen typically evoke fear by alluding to some "threat" from the outside. Thus, the justification for Pentagon budgets is imperiled by the possibility, not to mention the actuality, of a workable détente between the great powers.

The state-management has to obtain resources from a society that can sustain full employment through generally accepted civilian public policies. The attempt to preempt resources from a high employment economy for economically parasitic growth places great pressure on the relation between currency in circulation and the supply of goods, thereby generating unacceptable price inflation at home. Sustained high military expenditures threaten the value of the dollar at home and abroad. However, the state-management is not itself endangered by a diminution in the value of the dollar, whether from domestic or external causes. For whatever the relative value of the dollar may be, the state-management receives the goods and the services these dollars purchase, and for its purpose that is sufficient. . . .

The crucial role of the institution as against the individual is also seen in the way that the state-management institution has persistently rejected policy alternatives whose implementation would have halted or reversed the extension of the decision-power of that state-management. If the advice of men like Jerome Wiesner had been taken in 1961, an attempt would have been made to operate a strategic deterrent system based on a small number (say 200) of intercontinental missiles, without building the gigantic overkill force that now gives the United States a delivery capability of 4,200 intercontinental nuclear warheads. But that alternative would have limited the size of the strategic Air Force and also the aerospace industry, which had to be expanded to carry out the new missile program.

State-management control over the dissemination of information and the interpretation of information is far more important and subtle than simple "news management." As the Great Society legislative program began to unfold in 1965, the administration promised that all would proceed in good order, even while the Vietnam war continued and the military budget was enlarged. By the end of 1967, this estimate was revealed to be sharply contrary to economic feasibility and reality. Soon the Great Society became a not-so-great society. All the while, however, the state-management executives never relented in their public avowals of American ability to deliver both guns and butter to American society. An official myth was never publicly denied, even in the face of a sharp contrast between promise and performance. This could not be done because to erase the myth publicly would have required a reassessment of priorities, including the budget of the Department of Defense. It was left to a conservative Southern Democrat, Senator Ellender, in January, 1967, to tell the truth about the federal budget:

> The truth of the matter is that in many important respects, the Congress and the nation are in the hands of the military. Add to this group the Department of State and you have a combination that calls the shots. The Admirals and the Generals, strongly backed by the Department of State, seem to have the ways and means of getting just about what they want, regardless of the monetary difficulties

afflicting the nation. In contrast to the immensity of a $75.5 billion budget for the military, we need only take a glance at the budget estimates for the conservation and development of our natural resources. We find here a national commitment of only $2.5 billion. It is to the conservation of its land and water that the nation must look if we hope to remain strong and prosperous in the decades ahead, but our investment in this field will represent only a tiny portion of the huge sums to be expended by the military during fiscal 1968.

. . . For all its immense resources and access to high-grade personnel for its planning and operations management, the state-management has come to be a fundamentally fantasy-oriented organization. Its strategic military plans are oriented to nuclear supremacy, but the mutual attainment of overkill frustrates all ambitions of that sort. Its "conventional war" plans are oriented to winning guerrilla wars with immense firepower superiority, when the Vietnam war has shown this expectation to be only a Pentagon illusion. The Pentagon calculated that with superior military power, world political development could be substantially controlled, but American hegemony in critical places—as in much of Western Europe—has been leaking at the seams, just as Soviet hegemony has frayed in many parts of the world. Above all, the state-management has promised that, through its operations, the United States could be defended, and that is precisely what they have not been able to do. It took the Cuban missile crisis to produce the moment of truth: there is no shield when nation-states confront each other with great nuclear forces.

Structurally, the military economy is cross-class, that is, it represents a vertical slice of society, not simply a modern version of the celebrated "merchants of death" of the First World War vintage. While the top echelon of the state-management does the crucial planning and decision-making, its power depends upon the support and energetic participation of sub-managers, scientists, engineers, and trade union members in the great array of bases, research and development establishments, and weapons-manufacturing industries. One effect of this has been to produce a cross-class lobby for the Pentagon and its budgets. This cross-class bloc depletes the rest of the society.

There has been a similar pattern of cross political-ideological support for the operation of the state-management. Obviously, most conservatives have supported military budgets without limit in the name of defense against Communism. But an important bloc of support for the state-management is composed of moderates, political liberals, and leftists, whose ideology favors more authority for central government. Characteristically, this is justified by the proposition that central government alone has the capacity for regulating economic behavior and for planning and executing the economic amelioration which many liberals and leftists profess to desire. In the name of these ends, ever-increasing budgets for the federal government are supported, even though these growing budgets are for predominately military purposes. Thus, pro-big-government liberals and leftists, often critical of certain Pentagon policies, function as the loyal left opposition for the state-management.

The highly structured Pentagon, with its state-management, immense funds, collateral organizations in government and in industrial and other spheres of life, and its decisive influence on national and international affairs has become a true "state within a state," a para-state.

The normal operation and expansion of the para-state and its state-management has been based upon the wholesale selling of fear—fear of nuclear war, fear of Communism (even after the post-Stalin thaw)—as a lever for prying more and more support from the public and Congress for ever-larger military budgets. Here is the list of defense inadequacies that the operators of the most powerful military machine in the world claim have existed since 1960:

Missile gap
Bomber gap
Anti-ballistic missile gap
Fighter plane gap
Megatonnage gap
Submarine gap
Survival gap
Strategy gap
Security gap

Each of these claims evoked the genuine feelings of helplessness that ordinary people might have at the prospect of war in the nuclear age. However, the implied promise of the militarists is that they can erase the particular threat that is signaled by each "gap" and really provide security, if only they are granted more money for still another device or program. Whether explicit or merely implied, such claims are a cruel hoax. Military security in the nuclear era is obtainable only by workable agreements among states that weapons will not be used and that their actual numbers will be reduced. The very existence of quickly triggered, nuclear-powered antagonists, each prepared to use society-destroying weapons, is the final menace to the existence of the human species. This threat, which encourages antagonistic cooperation among

nuclear opponents, is the one military threat that the para-state systematically omits from its budget-supporting list of "threats."

The para-state, directed by its new class of managers and technolo-
gists, both breeds and needs foreign and domestic crises. The direction
of massive public funds towards parasitic growth and war-making helps
to create and sustain depletion in the value of the dollar; to create
inflation; to inflame race relations; to destroy morals; to cause serious
deficiencies in civilian technology, education, and health care; to sustain the draft; and to aid in the deterioration of domestic and international observance of lawful behavior.

16

Stanley M. Elkins

Slave Systems in North and South America

The basic reason for slavery in the New World can be summarized in one word—economics. The rising standard of living in Europe fostered a huge demand for tobacco, coffee, tea, and chocolate. The changing tastes in drinks stimulated the demand for cane sugar. The cultivation of both cane sugar and tobacco required vast armies of cheap, docile labor. As the New World became an agricultural periphery to the Old, plantation owners and developers turned increasingly to slaves as their source of labor.

Slave dealing centered around a triangle of trade which involved four continents. Goods manufactured in Europe were shipped to Africa and traded for slaves. The slaves were then shipped across the Atlantic to both North and South America, where they were used for growing crops. These crops were then shipped to Europe and exchanged for manufactured goods, and so on.

Slavery is anything but a new institution. Slavery goes back about as far as we have written records. But though it is given the same name, slavery was not the same around the world. Slavery can include the use of people as soldiers, eunuchs, wrestlers, or craftsmen, as well as field hands. Slavery can include being absorbed into an owner's family, being treated with kindness, and having the right to acquire wealth, even though the person is nonetheless a slave. Slavery can include the right to own property, the right to get married and raise a family, the right to serve as an equal witness before the law, and even the right

Reprinted from *Slavery* [pp. 53–55, 59–63, 72–77, 79–80] by Stanley M. Elkins by permission of The University of Chicago Press. Copyright © 1959 by The University of Chicago Press. All rights reserved.

to become the full heir of one's master. Slavery can, and has, included all these things, depending on how it was organized in a particular society.

Slavery in the United States, however, was among the worst the world has ever known. An American slave had none of the above rights. He was property before the law, not human. He was subject to the will of a single master who legally had complete control over his person. He was, moreover, a slave in perpetuity, as were his children and his children's children.

The American Colonies, however, were not the main recipients of the extensive traffic in black bodies. Only about 4.5 percent of the slaves exported from Africa were sent to what later became the United States, while approximately 90 percent were sent to tropical and subtropical America, which extends from Brazil to the Caribbean. Although slavery in this region was coterminous with slavery in the South, it was a different kind of slavery, as Elkins analyzes in the following article.

□ . . . That most ancient and intimate of institutional arrangements, marriage and the family, had long since been destroyed by the law, and the law never showed any inclination to rehabilitate it. Here was the area in which considerations of humanity might be expected most widely to prevail, and, indeed, there is every reason to suppose that on an informal daily basis they did: the contempt in which respectable society held the slave trader, who separated mother from child and husband from wife, is proverbial in Southern lore.[1] On the face of things, it ought to have been simple enough to translate this strong social sentiment into the appropriate legal enactments, which might systematically have guaranteed the inviolability of the family and the sanctity of the marriage bond, such as governed Christian polity everywhere. Yet the very nature of the plantation economy and the way in which the basic arrangements of Southern life radiated from it, made it inconceivable that the law should tolerate any ambiguity, should the painful clash between humanity and property interest ever occur. Any restrictions on the separate sale of slaves would have been reflected immediately in the market; their price would have dropped considerably.[2] Thus the law could permit no aspect of the slave's conjugal state to have an independent legal existence outside the power of the man who owned him: "The relation of master and slave is wholly incompatible with even the qualified relation of husband and wife, as it is supposed to exist among slaves. . . ."[3] Marriage, for them, was denied any standing in law. Accordingly, as T. R. R. Cobb of Georgia admitted, "The contract of marriage not being recognized among slaves, none of its consequences follow. . . ."[4] "The relation between slaves," wrote a North Carolina judge in 1858, "is essentially different from that of man and wife joined in lawful wedlock . . . [for] with slaves it may be dissolved at the pleasure of either party, or by the sale of one or both, depending on the caprice or necessity of the owners." [5]

It would thus go without saying that the offspring of such "contubernial relationships," as they were called, had next to no guaranties against indiscriminate separation from their parents.[6] Of additional interest is the fact that children derived their condition from that of their mother. This was not unique to American slavery, but it should be noted that especially in a system conceived and evolved exclusively on grounds of property there could be little doubt about how such a question would be resolved. Had status been defined according to the father's condition—as was briefly the case in seventeenth-century Maryland, following the ancient common law—there would instantly have arisen the irksome question of what to do with the numerous mulatto children born every year of white planter-fathers and slave mothers. It would have meant the creation of a free mulatto class, automatically relieving the master of so many slaves on the one hand, while burdening him on the other with that many colored children whom he could not own. Such equivocal relationships were never permitted to vex the law. That "the father of a slave is unknown to our law" was the universal understanding of Southern jurists.[7] It was thus that a father, among slaves, was legally "unknown," a husband without the rights of his bed,[8] the state of marriage defined as "only that concubinage . . . with which alone, perhaps, their condition is compatible," [9] and motherhood clothed in the scant dignity of the breeding function.[10] . . .

The rights of property, and all other civil and legal "rights," were everywhere denied the slave with a clarity that left no doubt of his utter dependency upon his master. "A slave is in absolute bondage; he has no civil right, and can hold no property, except at the will and pleasure of his master." [11] He could neither give nor receive gifts; he could make no will, nor could he, by will, inherit anything. He could not hire himself out or make contracts for any purpose—even including, as we have seen, that of matrimony—and thus neither his word nor his bond had any standing in law. He could buy or sell nothing at all, except as his master's agent, could keep no cattle, horses, hogs, or sheep and, in Mississippi at least, could raise no cotton. Even masters who permitted such transactions, except under express arrangement, were uniformly liable to fines.[12] It was obvious, then, that the case of a slave who should presume to buy his own freedom—he being unable to possess money —would involve a legal absurdity. "Slaves have no legal rights in things, real or personal; but whatever they may acquire, belongs, in point of law, to their masters." [13]

Such proscriptions were extended not only over all civil rights but even to the civic privileges of education and worship. Every Southern state except Maryland and Kentucky had stringent laws forbidding anyone to teach slaves reading and writing, and in some states the penalties applied to the educating of free Negroes and mulattoes as well. It was thought that "teaching slaves to read and write tends to dissatisfaction in their minds, and to produce insurrection and rebellion"; [14] in North Carolina it was a crime to distribute among them any pamphlet or book, not excluding the Bible. The same apprehensions applied to instruction in religion. Southern society was not disposed to withhold the consolations of divine worship from its slaves, but the conditions would have to be laid down not by the church as an institution, not even by the planters as laity, but by planters simply as masters. The conscientious master no doubt welcomed having the gospel preached to his slaves, provided that they should hear it, as J. W. Fowler of Coahoma County, Mississippi, specified, "in its original purity and simplicity." Fowler wrote to his overseer that "in view of the fanaticism of the age it behooves the Master or Overseer to be present on all such occasions." [15] Alexander Telfair, of Savannah, instructed his overseer that there should be "no night-meeting or preaching . . . allowed on the place, except on Saturday night & Sunday morn." [16] Similar restrictions found their way into the law itself. Typical were the acts of South Carolina forbidding religious meetings of slaves or free Negroes "either before the rising of the sun or after the setting of the same," and of Mississippi permitting slaves, if authorized by their masters, to attend the preaching of a *white* minister. It was a state of things deplored by the Southern churches, for the law had been none of their doing. "There are over *two millions* of human beings in the condition of heathen," lamented the Presbyterian Synod of South Carolina and Georgia in 1833, "and some of them in worse condition."

> In the present state of feeling in the South, a ministry of their own color could neither be obtained *nor tolerated*. But do not the negroes have access to the gospel through the stated ministry of the whites? We answer, No. The negroes have no regular and efficient ministry: as a matter of course, no churches; neither is there sufficient room in the white churches for their accommodation. [17]

But the church could do nothing. Its rural congregations were full of humane and decent Christians, but as an institution of authority and power it had no real existence.

It is true that among the most attractive features of the plantation legend, dear to every Southerner with a sense of his past, were the paternal affection of the good master for his blacks and the warm sentiments entertained in Southern society at large for the faithful slave. The other side of the coin, then, might appear as something of a paradox: the most implacable race-consciousness yet observed in virtually any society. It was evolved in the Southern mind, one might say, as a simple syllogism, the precision of whose terms paralleled the precision of the system itself. All slaves are black; slaves are degraded and contemptible; therefore all blacks are degraded and contemptible and should be kept in a state of slavery. How had the simple syllogism come into being? That very strength and bulwark of American society, capitalism, unimpeded by prior arrangements and institutions, had stamped the status of slave upon the black with a clarity which elsewhere could never have been so profound, and had further defined the institution of slavery with such nicety that the slave *was*, in fact, degraded. That the black, as a species, was thus contemptible seemed to follow by observation. This assumption took on a life of its own in the attitudes of the people, and the very thought of such a creature existing outside the pale of their so aptly devised system filled the most reasonable of Southerners with fear and loathing. Quite apart from the demands of the system itself, this may account for many of the subsidiary social taboos—the increasing severity of the laws against manumission, the horror of miscegenation, the depressed condition of the free Negro and his peculiar place in Southern society: all signs of how difficult it was to conceive a non-slave colored class. Nothing in their experience had prepared them for it; such a class was unnatural, logically awry, a blemish on the body politic, an anomaly for which there was no intellectual category.

There should be no such unresolved terms, no such unfactorable equations, in a society whose production economy had had such dynamic and unencumbered origins. Both reason and instinct had defined the Negro as a slave, and the slave as

. . . that condition of a natural person, in which, by the operation of law, the application of his physical and mental powers depends, as far as possible, upon the will of another who is himself subject to the supreme power of the state, and in which he is incapable, in the view of the law, of acquiring or holding property, and of sustaining those relations out of which *relative* rights . . . proceed, except as the agent or instrument of another. In slavery, strictly so called, the supreme power of the state, in ignoring the personality of the slave, ignores his capacity for moral action, and commits the control of his conduct as a moral agent, to the master, together with the power of transferring his authority to another.[18]

The basic fact was, of course, that the slave himself was property. He and his fellow bondsmen had long since become "chattels personal . . . to all intents, constructions and purposes whatsoever." [19]

In the slave system of the United States—so finely circumscribed and so cleanly self-contained—virtually all avenues of recourse for the slave, all lines of communication to society at large, originated and ended with the master. The system was unique, *sui generis*. The closest parallel to it at that time was to be found in the Latin-American colonies of Spain and Portugal. But the differences between the two systems are so much more striking than the similarities that we may with profit use them not as parallels but as contrasts. In the Spanish and Portuguese colonies, we are immediately impressed by the comparative lack of precision and logic governing the institution of slavery there; we find an exasperating dimness of line between the slave and free portions of society, a multiplicity of points of contact between the two, a confusing promiscuity of color, such as would never have been thinkable in our own country.[20] . . .

Neither in Brazil nor in Spanish America did slavery carry with it such precise and irrevocable categories of perpetual servitude, *"durante vita"* and "for all generations," as in the United States. The presumption in these countries, should the status of a colored person be in doubt, was that he was free rather than a slave.[21] There were in fact innumerable ways whereby a slave's servitude could be brought to an end. The chief of these was the very considerable fact that he might buy his own freedom. The Negro in Cuba or Mexico had the right to have his price declared and could, if he wished, purchase himself in instalments. Slaves escaping to Cuba to embrace Catholicism were protected by a special royal order of 1733 which was twice reissued. A slave unduly punished might be set at liberty by the magistrate. In Brazil the slave who was the parent of ten children might legally demand his or her freedom.[22] The medieval Spanish code had made a slave's service terminable under any number of contingencies—if he denounced cases of treason, murder, counterfeiting, or the rape of a virgin, or if he performed various other kinds of meritorious acts. Though all such practices did not find their way into the seventeenth- and eighteenth-century legal arrangements of Latin America, much of their spirit was perpetuated in the values, customs, and social expectations of that later period. It is important to appreciate the high social approval connected with the freeing of slaves. A great variety of happy family events—the birth of a son, the marriage of a daughter, anniversaries, national holidays—provided the occasion, and their ceremonial was frequently marked by the manumission of one or more virtuous servitors. It was considered a pious act to accept the responsibility of becoming godfather to a slave child, implying the moral obligation to arrange eventually for its freedom. Indeed, in Cuba and Brazil such freedom might be purchased for a nominal sum at the baptismal font.[23] All such manumissions had the strong approval of both church and state and were registered gratis by the government.[24]

In extending its moral authority over men of every condition, the church naturally insisted on bringing slave unions under the holy sacraments. Slaves were married in church and the banns published; marriage was a sacred rite and its sanctity protected in law. In the otherwise circumspect United States, the only category which the law could apply to conjugal relations between slaves—or to unions between master and slave—was concubinage. But concubinage, in Latin America, was condemned as licentious, adulterous, and immoral; safeguards against promiscuity were provided in the law,[25] and in Brazil the Jesuits labored mightily to regularize the libertinage of the master class by the sacrament of Christian marriage.[26] Moreover, slaves owned by different masters were not to be hindered from marrying, nor could they be kept separate after marriage. If the estates were distant, the wife was to go with her husband, and a fair price was to be fixed by impartial persons for her sale to the husband's master.[27] A slave might, without legal interference, marry a free person. The children of such a marriage, if the mother were free, were themselves free, inasmuch as children followed the condition of their mother.[28]

The master's disciplinary authority never had the completeness that it had in the United States, and nowhere did he enjoy powers of life and death over the slave's body. Under the Spanish code of 1789 slaves might be punished for failure to perform their duties, with prison, chains, or lashes, "which last must not exceed the number of twenty-five, and those must be given them in such manner as not to cause any contusion or effusion of blood: which punishments cannot be imposed on slaves but by their masters or the stewards." [29] For actual crimes a slave was to be tried in an ordinary court of justice like any free person,[30] and, conversely, the murder of a slave was to be prosecuted just as that of a free man would be.[31] Excessive punishments of slaves— causing "contusion, effusion of blood, or mutilation of members"—by plantation stewards were themselves punishable. Although gross violations of the law occurred, the law here was anything but the dead letter it proved to be in our own southern states. In the important administrative centers of both Brazil and the Spanish colonies there was an official protector of slaves, known variously as the syndic, procurador, or attorney-general, under whose jurisdiction came all matters relating to the treatment of slaves. His functions were nurtured by a well-articulated system of communications. The priests who made the regular rounds of the estates giving Christian instruction were required to obtain and render to him information from the slaves regarding their treatment, and investigation and the necessary steps would be taken accordingly. These priests were answerable to no one else for their activities. In addition, the magistrates were to appoint "persons of good character" to visit the estates thrice yearly and conduct similar inquiries on similar matters. A further ingenious provision in the Spanish code caused all fines levied, for mistreatment and other excesses against slaves, to be divided up three ways: one-third went to the judge, one-third to the informer, and one-third to the "Fines Chest." Finally, the attorney-general and the justices themselves were made accountable to the crown for failure to carry out these ordinances. An implicit royal threat underlay all this; should the fines not have the desired effect and should the ordinances continue to be broken, "I," His Majesty promised, "will take my measures accordingly." [32]

As was implied in his right to purchase his own freedom, the slave in the Spanish and Portuguese colonies had the right to acquire and hold property. This meant something specific; in Brazil a master was obliged by law to give liberty to his slaves on all Sundays and holidays—which totaled eighty-five in the year—during which a slave might work for himself and accumulate money for his purchase price,[33] and the Spanish code of 1789 provided that slaves must be allowed two hours each day in which to be employed in "occupations for their own advantage." [34] In many places slaves were encouraged to hire themselves out regularly (there were skilled artisans among them as well as ordinary laborers), an arrangement which was to the advantage of both the master and the slave himself, since the latter was allowed to keep a percentage of the wage. Slaves even in rural areas might sell the produce of their gardens and retain the proceeds.[35] For all practical purposes slavery here had become, as Mr. Tannenbaum puts it, a contractual arrangement: it could be wiped out by a fixed purchase price and leave no taint. "There may have been no written contract between the two parties, but the state behaved, in effect, as if such a contract did exist, and used its powers to enforce it." [36] It was a contract in which the master owned a man's labor but not the man.

As for the privileges of religion, it was here not a question of the planting class "permitting" the slave, under rigidly specified conditions, to take part in divine worship. It was rather a matter of the church's insisting—under its own conditions—that masters bring their slaves to church and teach them religion. Such a man as the Mississippi planter who directed that the gospel preached to his slaves should be "in its original purity and simplicity" would have courted the full wrath of the Latin church. A Caribbean synod of 1622, whose *sanctiones* had the force of law, made lengthy provisions for the chastisement of masters who prevented their slaves from hearing Mass or receiving instruction on feast days.[37] Here the power of the Faith was such that master and slave stood equally humble before it. "Every one who has slaves," according to the first item in the Spanish code, "is obliged to instruct them in the principles of the Roman Catholic religion and in the necessary truths in order that the slaves may be baptized within the (first) year of their residence in the Spanish dominions." [38] Certain assumptions were implied therein which made it impossible that the slave in this culture should ever quite be considered as mere property, either in law or in society's customary habits of mind. These assumptions, perpetuated and fostered by the church, made all the difference in his treatment by society and its institutions, not only while a slave, but also if and when he should cease to be one. They were, in effect, that he was a man, that he had a soul as precious as any other man's, that he had a moral nature, that he was not only as susceptible to sin but also as eligible for grace as his master—that master and slave were brothers in Christ. . . .

We are not, then, dealing with a society steeped, like our own, in traditions of political and economic democracy. We are concerned only with a special and peculiar kind of fluidity—that of their slave systems—and in this alone lay a world of difference. It was a fluidity that permitted a transition from slavery to freedom that was smooth, organic, and continuing. Manumitting slaves, carrying as it did such high social approval, was done often, and the spectacle of large numbers of freedmen was familiar to the social scene. Such opportunities as were open to any member of the depressed classes who had talent and diligence were open as well to the ex-slave and his descendants. Thus color itself was no grave disability against taking one's place in free society; indeed, Anglo-Saxon travelers in nineteenth-century Brazil were amazed at the thoroughgoing mixture of races there. "I have passed black ladies in silks and jewelry," wrote Thomas Ewbank in the 1850's "with male slaves in livery behind them. . . . Several have white husbands. The first doctor of the city is a colored man; so is the President of the Province." [39] Free Negroes had the same rights before the law as whites, and it was possible for the most energetic of their numbers to take immediate part in public and professional life. Among the Negroes and mulattoes of Brazil and the Spanish colonies—aside from the swarming numbers of skilled craftsmen—were soldiers, officers, musicians, poets, priests, and judges. "I am accustomed," said a delegate to the Cortes of Cádiz in 1811, "to seeing many engaged in all manner of careers." [40]

All such rights and opportunities existed *before* the abolition of slavery; and thus we may note it as no paradox that emancipation, when it finally did take place, was brought about in all these Latin-American countries "without violence, without bloodshed, and without civil war." [41] . . .

17

Robert Perrucci
Marc Pilisuk

Racism, Poverty, and Inequality

Slavery in the United States was not originally based on racism. The colonists at first preferred white indentured servants for their supply of cheap labor. Blacks were also indentured servants—at first. After serving their period of indentureship, as with white servants they were freed and able to take up land, to buy and sell property, and even to own indentured servants themselves. Later, however, the law was changed, and blacks became slaves for life. For what it cost to procure the services of an indentured servant for a period of but a few years, one became able to buy the services of a black for life. Where cheap labor was in short supply and high demand, as in the South, blacks were imported wholesale.

Thus out of slavery developed racism. Special laws were passed which applied or did not apply to people on the basis of their color. Solely on the basis of color some people possessed certain fundamental rights, while on the same basis those rights were denied others. An elaborately concocted doctrine was developed in order to justify the enslavement of some human beings by others. Into this ideology was poured human ingenuity, liberally mixed with political and theological affirmations. The result was a new doctrine of racism. Blacks became declared inferior to whites.

Note that this doctrine or ideology of racial superiority–inferiority was the purposefully contrived response to an economic system. It was the official justification for the enslavement of human beings by human beings. Yet, when pronounced by the respectable in society, officially supported by the law, and affirmed by theologians, the contrivance became reality. People perceived what the ideology taught. And they embraced it.

From this legacy of slavery our society has not yet recovered. Racism permeates our society even today. Racism has been with us in the past, it is with us now, and it seems likely to continue indefinitely into the future. It is some of the contemporary forms and consequences of racism which Perrucci and Pilisuk analyze in the following selection.

☐ Estimates of the number of poor in the United States range from a low of 20 million to a high of 40 million persons. The great variation in these estimates is due almost entirely to the definitions used to classify an individual or family above or below the poverty line. This reflects the relative nature of poverty (or luxury for that matter) and illustrates an important point: persons are classified as poor in relation to other persons and to a standard of living that is currently accepted as statistically normal. Failure to understand this basic fact often leads to efforts to show how America's "poor" earn more than the vast majority of persons in the rest of the world, or that the "poor" have television sets, cars, and other "luxuries." Such comparisons do not make use of some basic understandings concerning the *social* definitions of poverty.

In 1963 the Department of Health, Education and Welfare found that there were some 34½ million persons in the United States with incomes below a minimum budget; the budget is based on a minimum level of living for families and persons living alone (Miller, 1966). About 5 million of the poor lived alone, and 30 million, one-half of these being children, lived in families. Many of those families below the poverty line are not there because of unemployment. About one-half of the families are headed by males who had full-time employment at some point throughout the year. This indicates that many of the poverty families are working families with poor incomes and with little chance to improve their incomes because of limited skills and education.

In the last few years the number of families *defined* as poor (i.e., with income below the official poverty line) has decreased. This decrease is probably due to the effect of the poverty program in getting money and programs into low-income areas. Despite these gains, however, the rapidly rising cost of living in the last decade has virtually wiped out any of the apparent gains reflected in the declining number of poor families. In 1959, poverty was defined as income for a family of four below $3100, while the Bureau of Labor estimated that $7000 was needed for a "modest but adequate" living. In 1969, the poverty level for a family of four was $3335, and the "modest but adequate" living increased to $9200 (Reissman, 1969). In short, the gap between the poverty level and what is needed for an adequate living has increased quite sharply.

A substantial number of the poor are the older persons in our society. There are approximately 8 million Americans over 65 with incomes below the poverty line, with about 1.5 million of these who live alone on an income of less than $500 a year. The plight of the aged poor is described in the following account of a man on a pension.

Mr. MacIntosh depended on hard-boiled eggs because his hotel room has no refrigerator and he can't afford to eat out. He is trying to live on his $50-a-month Social Security check. Room rent is $38.50 a month, which provides a room with clean linen every two weeks and clean towels every day. The remainder goes for food and chewing tobacco. Every week friends on the same floor buy him two dozen eggs, seven small cans of V-8 juice, two cans of Spam, a carton of dry cereal (because the box says, "Minimum daily requirement of vitamins") and his tobacco. He boils his eggs at once and eats them morning and evening. He stretches a can of Spam for three days or so. It has cost him violent nausea to discover that hard-boiled eggs and opened Spam need refrigeration in warm weather. (Bagdikian, 1966.)

The effects of poverty are also revealed in the facts of hunger and malnutrition facing millions of Americans. The extent of hunger might still be secret but for the takeover of an abandoned Air Force base in Mississippi in 1965 by 35 Negroes whose leaflets said, "We are here because we are hungry and cold and we have no jobs or land." They were promptly evicted but a furor of federal food-stamp programs, replacing direct surplus-food distribution centers, were claiming success in eliminating hunger in Mississippi. Further investigation, however, showed the new food-stamp programs to be working to the detriment of people too poor to purchase the stamps. The wheels of the Department of Agriculture and the Congress grind slowly. Direct payments to assist people in purchase of food stamps was tried after some delays. Even with this, a team of doctors investigating the health of Mississippi children in 1967 made a report which stated:

In child after child we saw: evidence of vitamin and mineral deficiencies; serious untreated skin infestation and ulcerations; eye and ear diseases, also unattended bone diseases secondary to poor food intake; the prevalence of bacterial and parasitic disease as well as severe anemia, with resulting loss of energy and ability to live a normally active life; diseases of the heart and lungs—requiring surgery—which have gone undiagnosed and untreated; epileptic and other neurological disorders; severe kidney ailments, that in other children would warrant immediate hospitalization; and finally, in boys and girls in every county we visited, obvious evidence of severe malnutrition with injury to the body's tissues—its muscles, bones, and skin as well as an associated psychological state of fatigue, listlessness, and exhaustion.

We saw children afflicted with chronic diarrhea, chronic sores, chronic leg and arm (untreated) injuries and deformities. We saw homes without running water and live with germ-bearing mosquitoes and flies everywhere around. We saw homes with children who are lucky to eat one meal a day—and that one inadequate so far as vitamins, minerals, or protein is concerned. We saw children who don't get to drink milk, don't get to eat fruit, green vegetables, or meat. They live on starches—grits, bread, Kool Aid. Their parents may be declared ineligible for commodities, ineligible for the food stamp program, even though they have literally nothing. We saw children fed communally—that is, by neighbors who give scraps of food to children whose own parents have nothing to give them. (Quoted in Citizens' Board of Inquiry into Hunger and Malnutrition in the U.S., 1968.)

How the federal government operates in the face of such destitute conditions teaches us an important lesson about the workings of American government at all levels. At the county level, local control over food-assistance programs left local governments to request, pay for, and run the programs, thus putting those areas least responsive to their own poor in a position to deny those poor federally offered food. Control by local government is not the same as local democratic control by a community of program participants, and the latter rarely exists in this country.

The politics of the national failure to respond during the Johnson Administration are described in Elizabeth Drew's account of "Going Hungry in America." She summarizes:

Yet so little was accomplished not because of mechanical or industrial failures, but because of what can happen to men in policy-making positions in Washington. When they stay in a difficult job too long, they can be overwhelmed by the complexity of it all, and they become overly defensive. Man's pride, particularly the pride of a man who can tell himself he has done some good, can overtake his intellectual honesty. Thus, not Southern politicians, not Orville Freeman, not Lyndon Johnson could face the fact when it was pointed out that many people were hungry, that they weren't wearing clothes. In this they reflected a national trait: it has been easier to stir sustained national concern over hunger in Bihar or Biafra than places at home for which we are more directly responsible. The problems are looked at in terms of the workings of Washington, not in terms of the problems. Decent men could sit and discuss statistical reliability and administrative neatness and the importance of good precedents while people went hungry. (Drew, 1968, p. 61.)

An even more callous administrative response is found in President Nixon's administration as revealed by Nick Kotz's recent book so aptly titled *Let Them Eat Promises.* The contrast between bureaucratic political process and the reality of human need cannot be exaggerated. This gap is a measure of governmental failure. In the wealthiest nation in history there are babies who die in infancy because they cannot get milk; there are anemic children, and those with stunted growth stemming from protein deficiency; there are scurvy and rickets through lack of milk and citrus juice; there are the hookworms, roundworms, and other parasitic infections; and there are the thousands who go to school without breakfast and have no money for lunch. The shocking facts of starving children, adults, and old people are contained in *Hunger USA,* a report on the more than 14 million Americans without enough food to maintain health.

The impact of poverty upon the poor has been well documented. The sense of despair, alienation, and hopelessness combine to produce limited aspirations and a sense of powerlessness among the young. It is in the *adaptations* to poverty that these conditions are maintained and transmitted intergenerationally. Poverty does breed poverty! Other adaptations to poverty which have become part of the life style of the poor are often responded to as if they were the causes of the problems of the poor. Claude Brown (1965), in his personal account of growing up in Harlem, illustrates how the role of the "hustler" is simply one of many deviant occupations providing the outward symbols of success that are available to ghetto youth. Similarly, Gertrude Samuels' (1959) description of New York youth gangs reveals how gangs function to provide that sense of security and personal worth that their members cannot obtain in socially acceptable ways.

Yet we must be careful not to place too great an emphasis on the psychological impact of poverty which leads to self-defeating personal and cultural patterns. For to do so would turn our attention away from the more basic causes of poverty which are to be found in existing social institutions in American society. Moreover, an overemphasis on the pathological aspects of poverty leads us to neglect the stable patterns of social organization that are to be found in ghettos and low-income areas. In seeking out such existing strengths we may come to understand that there are many viable patterns of social life in American society in addition to the dominant middle-class patterns. In other words, the poor should not have to be required to be totally transformed in order to enjoy a decent standard of living and equal access to the rights guaranteed to all citizens.

Many of the issues raised here have been brought into very sharp focus within the context of the civil-rights movement. Black men have been given legal equality as many of the unequal-treatment laws have been declared unconstitutional and new legislation has provided guarantees of equality in education and voting. Yet while there have been great strides toward legal equality, the Negro has been denied the economic and political power necessary for social equality. It is hardly likely that Negroes derive any great satisfaction from knowing that racist explanations for his inferiority have been replaced by economic and political ones.

. . . The South has been the traditional setting in which the Negroes' quest for equality has taken place. The civil-rights movement as an organizational weapon had its greatest impact with the early boycotts and sit-ins. The nationally televised accounts of beating, police dogs, gas, and cattle prods as the Southern communities' response to the awakened Negro were sufficient to raise a national clamor for much of the civil-rights legislation currently in effect. The experience of the early years of the civil-rights movement has been vividly described by Peter Weiss (1964) in his account of a voter-registration project in Mississippi. He reveals the difficulties in voter registration of poor Negroes and whites after years of subordination and intimidation have left them apathetic or fearful, with little knowledge of their rights as citizens. It took great courage for civil-rights workers to enter Mississippi where the authorities were themselves lawless. Weiss recounts an incident in which a highway patrolman stopped a car with five SNCC workers inside, enroute to a meeting. The patrolman said, "You goddamn niggers want to change our way of life"; (hardly a traffic problem). Four of the occupants were delivered handcuffed to the sheriff at the Lowndes County Jail. The fifth, seventeen-year-old James Black, was taken to a spot a mile away by the patrolman. His affidavit dated June 8, 1964, reads:

> He told me to get out of the car; I refused to get out. So he pulled me out. He started hitting me with his fists, and after about twenty blows he got out his blackjack and hit me one time with it and knocked me down. Then he told me to get back in the car. While he was beating me, he asked if any white folks had ever treated me bad;

I told him yes, and he hit me again. He asked me again had any white folks in Mississippi treated me bad, and I told him no. At that point he helped me back into the car.

Then he took me to the county jail (Lowndes) where I was questioned by the sheriff. The sheriff asked for my driver's license and to take everything out of my pockets. . . . I had a friend's I.D. card in my pocket and he asked me if my friend was a Negro or a nigger. I told him a Negro. The same highway patrolman was there, and took out his blackjack and again asked if my friend was a Negro or a nigger. He started to hit me with the blackjack, and I told him my friend was a nigger.

The white Northerner's support of the civil-rights movement *in the South* was often accompanied by a smug complacency that the North was civilized and aware of human decency and the law of the land. The response of the white Northerners to the civil-rights movement was seen in Cicero, Illinois, and Milwaukee, Wisconsin, as Negroes sought to move into white workingclass neighborhoods; it was seen in the support received by George Wallace in Democratic primaries in Wisconsin and Indiana; it was seen in the repeal of an open-housing law by the voters of California. As the civil-rights movement attempted to deal with problems in the North, the moral superiority of the white Northerner over the white Southerner vanished. The comforting belief that racist America was only found in the South was shattered.

The response of the middle-class white Northerner to the growing consciousness and militancy of the Negro can only be understood in terms of the more general problem of poverty, inequality, and insecurity in American society. Poverty has to do with the inability of persons to achieve a level of income needed to live according to prevailing standards of living. As indicated earlier, the gap between the official poverty line and what is needed for a modest but adequate living has been increasing rather than shrinking. In contrast to poverty, inequality refers to the distribution of wealth or income among the general population. It is concerned with the relative share of total economic output that goes to different segments of the population. Thus, in 1960, the upper 20 percent of the population received 45 percent of total income, while the lower 20 percent received 5 percent of total income (Miller, 1964).

Unsure of his own economic and social status, the lower-middle class American feels his own chances for middle-class status restricted by technological change and a tightening opportunity structure. One consequence of this is that the workingclass white becomes both envious and resentful of the attention being given to the Negro at a time when no one seems concerned with his own plight. The combination of economic insecurity, resentment toward upper-middle-class whites, and envy over the growing consciousness of Negroes is revealed in the following statement by a mother from a working-class family that is barely able to make ends meet.

They may be poorer than a lot of white people, but not by very much. Anyway, what they don't get in money they more than gain in popularity these days. The papers have suddenly decided that the Negro is teacher's pet. Whatever he does good is wonderful, and we should clap. But if he does anything bad, it's our fault. I can't read the papers anymore when they talk about the race thing. I'm sick of their editorials. All of a sudden they start giving us a lecture every day on how bad we are. They never used to care about anything, the Negro or anything else. Now they're so worried. And the same goes with the Church. I'm as devout a Catholic as you'll find around. My brother is a priest, and I do more than go to Church once a week. But I just can't take what some of our priests are saying these days. They're talking as if we did something wrong for being white. I don't understand it at all. Priests never used to talk about the Negro when I was a child. Now they talk to my kids about them all the time. I thought the Church is supposed to stand for religion, and eternal things. They shouldn't get themselves into every little fight that comes along. The same goes with the schools. I went to school here in Boston, and nobody was talking about Negroes and busing us around. The Negroes were there in Roxbury and we were here.

Everybody can't live with you, can they? Everybody likes his own. But now even the school people tell us we have to have our kids with this kind and that kind of person, or else they will be hurt, or something. Now how am I supposed to believe everything all these people say? They weren't talking that way a few years ago. The governor wasn't either. Nor the mayor. They're all just like cattle stampeding to sound like one another. The same with those people out in the suburbs. Suddenly they're interested in the Negro. They worked and worked to get away from him, of course, and get away from us, too. That's why they moved so far, instead of staying here, where they can do something, if they mean so well. But no. They moved and now they're all ready to come back—but only to drive a few Negro kids out for a Sunday picnic. Who has to live with all this, and pay for it in taxes and everything? Whose kids are pushed around? And who gets called "prejudiced' and all the other sneery words? I've had enough of it. It's hypocrisy, right down the line. And we're the ones who get it; the final buck gets passed to us. (Quoted in Coles, 1956, p. 56.)

A detailed account of the facts of poverty and inequality is presented by Parker in the article "The Men of Middle America." Parker examines the contemporary versions of the Horatio Alger myth that has dominated America's beliefs about its progress and prosperity: we are the middle-class society, wallowing in the abundance of a technological miracle and distributing our material benefits to all regardless of status, class, or ethnic origin. Contrary to the myths, however, there are the tens of millions of Americans who, although above the official poverty line, are nonetheless "deprived." The myth of America as the middle-class affluent society is shattered in the face of its 30 million poor, its 70 million deprived, its inadequate health and welfare system, and its literacy and infant-mortality rates.

As the rich in America keep getting richer, even the liberal solutions of a guaranteed annual wage or negative income tax will not deal with the stubborn facts of poverty, deprivation, and inequality. Such solutions will only serve to institutionalize poverty and detract from the large-scale changes necessary for a more just distribution of the benefits of our economy. The particular relation between poverty and inequality in wealthy Western societies was captured in Paul Jacobs' study of business techniques designed to remove any money from the hands of the poor before it can be used for their betterment. His conclusion reflects the strain of being kept poor amidst apparent wealth.

All of us are born into a state of anxiety, and many, or even most, of us must cope, throughout our lives, with deep-rooted feelings of personal inadequacy. For the poor, these feelings are continuously reinforced by the economic circumstances in which they live and by their relationships with the rest of society. In an egalitarian society where everyone is living in poverty, being poor generates neither much anxiety nor strong feelings of inadequacy. But in a society such as ours, which measures achievement primarily by financial and material standards, to be poor is to be scorned by others, and even worse, by one's own self. It is for this reason that in America the taste and smell of poverty are so sour. (Jacobs, 1966, p. 27.)

Much of the difficulty in dealing with poverty among various subgroups in American society resides in the inability of existing social institutions to adapt to the patterns of life in the disadvantaged groups. Residents of urban ghettos are limited in their contacts with legal and welfare institutions to the policeman and social worker who come into their area but are not from their area. There is often little opportunity for the ghetto resident to make legal and welfare services more adaptable to his needs. The low-status client without power has great difficulty in influencing the professionals who come into the ghetto to serve him. Migratory poor have even less power. Truman Moore deals with the plight of the 2 million migrants who move about the country harvesting crops. For not only are the migrants without the power needed to influence state and federal agencies, but they are also transients who do not remain in an area long enough to be eligible to use existing services or to make agencies feel obligated to provide such services.

Moore indicates the failure of existing agencies at the state and national levels in providing minimum-wage protection, decent housing, health services, and schooling for children. The economic interests of the corporate farms that employ migrants are clearly of greater importance to those who make legislation than are the interests of the migrant. The vulnerability of an unprotected, economically disadvantaged group is probably found in more extreme form among migrants than among urban poor who at least have the *potential* for group power through their more stable residence patterns.

The question raised earlier in this essay—regarding whether one chooses to emphasize the barriers to full equality that reside within the disadvantaged group, or to emphasize the barriers that exist in the institutional structure which fails to adapt to the needs of the poor—remains as one of the persistent issues surrounding the causes of, and solutions to, poverty. The issue became a matter of public debate in 1965, with the appearance of a Department of Labor report entitled *The Negro Family: The Case for National Action*, written by Daniel P. Moynihan with the assistance of Paul Barton and Ellen Broderich. The essential argument of the Moynihan report was that the government efforts to lift the legal barriers in the area of discrimination would not lead to full equality for the Negro. Moynihan reasoned that the history of slavery and subordination had such a marked impact upon the Negro social structure (particularly the family) that many Negroes would be unable to take advantage of the new opportunities that were made available to them. As stated in the report: "at the heart of the deterioration of the fabric of Negro society is the deterioration of the Negro family." Moynihan used this argument to urge the establishment of a national family policy designed to enhance "the stability and resources of the Negro American family."

Controversy in government circles, the civil-rights movement, the press, and among academic social scientists followed this report. Many of the reactions to the report have been collected in a single volume by

Rainwater and Yancey (1967). The controversy over the objectives of the report is less pronounced than the disagreement over its emphasis on the pathology of the ghetto and the breakdown of the Negro family. Such emphases can often serve to turn attention away from the defective features of American society that have failed to provide full equality for the Negro. There is no doubt that black Americans bear some scars from a brutal history inflicted upon them. But the Moynihan report ignored three vital points. First, that female dominance of households in Ireland, Poland, and in Western society generally, has always followed (rather than caused) economic destitution (Carper, 1968). Second, who resides with whom, supports whom, marries whom, or has children with whom is none of the government's business. Diverse cultural life styles remain the right of the individual and the community. Third, Black people no less than women or other disadvantaged minority groups are not currently being victimized by the damage that was done to their ancestors 150 years earlier (about which nothing can be done). They are being damaged by the current racism and current inequitable distribution of wealth and power in American society (about which something must be done.

Despite the fact that the large majority of poor Americans are white, poverty is a condition that has come to be identified with black Americans, Mexican-Americans, and American Indians. It is this identification that is partly responsible for the way Americans continue to ignore the existence of the poor. The non-white poor can be ignored more easily when there are also justifying beliefs of the sort that sees non-white people as less worthy, less motivated, more immoral, or any other stereotype that goes into the construction of racist beliefs.

REFERENCES

BAGDIKIAN, BEN H., "Ed MacIntosh: Man on a Pension," in H. P. Miller (ed.), *Poverty, American Style* (Belmont, Calif.: Wadsworth, 1966).

BROWN, CLAUDE, *Manchild in the Promised Land* (New York: Macmillan, 1965).

CARPER, LAURA, "The Negro Family and the Moynihan Report," *Dissent* (March–April 1966), pp. 133–140; reproduced in R. Perrucci and M. Pilisuk (eds.), *The Triple Revolution: Social Problems in Depth* (Boston: Little, Brown, 1968), pp. 461–468.

CASAVANTES, EDWARD, "Pride and Prejudice: A Mexican American Dilemma," *Civil Rights Digest*, 3 (Winter 1970), pp. 22–27.

CLOWARD, RICHARD A., and FRANCES F. PIVAN, "Birth of a Movement," *Nation* (May 8, 1967).

COLES, ROBERT, "The White Northerner: Pride and Prejudice," *Atlantic* (June 1966), pp. 53–57; reproduced in R. Perrucci and M. Pilisuk (eds.), *The Triple Revolution: Social Problems in Depth* (Boston: Little, Brown, 1968), pp. 398–406.

COSER, LEWIS A., "The Sociology of Poverty," *Social Problems*, 13 (1965), pp. 140–145.

DREW, ELIZABETH, "Going Hungry in America," *Atlantic* (December 1968), pp. 33–61.

ELMAN, RICHARD M., *The Poorhouse State: The American Way of Life on Public Assistance* (New York: Pantheon, 1966).

FERMAN, LOUIS A., JOYCE L. KORNBLUH, and ALAN HABER (eds.), *Poverty in America* (Ann Arbor: Univ. of Michigan Press, 1965).

HARRINGTON, MICHAEL, *The Other America* (Baltimore: Penguin, 1962).

HAYDEN, TOM, "Colonialism and Liberation in America," *Viet-Report* (Summer 1968), pp. 32–39.

JACOBS, PAUL, "Keeping the Poor Poor," *New Politics*, 5 (1966), pp. 3–16, 19–20, 25–27.

KOPKIND, ANDREW, "Of, by, and for the Poor," *New Republic* (June 19, 1965), pp. 15–19; reproduced in R. Perrucci and M. Pilisuk (eds.), *The Triple Revolution: Social Problems in Depth* (Boston: Little, Brown, 1968), pp. 515–523.

KOTZ, NICK, *Let Them Eat Promises: The Politics of Hunger in America* (Englewood Cliffs, N.J.: Prentice-Hall, 1969).

MILLER, HERMAN P., "Facts about Poverty, Revised," in H. P. Miller (ed.), *Poverty, American Style* (Belmont, Calif.: Wadsworth, 1966).

MILLER, HERMAN P., *Rich Man, Poor Man* (New York: Crowell, 1964).

MILLER, S. M., "Poverty and Inequality in America: Implications for the Social Services," *Child Welfare*, 42:9 (November 1963), pp. 442–445; reproduced in R. Perrucci and M. Pilisuk (eds.), *The Triple Revolution: Social Problems in Depth* (Boston: Little, Brown, 1968), pp. 488–493.

MILLER, S. M., and PAMELA ROBY, *The Future of Inequality* (New York: Basic Books, 1970).

MONTEZ, PHILIP, "Will the Real Mexican American Please Stand Up," *Civil Rights Digest*, 3 (Winter 1970), pp. 28—31.

MOYNIHAN, DANIEL P., "The President and the Negro: The Moment Lost," *Commentary* (February 1967), pp. 3–17; reproduced in R. Perrucci and M. Pilisuk (eds.), *The Triple Revolution: Social Problems in Depth* (Boston: Little, Brown, 1968), pp. 431–460.

Negro Family, The: The Case for National Action (Moynihan Report) (Washington D.C.: U.S. Government Printing Office, March 1965).

Newsweek, "Tio Taco Is Dead" (June 29, 1970), pp. 22–28.

RAINWATER, LEE, and WILLIAM L. YANCEY, *The Moynihan Report and the Politics of Controversy* (Cambridge, Mass.: M. I. T. Press, 1967).

REISSMAN, LEONARD, *Urban Affairs Quarterly* (March 1969).

RUSTIN, BAYARD, "The 'Watts Manifesto' and the McCone Report," *Commentary* (March 1966), pp. 29–35; reproduced in R. Perrucci and M. Pilisuk (eds.), *The Triple Revolution: Social Problems in Depth* (Boston: Little, Brown, 1968), pp. 469–481.

SAMUELS, GERTRUDE, "Why 'The Assassins' Can't Be 'Punks,'" *New York Times Magazine* (August 16, 1959), p. 13ff.

SUTHERLAND, ELIZABETH (ed.), *Letters from Mississippi* (New York: McGraw-Hill, 1965).

U.S. Commission on Civil Rights, *The Mexican American* (Washington, D.C.: U.S. Government Printing Office, 1968).

WEISS, PETER, "Nightmare in Mississippi," *The Progressive* (September 1964), pp. 19–22; reproduced in R. Perrucci and M. Pilisuk (eds.), *The Triple Revolution: Social Problems in Depth* (Boston: Little, Brown, 1968), pp. 391–397.

18

Kate Millett

Theory of Sexual Politics

If racism is the assumption of the superiority of some and the inferiority of others on the basis of biology, then racism is an apt term to apply to the traditional ways men think of and treat women. On the basis of their biological inheritance, one group considers itself superior and plays the dominant role. On the same basis the first group considers the second inferior and discriminates against them by pushing them into subservient roles. Sexism is a form of racism.

Consequently, much of what sociologists have learned in their various studies of racism can be profitably applied to sexism. Here are just some of the many possible applications based on these studies, with some of the insights we can gain into the dynamics of sexism, especially the perpetuation of the discrimination–prejudice cycle:

1. Discrimination on the basis of sex is not simply a matter of individual sentiment. Rather, such discrimination is structurally based: It is part of the basic ordering of the sexes according to the way the social institutions are related.

2. The structural sources of discrimination lead to prejudice. Those who find themselves in the dominant sector tend to think of themselves as superior simply because they occupy the superior position. They also tend to think of those who occupy the subdominant position as inferior on the evidence that they are, after all, in the inferior position.

3. The resulting prejudice leads to further discrimination, tending to make the system self-maintaining.

4. Members of the dominant group also develop vested interests in maintaining the status quo of group relations. They feel that their security, primarily economic, is threatened if members of the subdominant group socially advance. Because they feel that others gain at a direct cost to themselves, they strive to maintain the status quo.

5. The "dirty work," tasks which are necessary but distasteful, is usually assigned to members of the minority group. Members of the dominant group do not care for these duties to become part of their lot in life. The jobs are frequently not only distasteful in themselves but have also become associated through the years with the "inferior" group. Members of the dominant group then feel that they would be degrading themselves if they were to perform these more menial tasks. Consequently, they have further reason to resist change.

6. Members of the group considered socially inferior tend to internalize the negative attitudes directed against them.

7. Internalizing negative self-attitudes leads to debilitating defeatism, to the feeling that (a) one has fewer abilities than members of the dominant group, and (b) it does little good to try because, even if one is an exception and has unusual abilities, one will ultimately be treated according to group membership and not according to individual talents and performance.

8. This defeatism, in turn, leads to performance below individual capacities.

9. Low performance, in turn, provides further justification by means of readily available evidence that the place the members of the subdominant group occupy is the right place for them.

10. To change attitudes, it is more effective to change structural conditions than it is to try first to change the "heart" of individuals. Attitudes, in other words, flow from social structure, not social structure from attitudes— though social structure will be reinforced by the attitudes it creates.

11. Possibly, structural change is best brought about by direct confrontation with the powers that are buttressing the structural status quo. (I say possibly because many other results can occur from direct confrontation, including greater repression. The results will depend on the circumstances within which the confrontation occurs.)

In the following article, Millett analyzes some of the bases underlying the historical suppression of women by men. Note especially her position that women constitute a separate social/sexual class within society, a class historically and contemporaneously exploited by those claiming dominance—indeed, mastery— on the basis of their sex.

☐ This essay does not define the political as that relatively narrow and exclusive world of meetings, chairmen, and parties. The term "politics" shall refer to power-structured relationships, arrangements whereby one group of persons is controlled by another. By way of parenthesis one might add that although an ideal politics might simply be conceived of as the arrangement of human life on agreeable and rational principles from whence the entire notion of power *over* others should be banished, one must confess that this is not what constitutes the political as we know it, and it is to this that we must address ourselves.

The following sketch, which might be described as "notes toward a theory of patriarchy," will attempt to prove that sex is a status category with political implications. Something of a pioneering effort, it must perforce be both tentative and imperfect. Because the intention is to provide an overall description, statements must be generalized, exceptions neglected, and subheadings overlapping and, to some degree, arbitrary as well.

The word "politics" is enlisted here when speaking of the sexes primarily because such a word is eminently useful in outlining the real nature of their relative status, historically and at the present. It is opportune, perhaps today even mandatory, that we develop a more relevant psychology and philosophy of power relationships beyond the simple conceptual framework provided by our traditional formal politics. Indeed, it may be imperative that we give some attention to defining a theory of politics which treats of power relationships on grounds less conventional than those to which we are accustomed.[1] I have therefore found it pertinent to define them on grounds of personal contact and interaction between members of well-defined and coherent groups: races, castes, classes, and sexes. For it is precisely because certain groups have no representation in a number of recognized political structures that their position tends to be so stable, their oppression so continuous.

In America, recent events have forced us to acknowledge at last that the relationship between the races is indeed a political one which involves the general control of one collectivity, defined by birth, over another collectivity, also defined by birth. Groups who rule by birthright are fast disappearing, yet there remains one ancient and universal scheme for the domination of one birth group by another—the scheme that prevails in the area of sex. The study of racism has convinced us that a truly political state of affairs operates between the races to perpetuate a series of oppressive circumstances. The subordinated group has inadequate redress through existing political institutions, and is deterred thereby from organizing into conventional political struggle and opposition.

Quite in the same manner, a disinterested examination of our system of sexual relationship must point out that the situation between the sexes now, and throughout history, is a case of that phenomenon Max Weber defined as *herrschaft,* a relationship of dominance and subordinance.[2] What goes largely unexamined, often even unacknowledged (yet is institutionalized nonetheless) in our social order, is the birthright priority whereby males rule females. Through this system a most ingenious form of "interior colonization" has been achieved. It is one which tends moreover to be sturdier than any form of segregation, and more rigorous than class stratification, more uniform, certainly more enduring. However muted its present appearance may be, sexual dominion obtains nevertheless as perhaps the most pervasive ideology of our culture and provides its most fundamental concept of power.

This is so because our society, like all other historical civilizations, is a patriarchy.[3] The fact is evident at once if one recalls that the military, industry, technology, universities, science, political office, and finance—in short, every avenue of power within the society, including the coercive force of the police, is entirely in male hands. As the essence of politics is power, such realization cannot fail to carry impact. What lingers of supernatural authority, the Deity, "His" ministry, together with the ethics and values, the philosophy and art of our culture—its very civilization—as T. S. Eliot once observed, is of male manufacture.

If one takes patriarchal government to be the institution whereby that half of the populace which is female is controlled by that half which is male, the principles of patriarchy appear to be two fold: male shall dominate female, elder male shall dominate younger. However, just as with any human institution, there is frequently a distance between the real and the ideal; contradictions and exceptions do exist within the system. While patriarchy as an institution is a social constant so deeply entrenched as to run through all other political, social, or economic forms, whether of caste or class, feudality or bureaucracy, just as it pervades all major religions, it also exhibits great variety in history and locale. In democracies,[4] for example, females have often held no office or do so (as now) in such minuscule numbers as to be below even token representation. Aristocracy, on the other hand, with its emphasis upon the magic and dynastic properties of blood, may at times permit women to hold power. The principle of rule by elder males is violated even more frequently. Bearing in mind the variation and degree in patriarchy—as say between Saudi Arabia and Sweden, Indonesia and Red China—we also recognize our own form in the U.S. and Europe to be much altered and attenuated by the reforms described in the next chapter [*i.e.,* Chapter Three in *Sexual Politics,* Doubleday & Company, Inc., 1970].

Ideological

Hannah Arendt [5] has observed that government is upheld by power supported either through consent or imposed through violence. Conditioning to an ideology amounts to the former. Sexual politics obtains consent through the "socialization" of both sexes to basic patriarchal polities with regard to temperament, role, and status. As to status, a pervasive assent to the prejudice of male superiority guarantees superior status in the male, inferior in the female. The first item, temperament, involves the formation of human personality along stereotyped lines of sex category ("masculine" and "feminine"), based on the needs and values of the dominant group and dictated by what its members cherish in themselves and find convenient in subordinates: aggression, intelligence, force, and efficacy in the male; passivity, ignorance, docility, "virtue," and ineffectuality in the female. This is complemented by a second factor, sex role, which decrees a consonant and highly elaborate code of conduct, gesture and attitude for each sex. In terms of activity, sex role assigns domestic service and attendance upon infants to the female, the rest of human achievement, interest, and ambition to the male. The limited role allotted the female tends to arrest her at the level of biological experience. Therefore, nearly all that can be described as distinctly human rather than animal activity (in their own way animals also give birth and care for their young) is largely reserved for the male. Of course, status again follows from such an assignment. Were one to analyze the three categories one might designate status as the political component, role as the sociological, and temperament as the psychological—yet their interdependence is unquestionable and they form a chain. Those awarded higher status tend to adopt roles of mastery, largely because they are first encouraged to develop temperaments of dominance. That this is true of caste and class as well is self-evident.

Biological

Patriarchal religion, popular attitude, and to some degree, science as well [6] assumes these psycho-social distinctions to rest upon biological differences between the sexes, so that where culture is acknowledged as shaping behavior, it is said to do no more than cooperate with nature. Yet the temperamental distinctions created in patriarchy ("masculine" and "feminine" personality traits) do not appear to originate in human nature, those of role and status still less.

The heavier musculature of the male, a secondary sexual characteristic and common among mammals, is biological in origin but is also
culturally encouraged through breeding, diet and exercise. Yet it is
hardly an adequate category on which to base political relations *within
civilization*.[7] Male supremacy, like other political creeds, does not finally
reside in physical strength but in the acceptance of a value system
which is not biological. Superior physical strength is not a factor in political relations—vide those of race and class. Civilization has always
been able to substitute other methods (technic, weaponry, knowledge)
for those of physical strength, and contemporary civilization has no
further need of it. At present, as in the past, physical exertion is very
generally a class factor, those at the bottom performing the most strenuous tasks, whether they be strong or not.

Not only is there insufficient evidence for the thesis that the present
social distinctions of patriarchy (status, role, temperament) are physical
in origin, but we are hardly in a position to assess the existing differen-
tiations, since distinctions which we know to be culturally induced at
present so outweigh them. Whatever the "real" differences between the
sexes may be, we are not likely to know them until the sexes are treated
differently, that is alike. And this is very far from being the case at
present. Important new research not only suggests that the possibilities
of innate temperamental differences seem more remote than ever, but
even raises questions as to the validity and permanence of psycho-sex-
ual identity. In doing so it gives fairly concrete positive evidence of the
overwhelmingly *cultural* character of gender, i.e. personality structure
in terms of sexual category.

Because of our social circumstances, male and female are really two
cultures and their life experiences are utterly different—and this is
crucial. Implicit in all the gender identity development which takes
place through childhood is the sum total of the parents', the peers', and
the culture's notions of what is appropriate to each gender by way of
temperament, character, interests, status, worth, gesture, and expression. Every moment of the child's life is a clue to how he or she must
think and behave to attain or satisfy the demands which gender places
upon one. In adolescence, the merciless task of conformity grows to
crisis proportions, generally cooling and settling in maturity.

Since patriarchy's biological foundations appear to be so very insecure, one has some cause to admire the strength of a "socialization"
which can continue a universal condition "on faith alone," as it were, or
through an acquired value system exclusively. What does seem decisive
in assuring the maintenance of the temperamental differences between
the sexes is the conditioning of early childhood. Conditioning runs in a
circle of self-perpetuation and self-fulfilling prophecy. To take a simple

example: expectations the culture cherishes about his gender identity encourage the young male to develop aggressive impulses, and the female to thwart her own or turn them inward. The result is that the male tends to have aggression reinforced in his behavior, often with significant anti-social possibilities. Thereupon the culture consents to believe the possession of the male indicator, the testes, penis, and scrotum, in itself characterizes the aggressive impulse, and even vulgarly celebrates it in such encomiums as "that guy has balls." The same process of reinforcement is evident in producing the chief "feminine" virtue of passivity.

In contemporary terminology, the basic division of temperamental trait is marshaled along the line of "aggression is male" and "passivity is female." All other temperamental traits are somehow—often with the most dexterous ingenuity—aligned to correspond. If aggressiveness is the trait of the master class, docility must be the corresponding trait of a subject group. The usual hope of such line of reasoning is that "nature," by some impossible outside chance, might still be depended upon to rationalize the patriarchal system. An important consideration to be remembered here is that in patriarchy, the function of norm is unthinkingly delegated to the male—were it not, one might as plausibly speak of "feminine" behavior as active, and "masculine" behavior as hyperactive or hyperaggressive.

Sociological

Patriarchy's chief institution is the family. It is both a mirror of and a connection with the larger society; a patriarchal unit within a patriarchal whole. Mediating between the individual and the social structure, the family effects control and conformity where political and other authorities are insufficient.[8] As the fundamental instrument and the foundation unit of patriarchal society the family and its roles are prototypical. Serving as an agent of the larger society, the family not only encourages its own members to adjust and conform, but acts as a unit in the government of the patriarchal state which rules its citizens through its family heads. Even in patriarchal societies where they are granted legal citizenship, women tend to be ruled through the family alone and have little or no formal relation to the state.[9]

As co-operation between the family and the larger society is essential, else both would fall apart, the fate of three patriarchal institutions, the family, society, and the state are interrelated. In most forms of patriarchy this has generally led to the granting of religious support in statements such as the Catholic precept that "the father is head of the family," or Judaism's delegation of quasi-priestly authority to the male parent. Secular governments today also confirm this, as in census practices of designating the male as head of household, taxation, passports etc. Female heads of household tend to be regarded as undesirable; the phenomenon is a trait of poverty or misfortune. The Confucian prescription that the relationship between ruler and subject is parallel to that of father and children points to the essentially feudal character of the patriarchal family (and conversely, the familial character of feudalism) even in modern democracies.[10]

The chief contribution of the family in patriarchy is the socialization of the young (largely through the example and admonition of their parents) into patriarchal ideology's prescribed attitudes toward the categories of role, temperament, and status. Although slight differences of definition depend here upon the parents' grasp of cultural values, the general effect of uniformity is achieved, to be further reinforced through peers, schools, media, and other learning sources, formal and informal. While we may niggle over the balance of authority between the personalities of various households, one must remember that the entire culture supports masculine authority in all areas of life and—outside of the home—permits the female none at all.

To insure that its crucial functions of reproduction and socialization of the young take place only within its confines, the patriarchal family insists upon legitimacy. Bronislaw Malinowski describes this as "the principle of legitimacy" formulating it as an insistence that "no child should be brought into the world without a man—and one man at that—assuming the role of sociological father." [11] By this apparently consistent and universal prohibition (whose penalties vary by class and in accord with the expected operations of the double standard) patriarchy decrees that the status of both child and mother is primarily or ultimately dependent upon the male. And since it is not only his social status, but even his economic power upon which his dependents generally rely, the position of the masculine figure within the family—as without—is materially, as well as ideologically, extremely strong.

Class

It is in the area of class that the castelike status of the female within patriarchy is most liable to confusion, for sexual status often operates in a superficially confusing way within the variable of class. In a society where status is dependent upon the economic, social, and educational circumstances of class, it is possible for certain females to appear to stand higher than some males. Yet not when one looks more closely at the subject. This is perhaps easier to see by means of analogy: a black doctor or lawyer has higher social status than a poor white sharecropper. But race, itself a caste system which subsumes class, persuades the latter citizen that he belongs to a higher order of life, just as it oppresses the black professional in spirit, whatever his material success may be. In much the same manner, a truck driver or butcher has always his "manhood" to fall back upon.

The function of class or ethnic mores in patriarchy is largely a matter of how overtly displayed or how loudly enunciated the general ethic of masculine supremacy allows itself to become. Here one is confronted by what appears to be a paradox: while in the lower social strata, the male is more likely to claim authority on the strength of his sex rank alone, he is actually obliged more often to share power with the women of his class who are economically productive; whereas in the middle and upper classes, there is less tendency to assert a blunt patriarchal dominance, as men who enjoy such status have more power in any case.[12]

One of the chief effects of class within patriarchy is to set one woman against another, in the past creating a lively antagonism between whore and matron, and in the present between career woman and housewife. One envies the other her "security" and prestige, while the envied yearns beyond the confines of respectability for what she takes to be the other's freedom, adventure, and contact with the great world. Through the multiple advantages of the double standard, the male participates in both worlds, empowered by his superior social and economic resources to play the estranged women against each other as rivals. One might also recognize subsidiary status categories among women: not only is virtue class, but beauty and age as well.

Perhaps, in the final analysis, it is possible to argue that women tend to transcend the usual class stratifications in patriarchy, for whatever the class of her birth and education, the female has fewer permanent class associations than does the male. Economic dependency renders her affiliations with any class a tangential, vicarious, and temporary matter. Aristotle observed that the only slave to whom a commoner might lay claim was his woman, and the service of an unpaid domestic still provides working-class males with a "cushion" against the buffets of the class system which incidentally provides them with some of the psychic luxuries of the leisure class. Thrown upon their own resources, few women rise above working class in personal prestige and economic power, and women as a group do not enjoy many of the interests and benefits any class may offer its male members. Women have therefore less of an investment in the class system. But it is important to understand that as with any group whose existence is parasitic to its rulers, women are a dependency class who live on surplus. And their marginal life frequently renders them conservative, for like all persons in their situation (slaves are a classic example here) they identify their own survival with the prosperity of those who feed them. The hope of seeking liberating radical solutions of their own seems too remote for the majority to dare contemplate and remains so until consciousness on the subject is raised.

Economic

One of the most efficient branches of patriarchal government lies in the agency of its economic hold over its female subjects. In traditional patriarchy, women, as non-persons without legal standing, were permitted no actual economic existence as they could neither own nor earn in their own right. Since women have always worked in patriarchal societies, often at the most routine or strenuous tasks, what is at issue here is not labor but economic reward. In modern reformed patriarchal societies, women have certain economic rights, yet the "woman's work" in which some two thirds of the female population in most developed countries are engaged is work that is not paid for. In a money economy where autonomy and prestige depend upon currency, this is a fact of great importance. In general, the position of women in patriarchy is a continuous function of their economic dependence. Just as their social position is vicarious and achieved (often on a temporary or marginal basis) though males, their relation to the economy is also typically vicarious or tangential.

In modern capitalist countries women also function as a reserve labor force, enlisted in times of war and expansion and discharged in times of peace and recession. In this role American women have replaced immigrant labor and now compete with the racial minorities. In socialist countries the female labor force is generally in the lower ranks as well, despite a high incidence of women in certain professions such as medicine. The status and rewards of such professions have declined as women enter them, and they are permitted to enter such areas under a rationale that society or the state (and socialist countries are also patriarchal) rather than woman is served by such activity.

In terms of industry and production, the situation of women is in many ways comparable both to colonial and to pre-industrial peoples. Although they achieved their first economic autonomy in the industrial

revolution and now constitute a large and underpaid factory population, women do not participate directly in technology or in production.
What they customarily produce (domestic and personal service) has no
market value and is, as it were, pre-capital. Nor, where they do participate in production of commodities through employment, do they own
or control or even comprehend the process in which they participate.
An example might make this clearer: the refrigerator is a machine all
women use, some assemble it in factories, and a very few with scientific
education understand its principles of operation. Yet the heavy industries which roll its steel and produce the dies for its parts are in male
hands. The same is true of the typewriter, the auto, etc. Now, while
knowledge is fragmented even among the male population, collectively
they could reconstruct any technological device. But in the absence of
males, women's distance from technology today is sufficiently great that
it is doubtful that they could replace or repair such machines on any
significant scale. Woman's distance from higher technology is even
greater: large-scale building construction; the development of compu-
ters; the moon shot, occur as further examples. If knowledge is power,
power is also knowledge, and a large factor in their subordinate position is the fairly systematic ignorance patriarchy imposes upon women.

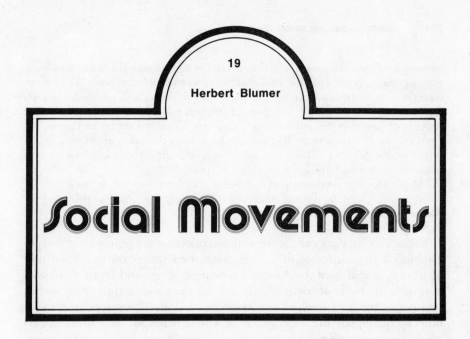

19

Herbert Blumer

Social Movements

Contemporary society is characterized by social change. We are constantly immersed in change. Little appears to remain the same over the years. New gadgets. Inflation. Economic recessions and booms. Wars or "peace-keeping" operations, as the case may be. Changing patterns of education, child raising, marriage. Cold wars, and their thaws deliberately timed. Political upheaval. Watergates. New weapons and deployment systems. Energy crises. Riots. Sexual "revolutions." The "new" morality. Zero population growth. Legalized abortion. The Pill. Hippies. Psychedelics. Grass in place of cocktails. And on and on.

When vague dissatisfactions felt by large numbers of people become focused, we have the potential of a social movement. When general ideas that people hold concerning the place they occupy in life fail to match what they think should legitimately be theirs, the potential of a social movement is present. Leadership must emerge, however, to crystallize dissatisfactions, to provide direction, to agitate, and to develop shared sentiments in order for the potential to become actuality.

Because social definitions determine how people view reality, those who control definitional processes to a large extent control people. If definitions can be fostered to make people think that the dissatisfactions they experience are due to some fault within them, that what they experience is an individualistic matter having little or nothing to do with others, dissatisfactions can be kept from crys-

From pp. 99–105 and 114–120 of "Social Movements" by Herbert Blumer from *Principles of Sociology,* 3rd Edition, edited by Alfred McClung Lee. Copyright © 1969 by Barnes & Noble, Inc. By permission of Harper & Row, Publishers, Inc.

tallizing into cooperative social action geared to challenging the status quo. So it was for many years with the dissatisfactions women experienced. They were thought to be individual matters, problems of the individual, problems, in fact, due to some lack within the individual. But these dissatisfactions are now in the process of being redefined as originating not from individual situations but from the social structure itself, from the basic ways the sexes are structured to relate to one another. The status quo has now been directly challenged, and oppositional forces have been brought into play.

The women's movement, and the other social movements in their role in social change, can be better understood through the analysis provided by Blumer in this final article in this section.

☐ Social movements can be viewed as collective enterprises seeking to establish a new order of life. They have their inception in a condition of unrest, and derive their motive power on one hand from disatisfaction with the current form of life, and on the other hand, from wishes and hopes for a new scheme or system of living. The career of a social movement depicts the emergence of a new order of life. In its beginning, a social movement is amorphous, poorly organized, and without form; the collective behavior is on the primitive level that we have already discussed, and the mechanisms of interaction are the elementary, spontaneous mechanisms of which we have spoken. As a social movement develops, it takes on the character of a society. It acquires organization and form, a body of customs and traditions, established leadership, an enduring division of labor, social rules and social values—in short, a culture, a social organization, and a new scheme of life.

Our treatment of social movements will deal with three kinds—general social movements, specific social movements, and expressive social movements.[1]

General Social Movements

By general social movements we have in mind movements such as the labor movement, the youth movement, the women's movement, and the peace movement. Their background is constituted by gradual and pervasive changes in the values of people—changes which can be called cultural drifts. Such cultural drifts stand for a general shifting in the ideas of people particularly along the line of the conceptions which people have of themselves, and of their rights and privileges. Over a period of time many people may develop a new view of what they believe they are entitled to—a view largely made up of desires and hopes. It signifies the emergence of a new set of values which influence people in the way in which they look upon their own lives. Examples of such cultural drifts in our own recent history are the increased value of health, the belief in free education, the extension of the franchise, the emancipation of women, the increasing regard for children, and the increasing prestige of science.

Indefinite Images and Behavior

The development of the new values which such cultural drifts bring forth involve some interesting psychological changes which provide the motivation for general social movements. They mean, in a general sense, that people have come to form new conceptions of themselves which do not conform to the actual positions which they occupy in their life. They acquire new dispositions and interests and, accordingly, become sensitized in new directions; and, conversely, they come to experience dissatisfaction where before they had none. These new images of themselves, which people begin to develop in response to cultural drifts, are vague and indefinite; and correspondingly, the behavior in response to such images is uncertain and without definite aim. It is this feature which provides a clue for the understanding of general social movements.

Characteristics of General Social Movements

General social movements take the form of groping and unco-ordinated efforts. They have only a general direction, toward which they move in a slow, halting, erratic yet persistent fashion. As movements they are unorganized, with neither established leadership nor recognized membership, and little guidance and control. Such a movement as the women's movement, which has the general and vague aim of the emancipation of women, suggests these features of a general social movement. The women's movement, like all general social movements, operates over a wide range—in the home, in marriage, in education, in industry, in politics, in travel—in each area of which it represents a search for an arrangement which will answer to the new idea of status being formed by women. Such a movement is episodic in its career, with very scattered manifestations of activity. It may show considerable enthusiasm at one point and reluctance and inertia at another; it may experience success in one area, and abortive effort in another. In general, it may be said that its progress is very uneven with setbacks, reverses, and frequent retreading of the same ground. At one time the impetus to the movement may come from people in one place, at another time in another place. On the whole the movement is likely to be carried on by many unknown and obscure people who struggle in different areas without their striving and achievements becoming generally known.

A general social movement usually is characterized by a literature, but the literature is as varied and ill-defined as is the movement itself. It is likely to be an expression of protest, with a general depiction of a kind of utopian existence. As such, it vaguely outlines a philosophy based on new values and self-conceptions. Such a literature is of great importance in spreading a message or view, however imprecise it may be, and so in implanting suggestions, awakening hopes, and arousing dissatisfactions. Similarly, the "leaders" of a general social movement play an important part—not in the sense of exercising directive control over the movement, but in the sense of being pace-makers. Such leaders are likely to be "voices in the wilderness," pioneers without any solid following, and frequently not very clear about their own goals. However, their example helps to develop sensitivities, arouse hopes, and break down resistances. From these traits one can easily realize that the general social movement develops primarily in an informal, inconspicuous, and largely subterranean fashion. Its media of interaction are primarily reading, conversations, talks, discussions, and the perception of examples. Its achievements and operations are likely to be made primarily in the realm of individual experience rather than by noticeable concerted action of groups. It seems evident that the general social movement is dominated to a large extent by the mechanisms of mass behavior, such as we have described in our treatment of the mass. Especially in its earlier stages, general social movements are likely to be merely an aggregation of individual lines of action based on individual decisions and selections. As is characteristic of the mass and of mass behavior, general social movements are rather formless in organization and inarticulate in expression.

The Basis for Specific Social Movements

Just as the cultural drifts provide the background out of which emerge general social movements, so the general social movement constitutes the setting out of which develop specific social movements. Indeed, a specific social movement is usually a crystallization of much of the motivation of dissatisfaction, hope, and desire awakened by the general social movement and the focusing of this motivation on some specific objective. A convenient illustration is the anti-slavery movement, which was, to a considerable degree, an individual expression of the widespread humanitarian movement of the nineteenth century. With this recognition of the relation between general and specific social movements, we can turn to a consideration of the latter.

Specific Social Movements

The outstanding instances of this type of movement are reform movements and revolutionary movements. A specific social movement is one which has a well-defined objective or goal which it seeks to reach. In this effort it develops an organization and structure, making it essentially a society. It develops a recognized and accepted leadership and a definite membership characterized by a "we-consciousness." It forms a body of traditions, a guiding set of values, a philosophy, sets of rules, and a general body of expectations. Its members form allegiances and loyalties. Within it there develops a division of labor, particularly in the form of a social structure in which individuals occupy status positions. Thus, individuals develop personalities and conceptions of themselves, representing the individual counterpart of a social structure.

A social movement, of the specific sort, does not come into existence with such a structure and organization already established. Instead, its organization and its culture are developed in the course of its career. It is necessary to view social movements from this temporal and developmental perspective. In the beginning a social movement is loosely organized and characterized by impulsive behavior. It has no clear objective; its behavior and thinking are largely under the dominance of restlessness and collective excitement. As a social movement develops, however, its behavior, which was originally dispersed, tends to become organized, solidified, and persistent. It is possible to delineate stages roughly in the career of a social movement which represent this increasing organization. One scheme of four stages has been suggested by Dawson and Gettys.[2] These are the stage of social unrest, the stage of popular excitement, the stage of formalization, and the stage of institutionalization.

Stages of Development

In the first of these four stages people are restless, uneasy, and act in the random fashion that we have considered. They are susceptible to appeals and suggestions that tap their discontent, and hence, in this stage, the agitator is likely to play an important role. The random and erratic behavior is significant in sensitizing people to one another and so makes possible the focusing of their restlessness on certain objects. The stage of popular excitement is marked even more by milling, but it is not quite so random and aimless. More definite notions emerge as to the cause of their condition and as to what should be done in the way of social change. So there is a sharpening of objectives. In this stage the leader is likely to be a prophet or a reformer. In the stage of formalization the movement becomes more clearly organized with rules, policies, tactics, and discipline. Here the leader is likely to be in the nature of a statesman. In the institutional stage, the movement has crystallized into a fixed organization with a definite personnel and structure to carry into execution the purposes of the movement. Here the leader is likely to be an administrator. In considering the development of the specific social movement our interest is less in considering the stages through which it passes than in discussing the mechanisms and means through which such a movement is able to grow and become organized. It is convenient to group these mechanisms under five heads: (1) agitation, (2) development of *esprit de corps,* (3) development of morale, (4) the formation of an ideology, and (5) the development of operating tactics.

The Role of Agitation

Agitation is of primary importance in a social movement. It plays its most significant role in the beginning and early stages of a movement, although it may persist in minor form in the later portions of the life-cycle of the movement. As the term suggests, agitation operates to arouse people and so make them possible recruits for the movement. It is essentially a means of exciting people and of awakening within them new impulses and ideas which make them restless and dissatisfied. Consequently, it acts to loosen the hold on them of their previous attachments, and to break down their previous ways of thinking and acting. For a movement to begin and gain impetus, it is necessary for people to be jarred loose from their customary ways of thinking and believing, and to have aroused within them new impulses and wishes. This is what agitation seeks to do. To be successful, it must first gain the attention of people; second, it must excite them, and arouse feelings and impulses; and third, it must give some direction to these impulses and feelings through ideas, suggestions, criticisms, and promises.

Agitation operates in two kinds of situations. One is a situation marked by abuse, unfair discrimination, and injustice, but a situation wherein people take this mode of life for granted and do not raise questions about it. Thus, while the situation is potentially fraught with suffering and protest, the people are marked by inertia. Their views of their situation incline them to accept it; hence the function of the agitation is to lead them to challenge and question their own modes of living. It is in such a situation that agitation may create social unrest where none existed previously. The other situation is one wherein people are already aroused, restless, and discontented, but where they either are too timid to act or else do not know what to do. In this situation the function of agitation is not so much to implant the seeds of unrest, as to intensify, release, and direct the tensions which people already have.

Agitators seem to fall into two types corresponding roughly to these two situations. One type of agitator is an excitable, restless, and aggressive individual. His dynamic and energetic behavior attracts the attention of people to him; and the excitement and restlessness of his behavior tends to infect them. He is likely to act with dramatic gesture and to talk in terms of spectacular imagery. His appearance and behavior foster the contagion of unrest and excitement. This type of agitator is likely to be most successful in the situation where people are already disturbed and unsettled; in such a situation his own excited and energetic activity can easily arouse other people who are sensitized to such behavior and already disposed to excitability.

The second type of agitator is more calm, quiet, and dignified. He stirs people not by what he does, but what he says. He is likely to be a man sparing in his words, but capable of saying very caustic, incisive, and biting things—things which get "under the skin" of people and force them to view things in a new light. This type of agitator is more suited to the first of the social situations discussed—the situation where people endure hardships or discrimination without developing attitudes of resentment. In this situation, his function is to make people aware of their own position and of the inequalities, deficiencies, and injustices that seem to mark their lot. He leads them to raise questions about what they have previously taken for granted and to form new wishes, inclinations, and hopes.

The function of agitation, as stated above, is in part to dislodge and stir up people and so liberate them for movement in new directions. More specifically, it operates to change the conceptions which people have of themselves, and the notions which they have of their rights and dues. Such new conceptions involving beliefs that one is justly entitled to privileges from which he is excluded, provide the dominant motive force for the social movement. Agitation, as the means of implanting these new conceptions among people, becomes, in this way, of basic importance to the success of a social movement.

A brief remark relative to the tactics of agitation may be made here. It is sufficient to say that the tactics of agitation vary with the situation, the people, and the culture. A procedure which may be highly successful in one situation may turn out to be ludicrous in another situation. This suggests the problem of identifying different types of situations and correlating with each the appropriate form of agitation. Practically no study has been conducted on this problem. Here, one can merely state the truism that the agitator, to be successful, must sense the thoughts, interests, and values of his listeners. . . .

Expressive Movements

The characteristic feature of expressive movements is that they do not seek to change the institutions of the social order or its objective character. The tension and unrest out of which they emerge are not focused upon some objective of social change which the movement seeks collectively to achieve. Instead, they are released in some type of expressive behavior which, however, in becoming crystallized, may have profound effects on the personalities of individuals and on the character of the social order. We shall consider two kinds of expressive movements: religious movements and fashion movements.

Religious Movements

Genuine religious movements are to be distinguished from reform movements and factional splits that take place inside of an established religious body. Religious movements begin essentially as cults; they have their setting in a situation which, psychologically, is like that of the dancing crowd. They represent an inward direction of unrest and tension in the form of disturbed feelings which ultimately express themselves in movement designed to release the tension. The tension does not then go over into purposive action but into expression. This characteristic suggests the nature of the situation from which religious movements emerge. It is a situation wherein people are upset and disturbed, but wherein they cannot act; in other words, a situation of frustration. The inability to release their tension in the direction of some actual change in the social order leaves as the alternative mere expressive behavior.

It is well to recall here the most prominent features of the dancing crowd. One of these is a feeling of *intense intimacy* and *esprit de corps*. Another is a heightened feeling of *exaltation* and ecstasy which leads individuals to experience personal expansion and to have a sense of being possessed by some transcendental spirit. Individuals feel inspired and are likely to engage in prophetic utterances. A third mark is the *projection of the collective feelings on outside objects*—persons, behavior, songs, words, phrases, and material objects—which thereby take on a sacred character. With the recurrence and repetition of this crowd behavior, the *esprit de corps* becomes strengthened, the dancing behavior formalized and ritualized, and the sacred objects reinforced. It is at this stage that the sect or cult appears. Since the growth of a religious movement is patterned after that of the sect, let us consider some of the important features of the sect.

First it should be noted that the members of a sect may be recruited from a heterogeneous background, showing differences in wealth, rank, education, and social background. These differences and distinctions have no significance in the sect. In the milling and in the development of rapport everyone is reduced to a common level of brotherhood. This fact is shown not only by the feelings and attitudes which the members have for one another, but also by the manner in which they refer to one another and the way in which they address one another.

Around the feelings of exaltation and the sacred symbols in which these feelings become crystallized, there grow up a series of beliefs and rites which become the *creed and the ritual of the sect*. The whole life of the sect becomes centered around this creed and ritual which, in themselves, come to acquire a sacred character. Since they symbolize the intense feelings of the group, they become absolute and imperative. The prophet plays an important role here. He is a sacred personage and he tends to symbolize in himself the creed and ritual of the group. Also, he is the primary guardian of this creed and ritual.

The creed of the group becomes elaborated into an extensive body of doctrine as the sect becomes cognizant of criticisms made by outsiders and as it seeks to justify its views. It is in this way that a *theology* arises; a large part of it is in the form of an apologia. Accompanying this is some change in the ritual. Those features of its practices and modes of living which subject the sect to criticism and even persecution at the hands of outsiders are likely to be cherished by the sect as the marks of its own identity and thus acquire a special significance.

Another important feature of the sect that arises from its peculiar experience and sacred character is the belief that it is divinely favored, and that it consists of a *select group of sacred souls*. The personal transformation experienced by members of the sect and the new moral and communal vistas that it yields, readily lead them to this conviction. People on the outside of the sect are regarded as lost souls; they have not been blessed with this rectifying experience.

The feeling which the sect has of itself as a community of saved souls easily disposes it to aggressive proselytizing of outsiders. Frequently, it feels it has a divine mission to save others and to "show them the light." Hence it seeks *converts*. In order to become a member, an outsider has to have a conversion experience—a moral transformation similar in character to that of the original members. The public confession is a testimonial of such an experience, and is a sign that the individual is a member of the select. These remarks point to a particularly significant characteristic of the sect—the intense conflict relation in which the sect stands with reference to the outside world. The sect may be said to be at war with the outside world, yet it is a peculiar kind of conflict relation, in that the sect is not concerned with seeking to change the institutions or the objective social order, but instead seeks the moral regeneration of the world. It aims, at least originally, not to change the outside existence, but to change the inner life. In this sense, the sect might be thought of as profoundly revolutionary, in that it endeavors to inculcate a new conception of the universe instead of merely seeking to remake institutions or the objective structure of a social order.

A religious movement tends to share these features of the sect. Its program represents a new way of living and it aims at a moral regeneration of the world. As it develops from the amorphous state that it is likely to have in the situation of the dancing crowd, it tends to acquire a structure like that of the sect, and so develops into a society. In this way it becomes analogous to specific social movements except that its aims are of a profoundly different nature.[3]

Fashion Movements

While fashion is thought of usually in relation to clothing, it is important to realize that it covers a much wider domain. It is to be found in manners, the arts, literature, and philosophy, and may even reach into certain areas of science. In fact, it may operate in any field of group life, apart from the technological and utilitarian area and the area of the sacred. Its operation requires a class society, for in its essential character it does not occur either in a homogeneous society like a primitive group, or in a caste society.

Fashion behaves as a movement, and on this basis it is different from custom which, by comparison, is static. This is due to the fact that fashion is based fundamentally on differentiation and emulation. In a class society, the upper classes or so-called social elite are not able to differentiate themselves by *fixed* symbols or badges. Hence the more external features of their life and behavior are likely to be imitated by classes immediately subjacent to them, who, in turn, are imitated by groups immediately below them in the social structure. This process gives to fashion a vertical descent. However, the elite class finds that it is no longer distinguishable, by reason of the imitation made by others, and hence is led to adopt new differentiating criteria, only to displace these as they in turn are imitated. It is primarily this feature that makes fashion into a movement and which has led one writer to remark that a fashion, once launched, moves to its doom.

As a movement, fashion shows little resemblance to any of the other movements which we have considered. While it occurs spontaneously and moves along in a characteristic cycle, it involves little in the way of crowd behavior and it is not dependent upon the discussion process and the resulting public opinion. It does not depend upon the mechanisms of which we have spoken. The participants are not recruited through agitation or proselytizing. No *esprit de corps* or morale is built up among them. Nor does the fashion movement have, or require, an ideology. Further, since it does not have a leadership imparting *conscious* direction to the movement, it does not build up a set of tactics.[4] People participate in the fashion movement voluntarily and in response to the interesting and powerful kind of control which fashion imposes on them.

Not only is the fashion movement unique in terms of its character, but it differs from other movements in that it does not develop into a society. It does not build up a social organization; it has no personnel or functionaries; it does not develop a division of labor among its participants with each being assigned a given status; it does not construct a set of symbols, myths, values, philosophy, or set of practices, and in this sense does not form a culture; and finally, it does not develop a set of loyalties or form a we-consciousness.

Nevertheless, the movement of fashion is an important form of collective behavior with very significant results for the social order. First, it should be noted that the fashion movement is a genuine expressive movement. It does not have a conscious goal which people are trying to reach through collective action, as is true in the case of the specific social movements. Nor does it represent the release of excitement and tension generated in a dancing crowd situation. It is expressive, however, of certain fundamental impulses and tendencies, such as an inclination toward novel experience, a desire of distinction, and an urge to conform. Fashion is important especially in providing a means for the expression of developing tastes and dispositions; this feature establishes it as a form of expressive behavior.

The latter remark provides a cue for understanding the role of fashion and the way in which it contributes to the formation of a new social order. In a changing society, such as is necessarily presupposed for the operation of fashion, people are continually having their subjective lives upset; they experience new dispositions and tastes which, however, are vague and ill-defined. It seems quite clear that fashion, by providing an opportunity for the expression of dispositions and tastes, serves to make them definite and to channelize them and, consequently, to fix and solidify them. To understand this, one should appreciate the fact that the movement and success of fashion are dependent upon the acceptance of the given style or pattern. In turn, this acceptance is based not merely upon the prestige attached to the style but also upon whether the style meets and answers to the dispositions and developing tastes of people. (The notorious failures that attend efforts to make styles fashionable upon the basis of mere prestige provide some support for this point.) From this point of view, we can regard fashion as arising and flourishing in response to new subjective demands. In providing means for the expression of these dispositions and tastes, fashion acts, as suggested before, to shape and crystallize these tastes. In the long run fashion aids, in this manner, to construct a *Zeitgeist* or a common subjective life, and in doing so, helps to lay the foundation for a new social order.

Revival Movements and Nationalist Movements

In our discussion so far, we have been treating separately specific social movements, religious movements, and fashion movements. Yet it should be clear that they can be merged, even though in very different degrees. Thus a revolutionary movement may have many of the features of a religious movement, with its success dependent to some extent upon the movement's becoming fashionable.

Revival Movements

Revival movements and nationalist movements are particularly likely to have this mixed character. We shall devote a few remarks to them. In revival movements people idealize the past, venerate the ideal picture that they have, and seek to mold contemporary life in terms of this ideal picture. Such movements are explainable, apparently, as a response to a situation of frustration. In this situation people are experiencing a loss of self-respect. Since the future holds no promise for them to form a new respectful conception of themselves, they turn to the past in an effort to do so. By recalling past glories and achievements they can regain a modicum of self-respect and satisfaction. That such movements should have a strong religious character is to be expected. Nationalist movements are very similar in these respects.

Nationalist Movements

Movements of nationalism are exceedingly pronounced in our current epoch. They represent efforts of a given people sharing some sense of common identity and historical lineage to gain independent status inside of an international order of sovereign bodies. They seek to guide their own destiny in place of being subservient to the control of an alien group. "Liberty" and "freedom" thus become both the goal and the inspiring clarion calls of nationalist movements. This type of movement has its source in distressing personal experiences in which individuals are made to feel inferior because of the subordinate status of the people to which they belong. They seek, accordingly, to raise the status of their group. While usually beginning as reform movements nationalist movements generally become revolutionary in character. Barred from the institutions and channels of the dominant group they resort to the use of revolutionary tactics, carrying on their agitation and planning inside of their own separate institutions, frequently their native church. At the same time, like a reform movement, they solicit the favorable opinion of outside peoples. Thus, nationalist movements rely on the use of the mechanisms previously discusssed in the case of specific social movements. One should note, in addition, the strong revivalistic slant that nationalist movements usually take; such movements seek to glorify the past of the people and eulogize the distinctive culture of the people, particularly their language. Where there is no sense of a common past or the sharing of a common language, as in the case of many recent nationalist movements in present-day Africa, a nationalist movement has to depend primarily on cultivating and using the ingroup-out-group mechanism as the means of developing unity and persistence.

5

The Social Fabric

As we have covered in preceding selections, many groups compete with one another for scarce resources. Some come into direct conflict with one another as they jockey for a better shake for themselves and as other groups fend them off. The poor, blacks, and women, among others, are involved in concerted efforts at bringing about sweeping change in the structure of American society. Similarly, subcultures come into conflict: heterosexuals with homosexuals, violence-oriented gangs with other gangs and with the public, and so on.

With many forces threatening to rip society asunder, what holds it together? It is this basic question of social life to which Bartlett addresses himself in the concluding selection in this volume. Bartlett focuses on socialization into a belief system, into ideologies which unify by giving people common perspectives from which to view the world. It is here, within the symbolic systems which human beings develop and by which they interpret reality and interact with one another, that the answer lies.

20

Randall Bartlett

The Role of Ideology in Political Power

What keeps a pluralistic society from separating into hundreds of warring factions? This is a question with which scholars have wrestled for many years, and for which no completely satisfactory answer has been developed. First of all, force and the threat of force are obviously used to maintain social order. The legitimate means of violence are concentrated in the hands of a select few who can direct those powers against persons and groups which threaten the social system. Our social system is always underpinned by forms of power ready to be unleashed against those who disturb and threaten. But few of us live in slave states in which we are driven to cooperation by the lash. Most of us are not ready to rebel—rather, we usually quietly acquiesce to the larger social system in which we are immersed. The vast majority of us actively participate in our social system, engaging in cooperative acts which benefit many besides ourselves. Yet even if we are not rebellious, neither are most of us unusually eager to participate.

Whence, then, is the source of our cooperation? Among other factors, the following appear to be significant. First, commonalities in our language bind us to other members of our linguistic community. Our language provides shared perceptions and ways of evaluating life. It paints basic pictures of the world. Language is a major orienting device with which we approach the world. It is much more significant than most of us think, as few of us ever learn a second language and, consequently, few of us acquire comparative tools for examining the pervasive effects of our language. Second, the taken-for-granted background assumptions we share unite us into a cultural community. They provide us an identity which unites us in behavior while separating us from members of other cultures and subcultures. Third, we learn to accept an authority system because of our childhood socialization. We learn to take it for granted that others have power over us. Fourth, at an early point in our lives we learn that it is right, normal, and expected of us that we should exchange our labor for money. Fifth, we early develop the need to maintain a supply of money in order to satisfy both our basic biological and our socially derived needs. To satisfy these needs, we relegate many personal desires to a secondary position and exchange our labor for money under an occupational hierarchy. Sixth, we early in life learn to accept unquestioningly inequality as a natural part of the world. This helps justify whatever place we find ourselves in life, further stabilizing the social system by gaining our acquiescence to the status quo. Seventh, we are united by a larger, encompassing, and sometimes overwhelming symbolic system which joins us to others. These symbols are regularly manipulated, in interaction and by the mass media, bringing our behavior in line with the expectations of others.

In this final selection, Bartlett focuses on socialization into ideologies as a partial solution to this basic question of what keeps pluralistic societies from ripping apart.

> The rich man in his castle
> The poor man at his gate
> God made them high and lowly
> And ordered their estate

TRADITIONAL HYMN

Whether or not ideology can be eliminated from the world of thought in the social sciences, it is certainly indispensable in the world of action in social life. A society cannot exist unless its members have common feelings about what is the proper way of conducting its affairs, and these common feelings are expressed in ideology.

JOAN ROBINSON

Any economic system requires a set of rules, an ideology to justify them, and a conscience in the individual which makes him strive to carry them out.

JOAN ROBINSON

We can observe systems of belief in all societies. Groups of men who tend to identify themselves as distinct groups have certain perceptions of the world in common. Often it is the sharing of these perceptions which defines the membership of the group. These common thoughts and values can be systematically interwoven to form an ideology, the common doctrines of a people. . . .

Ideological Justification of Value Distribution

The basic precepts of any national ideology tend to provide philosophical explanations of the discrepancies in value endowments which the mass may observe. For example, the strong emphasis upon individual responsibility and equality of opportunity in American society creates a belief that the relative positions of different individuals depend upon their efforts. Hard work merits and will receive large rewards; a lack of productivity brings with it well-deserved poverty. Individuals are paid according to the amount they contribute to the production of real goods and services and hence those with the highest rewards are regarded as having contributed the most whether this is objectively verifiable or not. It is regarded as "un-American" to suggest depriving a man of the fruits of his labors, particularly if they are to be shared with "less productive" individuals. The question here is not one of the value of these precepts in terms of some absolute standards of "good" and "bad," or even one of their validity. What is important here is that they are widely held and strongly believed, and that they do provide a justification for the inequality in the distribution of values.

. . . All societies have a set of values justifying what is. It is easy to see these aspects of ideologies in "opposing" societies even if it is less obvious in the case of one's own. The organic view of society which is typical of fascist states such as Nazi Germany is built around the concept that individuals act as cells in the body of the total state. They perform specialized functions which benefit the whole rather than themselves. In this type of value system equality is of little importance since the welfare of the individual derives directly from the welfare of the whole. As long as the state in its entirety is enjoying the maximum possible vitality, the individual should be satisfied. To the extent that this ideology is believed, it provides a justification for the inequality in the distribution of values and will lead the mass to accept, and perhaps even defend it. Again, it matters not whether this view of society is correct, or even if there is any such thing as "correct" with regard to ideologies; all that matters is that it be believed.

The ideology of a truly communistic state also serves this same purpose of providing justification. "From each according to his ability; to each according to his need." To the extent that people believe this principle and the fact that needs may differ, they will accept and defend inequality in the distribution of values. Since, in practice, the determination of "needs" would probably be made by the elite, we might expect them to weight their own relatively heavily.

Justification of the status quo by national ideologies is by no means a new development in human society. It is probably most easily seen and accepted in the historical past, perhaps because we have not been exposed to any "acculturation" of now obsolete ideologies. For centuries, monarchs ruled with absolute power in both the east and the west under the banner of the "divine right of kings." Having been granted wealth and power by God himself, monarchs could regard challenges to their privilege as both treasonable and sacrilegious. To the extent that the mass *believed* this justification of the situation, it was satisfied that the distribution of values was both inevitable and just.

A further point has been suggested here and its importance is great—the *elite* will often believe and defend the ideology just as strongly as the mass. It is seldom an act of conscious deception when the elite stresses the sanctity of the national ideology. It is accepted and believed by them as well. As members of a society they learn to adhere to its basic philosophy as a matter of course, just as does the mass.

> The ethical system implanted in each of us by our upbringing (even a rebel is influenced by what he rebels against) was not derived from any reasonable principles; those who conveyed it to us were rarely able to give any rational account of it, or indeed to formulate it explicitly at all. They handed on to us what society had taught them, in the same way as they handed on to us the language they had learned to speak.[1]

The Imposition of Ideology

. . . The central ideas of any society are instilled in its members through an extensive program of acculturation. This takes place in societies which have known ideological stability for years, but it also takes place, and is more obvious, in societies which have experienced a recent change in elites necessitating an alteration of the national ideology. A commonly noted characteristic of post-revolutionary governments is a program of "re-educating" the people and of suppressing "counter-revolutionary" thought. This often involves a degree of coercion in the sense that people may suffer real punishments for rejecting the new "truth" while they are often rewarded for openly accepting it.

It also includes alterations in the relative prices of different bits of information with respect to the pre-revolutionary ratios. The good points of the new elite are stressed, along with the reasons for the revolution; the evils of the old and its injustices are often mentioned. This information will be provided at a subsidized rate to the entire society. Such a process is often condemned as a form of thought control, and indeed it is that, but it is by no means limited to revolutionary governments and societies. It is merely most obvious there.

A further example of the explicit manipulation of national ideologies to justify a new elite may be seen in Nazi Germany. Hitler's vast campaigns of propaganda, his organization of the "Hitler Youth," his emphasis on Naziism in the curriculum of German schools, and his massive rallies and insistence upon an organic view of the state and its mission were all attempts to affect the perceptions of the German mass and hence its ideology. These all involved alteration of the relative prices of information, partly through subsidization, and partly by raising the price of acquiring unfavorable information with the threat of violence. To a rather significant degree he was successful in his attempts.

In well-established societies, enjoying ideological stability, this process of acculturation still occurs, but it takes less obvious forms and requires less coercion and also less expenditure of resources by the elite.

> An ideology, once accepted, perpetuates itself with remarkable vitality. The individuals born into the state direct some of their love toward the symbols which sustain the system: the common name, the common heroes, the common mission, the common demands. Some destructive tendencies are directed against rivals, traitors, heresies and counterdemands.[2]

As soon as one generation comes to accept the ideology, then the task of instilling it in the next passes out of the hands of the elite and becomes an automatic activity of the mass itself. Parents teach their children to accept certain concepts as true and good, others as false and evil. Schools spend a great deal of time and effort educating children about the requirements and responsibilities of good citizenship. They teach that the existing society is the best of all possible ones. They teach children to revere the symbols of the ideology and its catchwords—whether these be the American flag or the swastika, the Pledge of Allegiance or the Communist Manifesto, George Washington or Mao Tse-tung. It is not coincidental that American children tend to regard Lenin as evil and Russian children to regard him as good. They are both taught to do so.

Moreover, the entire culture of the society will come to reflect and glorify the ideological principles without any conscious guidance by the elite. In the United States:

> Gossip, fiction, motion pictures sustain the thesis of personal responsibility for failure or success. He failed because he lacked tact or had halitosis or didn't finish his education. . . . She was successful because she got the right shade of lipstick, took French lessons at home on the phonograph, kept the skin you love to touch. . . . In "I'm No Angel" the ex-carnival girl marries a society man. In "Morning Glory" a stage-struck country girl is shoved into the star part on the opening night of a play and makes a hit. . . .

while in the Soviet Union:

> Group tasks supplant individual tasks in order to keep collective enterprises rather than ambitious persons at the center of attention. Theatricals emphasize the play and not the star, and treat the fate of movements rather than the problems of the individual person.[3]

In all societies there is an ideology which arises and is perpetuated either through a conscious program directed by an elite, or through the automatic process of acculturating each new generation to the dominant beliefs of its society. Whether one ideology is better than another in some absolute sense is a value judgment we are unqualified to make. We claim only that each society has an ideology which provides a justification for the status quo, and that it is a learned ideology. . . .

Rational Response to Ideology

The individual human organism at birth is essentially an ideological and factual blank. On the basis of his experiences and the information he acquires from other humans regarding their experiences and knowledge he begins to form his own view of the world. Different inputs into this process will result in different philosophical and ideological outputs. Children, if they are rational, will accept as inputs into the formation of their personalities and ideologies those informational items which are offered at the lowest cost. Few American children have the desire or the ability to travel to the Soviet Union or China to be told what values are important in society. If they are trying to minimize the costs and discomfort of learning (and what child isn't) they will be content to acquire that information from their parents since it is available at a much lower relative price.

Similarly, since the experience of children is inevitably limited they will be unable to form an effective discount to be applied to the information received from their home culture. However, one aspect of the home culture is the formation of discount factors which are applied to foreign ideologies. It is rational to assimilate the domestic ideology and rational to be unaware of, or reject, opposing ideologies strictly on the basis of cost minimization.

As children mature and become adults they must continue to formulate and re-evaluate their particular ideology on the basis of past experience, the information they have accumulated in this way in the past, and upon newly acquired information. As in all previous cases of decision making in the face of uncertainty, information will be acquired according to the relative costs of various items, though certain sources of information may call into play a discount factor which lowers the perceived value of information from that source. The dominant ideology will be perpetuated, or a new one will replace it, on the basis of the relative price schedules for informational items and the scale of discount factors. The control of information and the ability to influence the prices of various items carries with it the ability to influence ideological belief. This is particularly true since information in this type of process can and will include not only facts (if such exist) but also interpretations of facts and systems of thought for analyzing them.

For example, each society has a particular view of history that it teaches to each succeeding generation. History is never totally objective, however, for it is always recorded from the point of view of an observer. People studying the record of history are presented explicitly with a sequence of events and either implicitly or explicitly with this particular point of view. American students of the Russian revolution are presented with low cost facts as to the casualties caused by the Bolsheviks in their bloody "purges" and with explanations of the failure of the revolution from the capitalistic point of view. Russian students are presented with low cost facts as to the corruption of the Czar, his oppression of the masses, and the necessity and success of the revolution from the socialist viewpoint. To either group, the costs of understanding the opposite interpretation are substantially raised since it requires direct research outside of the normal process of education, utilizing sources to which a significant discount factor is normally affixed.

Similarly, Americans are presented with low cost information as to the necessity of American intervention in Southeast Asia for the preservation of freedom and the containment of communistic slavery. People in the Socialist countries receive subsidized information stressing the role of the United States in crushing the freedom of already oppressed peoples in order to protect American investments and profits. Facts carry not only objective information, but they are generally accompanied by interpretations and explanations of phenomena. . . .

"Fringe Benefits" of Ideologies

In addition to allowing long run inequality in the distribution of values within a society, an ideology also provides a method of cost minimization with regard to short term decisions, as seen by both the decider and those who may wish to influence the decision. There are certain symbols associated with an ideology which take on high importance and lend credence and desirability to any position which can be associated with them. "By the use of sanctioned words and gestures the elite elicits blood, work, taxes, applause from the masses." [4] It is far cheaper to influence the actions of the mass by appealing to "patriotic duty" and "national tradition" than it is to provide extensive amounts of subsidized information as to the "objective" advisability of those actions. Once an ideology has been accepted, its symbols and precepts provide low-cost methods of influencing short-run decisions on particular issues.

There are also benefits for the mass, or other deciders as well, in terms of cost minimization with regard to particular issues. These fall closely in line with Downs' analysis of ideologies' role in voting decisions. He claimed that voters could compare their personal philosophies with party ideologies and vote on that basis without having to compare a vast number of policy positions. This same idea can be applied to non-voting decisions as well. Once it has accepted an ideology, it is far cheaper for the mass to decide on actions in support of policies on the basis of appeals to this "patriotic duty" than on the basis of analyzing much larger amounts of factual information even if it is provided at a subsidized rate. Ideologies reduce the costs faced by influencer and influenced once they have been accepted as the correct view of the world.

Masses can thus be called forth to action by the mere use of symbols in a sort of conditioned response. American soldiers fight wars in the defense of "apple pie and motherhood" but in the entire scope of human history there has never been a war fought over anything as mundane as an apple pie. Not even Ho Chi Minh represented any significant threat to American apple pies. Wars are fought over conflicts of power as elites and countries try to re-allocate the international distribution of values. But it is cheaper to recruit soldiers on the basis of glory and apple pie than it is on the basis of creating a belief in the desirability of altering an elite's international position. This is of course most apparent in the case of offensive as opposed to defensive wars, since in this case it is most obviously the elite which benefits while it is the mass which bears the burden of the actual fighting.

Conclusions

An ideology is a system of thought underlying a society which justifies the rules by which that society operates and hence also justifies the outcome of that operation. It provides a rationale for the status quo and its perpetuation. Some ideologies may be better than others; or they may not. They are based upon normative precepts which cannot be judged in a truly objective treatise. The choice among ideologies must be a problem for philosophers. What is important at this point is that they all provide an explanation for the distribution of values which, in the real world, implies an explanation of a greater or lesser degree of inequality in the distribution. To the extent that the ideology is believed, it can assure the long-term continuation of the inequality. . . .

Notes

4: The Influence of Language (pp. 47–53)

1. This excellent term was used by Joseph Church, *Language and the Discovery of Reality: A Developmental Psychology of Cognition* (New York: Random House, 1961), pp. 86–87.

2. These ideas have been suggested in part by Arnold W. Green, *Sociology* (New York: McGraw-Hill Book Co., 1960), p. 71.

3. Cf. Green, pp. 72–75. See also Walter R. Goldschmidt (ed.), *Exploring the Ways of Mankind* (New York: Holt, Rinehart & Winston, 1960), Introduction to Chap. II, p. 67.

4. Cf. Robert M. Estrich and Hans Sperber, *Three Keys to Language* (New York: Rinehart, 1952), pp. 337–338.

6: The Social Origins of the Self (pp. 71–78)

1. The foregoing distinctions can also be expressed in terms of the differences between "signs," or "signals," and symbols. A sign stands for something else because of the fact that it is present at approximately the same time and place with that "something else." A symbol, on the other hand, stands for something else because its users have agreed to let it stand for that "something else." Thus, signs are directly and intrinsically linked with present or proximate situations; while symbols, having arbitrary and conventional, rather than intrinsic, meanings, transcend the immediate situation. (We shall return to this important point in our discussion of "mind.") Only symbols, of course, involve interpretation, self-stimulation and shared meaning.

2. To anyone who has taken even one course in sociology it is probably superfluous to stress the importance of symbols, particularly language, in the acquisition of all other elements of culture. The process of socialization is essentially a
process of symbolic interaction.

7: Presenting the Self to Others (pp. 79–89)

1. Gustav Ichheiser, "Misunderstandings in Human Relations," Supplement to
The American Journal of Sociology, 55 (September, 1949): 6–7.

2. Quoted in E. H. Volkart, editor, *Social Behavior and Personality*, Contributions of W. I. Thomas to Theory and Social Research (New York: Social
Science Research Council, 1951), p. 5.

3. Here I owe much to an unpublished paper by Tom Burns of the University
of Edinburgh. He presents the argument that in all interaction a basic underlying theme is the desire of each participant to guide and control the responses
made by the others present. A similar argument has been advanced by Jay
Haley in a recent unpublished paper, but in regard to a special kind of control,
that having to do with defining the nature of the relationship of those involved
in the interaction.

4. Willard Waller, "The Rating and Dating Complex," *American Sociological
Review*, 2: 730.

5. William Sansom, *A Contest of Ladies* (London: Hogarth, 1956), pp. 230–32.

6. The widely read and rather sound writings of Stephen Potter are concerned
in part with signs that can be engineered to give a shrewd observer the apparently incidental cues he needs to discover concealed virtues the gamesman
does not in fact possess.

7. An interaction can be purposely set up as a time and place for voicing differences in opinion, but in such cases participants must be careful to agree not
to disagree on the proper tone of voice, vocabulary, and degree of seriousness
in which all arguments are to be phrased, and upon the mutual respect which
disagreeing participants must carefully continue to express toward one another. This debaters' or academic definition of the situation may also be in-
voked suddenly and judiciously as a way of translating a serious conflict of
views into one that can be handled within a framework acceptable to all
present.

8. W. F. Whyte, "When Workers and Customers Meet," Chap. VII, *Industry
and Society*, ed. W. F. Whyte (New York: McGraw-Hill, 1946), pp. 132–33.

9. Teacher interview quoted by Howard S. Becker, "Social Class Variations in
the Teacher-Pupil Relationship," *Journal of Educational Sociology*, 25: 459.

10. Harold Taxel, "Authority Structure in a Mental Hospital Ward" (unpublished Master's thesis, Department of Sociology, University of Chicago,
1953).

11. This role of the witness in limiting what it is the individual can be has been

stressed by Existentialists, who see it as a basic threat to individual freedom. See Jean-Paul Sartre, *Being and Nothingness,* trans. by Hazel E. Barnes (New York: Philosophical Library, 1956), p. 365 ff.

12. Goffman, *op. cit.,* pp. 319–27.

13. Peter Blau, "Dynamics of Bureaucracy" (Ph.D. dissertation, Department of Sociology, Columbia University, forthcoming, University of Chicago Press), pp. 127–29.

14. Walter M. Beattie, Jr., "The Merchant Seaman" (unpublished M.A. Report, Department of Sociology, University of Chicago, 1950), p. 35.

15. Sir Frederick Ponsonby, *Recollectitons of Three Reigns* (New York: Dutton, 1952), p. 46.

8: Protecting the Self (pp. 90–96)

1. Compare the somewhat similar approach in Paul F. Secord and Carl W. Backman, "Personality Theory and the Problem of Stability and Change in Individual Behavior: An Interpersonal Approach," *Psychological Review,* 68 (January, 1961), 21–33.

2. For a more thorough discussion of selective perception, see Chapter 5 of George J. McCall and J. L. Simmons, *Identities and Interactions,* New York: The Free Press, 1966.

3. Selective interpretation is discussed in more detailed fashion in Chapter 5, *ibid.*

4. Kurt Lewin, *Field Theory in Social Science,* New York: Harper, 1951, p. 262.

5. *Cf.* E. J. Cleveland and W. D. Longaker, "Neurotic Patterns in the Family," in Alexander H. Leighton, John A. Clausen, and Robert N. Wilson, editors, *Explorations in Social Psychiatry,* New York: Basic Books, 1957, pp. 167–200, especially pp. 184–194.

6. Tamotsu Shibutani, "Reference Groups and Social Control," in Arnold M. Rose, editor, *Human Behavior and Social Processes,* Boston: Houghton Mifflin, 1962, pp. 128–147.

7. This sacrifice is represented more specifically in the pronounced drop in immediate desire for support of that identity that results from an extreme negative discrepancy between obtained and desired support, as discussed on p. 89 of McCall and Simmons, *op. cit.*

8. Emile Durkheim, *Suicide* (trans. John A. Spaulding and George Simpson), New York: Free Press, 1951; and Bronislaw Malinowski, *Crime and Custom in Savage Society,* New York: Humanities Press, 1926, pp. 77–80.

9. Claude C. Bowman, "Distortion of Reality as a Factor in Morale," in Rose, editor, *Mental Health and Mental Disorder,* New York: Norton, 1955, pp. 393–407.

10. Merton, *Social Theory and Social Structure* (rev. ed.), New York: Free Press, 1957, pp. 421–436.

9: Distorting Reality (pp. 97–106)

1. Karl Mannheim, *Ideology and Utopia* (London: Routledge and Kegan Paul, Ltd., 1953), pp. 49–53.

2. Mannheim dealt primarily with the cognitive categories unconsciously accepted by the group. By contrast, he did on occasion analyze valuations as well; and when he did, his definitions of "utopias" resembled those associated with counter-culture, a term in turn derived from the circumscribed definition of culture. The circumscribed definition of culture denotes the beliefs, values, and norms common to a society. By contrast, the all-encompassing specification, one for example accepted by the Leslie White school of anthropology, would include "everything" but habitat. By "everything" is meant not only ideas, but the organizational and technological systems as well.

3. Harry Brill, "Unemployment: Official and Real," *The Nation*, Vol. 212, January 25, 1971, p. 100.

4. I was able to obtain this information on unadjusted comparisons plus the option of do-it-yourself adjusted comparisons from Miss Kohlnieser of the New York office of the Bureau of Labor Statistics.

5. "How the Government Measures Unemployment," Bureau of Labor Statistics Report Number 312, June 1967, pp. 7–8. The now-used definition of participation in the labor force is more narrow than it was prior to 1967, when groups such as fourteen- and fifteen-year-olds were included. Briefly put, the labor force consists of the employed and the unemployed persistently seeking work. The BLS has evolved certain standard techniques for obtaining information on these groups:

> Statistics on the employment status of the population, the personal, occupational, and other characteristics of the employed, the unemployed, and persons not in the labor force, and related data are compiled for the BLS by the Bureau of the Census in its Current Population Survey (CPS). A detailed description of this survey appears in *Concepts and Methods Used in Manpower Statistics from the Current Population Survey*, BLS Report 313. This report is available from BLS on request.
>
> These monthly surveys of the population are conducted with a scientifically selected sample designed to represent the civilian noninstitutional population sixteen years and over. Respondents are interviewed to obtain information about the employment status of each member of the household sixteen years of age and over. The inquiry relates to activity or status during the calendar week, Sunday through Saturday, which includes the 12th of the month. This is known as the survey week. Actual field interviewing is conducted in the following week.
>
> Inmates of institutions and persons under sixteen years of age are not covered in the regular monthly enumerations and are excluded from the population and labor force statistics shown in this report. Data on members of the Armed Forces, who are included as part of the categories "total noninstitutional population" and "total labor force," are obtained from the Department of Defense.

Each month, 50,000 occupied units are designated for interview. About 2,250 of these households are visited but interviews are not obtained because the occupants are not found at home after repeated calls or are unavailable for other reasons. This represents a noninterview rate for the survey of about 4.5 percent. In addition to the 50,000 occupied units, there are 8,500 sample units in an average month which are visited but found to be vacant or otherwise not to be enumerated. Part of the sample is changed each month. The rotation plan provides for three-fourths of the sample to be common from one month to the next, and one-half to be common with the same month a year ago.

See "Labor Force Data," *Employment and Earnings,* Vol. 18, No. 3, September 1971. U.S. Department of Labor, Bureau of Labor Statistics.

6. *Ibid.,* p. 5. See also *Employment and Earnings, op. cit.,* p. 140.

7. *Ibid.,* p. 4. See also *Employment and Earnings, op. cit.,* p. 140.

8. In communities such as Detroit, this matter of counting the unemployed strikers as employed involves not a few people. In metropolitan Detroit, for example, in 1964 there were 95 work stoppages involving 114,000 workers who were idle a total of 2,060,000 work days. Were the BLS to count these workers as unemployed or non-participants in the labor force, the overall incidence of unemployment would undoubtedly increase significantly. See U.S. Department of Labor, Bureau of Labor Statistics, *Analysis of Work Stoppages,* Bulletin No. 1460, October 1965, p. 17.

9. Since 1967, the technique used to count the unemployed has been one of including those who have sought work in the last twenty-eight days. Excluded from this category, however, are people who have sought work in the last twenty-eight days but not been available to take a job in the week prior to the interview because they were attending school. For a more precise idea on the fact-gathering questions used in collecting materials, see Office of Statistical Policy, Bureau of the Budget, *Household Survey Manual* (Washington: Office of Statistical Policy, 1969), pp. 13–17.

10. Harry Brill, "Can We Train Away the Unemployed?" *The Feedback,* Vol. III, November–December 1965, pp. 5–12.

11. Paul O. Flaim and Paul M. Schwab have observed that:

Most of the persons who became unemployed in 1970 managed to find work after a relatively short period of job hunting. Thus, the average duration of unemployment increased only moderately during the year. At an 8.8 week average, it was only one week higher than in 1969, but well below the levels that in earlier years had been associated with unemployment rates of the magnitude reached in 1970. Nevertheless, a gradually higher proportion of the unemployed (about one-fifth at year's end) had been jobless for at least fifteen weeks, while a limited number apparently had left the labor force.

See their "Changes in Employment and Unemployment in 1970," *Monthly Labor Review,* Volume 94, February 1971, p. 13.

12. "The 'Hidden' Jobless Figures," The San Francisco *Chronicle,* March 11, 1964, p. 14.

10: The Homosexual Role (pp. 107–119)

1. Irving Bieber, "Clinical Aspects of Male Homosexuality," in Judd Marmor, editor, *Sexual Inversion,* New York: Basic Books, 1965, p. 248; this is but one example among many.

2. R. von Krafft-Ebing, *Psychopathia Sexualis,* 1889.

3. Later published in H. Ellis, *Studies in the Psychology of Sex,* Vol. 2, New York: Random House, 1936.

4. This is a grossly simplified account. Edwin Lemert provides a far more subtle and detailed analysis in *Social Pathology,* New York: McGraw-Hill, 1951, ch. 4, "Sociopathic Individuation."

5. For discussion of situations in which deviants can lay claim to legitimacy, see Talcott Parsons, *The Social System,* New York: Free Press, 1951, pp. 292–293.

6. The position taken here is similar to that of Erving Goffman in his discussion of becoming a mental patient; *Asylums,* Garden City, N.Y.: Doubleday-Anchor, 1961, pp. 128–146.

7. For evidence that many self-confessed homosexuals in England are not effeminate and many are not interested in boys, see Michael Schofield, *Sociological Aspects of Homosexuality,* London: Longmans, 1965.

8. Marc Daniel, "Essai de méthodologie pour l'étude des aspects homosexuels de l'histoire," *Arcadie,* 133 (January, 1965), pp. 31–37.

9. Marvin Opler, "Anthropological and Cross-Cultural Aspects of Homosexuality," in Marmor, editor, *op. cit.,* p. 174.

10. *Ibid.,* p. 117.

11. C. S. Ford and F. A. Beach, *Patterns of Sexual Behavior,* New York: Harper, 1951, ch. 7.

12. George Devereux, "Institutionalized Homosexuality of the Mohave Indians," *Human Biology,* Vol. 9, 1937, pp. 498–527; reprinted in Hendrik M. Ruitenbeek, editor, *The Problem of Homosexuality in Modern Society,* New York: Dutton, 1963.

13. The lack of cultural distinction is reflected in behavior; Gordon Westwood found that only a small proportion of his sample of British homosexuals engaged in anal intercourse and many of these had been both active and passive and did not have a clear preference. See *A Minority,* London: Longmans, 1960, pp. 127–134.

14. Gordan Rattray Taylor, "Historical and Mythological Aspects of Homosexuality," in Marmor, *op. cit.;* Fernando Henriques, *Prostitution and Society,* Vol. 1, London: MacGibbon and Kee, 1962, pp. 341–343.

15. Ford and Beach, *op. cit.,* p. 132.

16. *Ibid.,* pp. 131–132.

17. Geoffrey May, *Social Control of Sex Expression,* London: Allen and Unwin, 1930, pp. 65 and 101.

18. Especially Havelock Ellis, *Sexual Inversion,* London: Wilson and Macmillan,

1897; Iwan Bloch (E. Dühren, pseud.), *Sexual Life in England Past and Present,* English translation, London: Francis Aldor, 1938; German edition, Charlottenberg, Berlin, 1901–03; Gordon Rattray Taylor, *Sex in History,* London: Thames and Hudson, 1953; Noel I. Garde, *Jonathan to Gide: The Homosexual in History,* New York: Vantage, 1964.

19. Dr. Evelyn Hooker has suggested that in a period when homosexual grouping and a homosexual subculture have not yet become institutionalized, homosexuals are likely to behave in a more distinctive and conspicuous manner because other means of making contact are not available. This is confirmed by the fact that lesbians are more conspicuous than male homosexuals in our society, but does not seem to fit the 17th century, where the groups are already described as "clubs."

20. However, "fairy" and "pansy," the commonest slang terms used by non-homosexuals, have the same meaning of effeminate as the earlier terms.

21. Bloch, *op. cit.,* p. 328, gives several examples, but attributes their emergence to the fact that "the number of homosexuals increased."

22. Quoted in *ibid.,* pp. 328–329.

23. Anon, *Hell upon Earth: or the Town in an Uproar,* London, 1729, quoted by G. R. Taylor in Marmor, editor, *op. cit.,* p. 142.

24. Bloch, *op. cit.,* p. 334.

25. Alfred C. Kinsey *et al., Sexual Behavior in the Human Male,* Philadelphia and London: Saunders, 1948; and Kinsey *et al., Sexual Behavior in the Human Female,* Philadelphia and London: Saunders, 1953.

26. Kinsey *et al., Sexual Behavior in the Human Male,* pp. 636–37.

27. *Ibid.,* ch. 21, pp. 610–666.

28. The more general drawbacks of Kinsey's data, particularly the problem of the representativeness of his sample, have been thoroughly canvassed in a number of places; see especially William G. Cochran *et al., Statistical Problems of the Kinsey Report on Sexual Behavior in the Human Male,* Washington: American Statistical Society, 1954.

29. This cannot be taken in a rigorously statistical sense, since the categories are arbitrary and do not refer to numbers, or even proportions, of actual sexual acts.

30. But an interesting beginning has been made by Evelyn Hooker in "The Homosexual Community," *Proc. XIVth Int. Congr. Appl. Psychol. Personality Research,* Vol. 2, Copenhagen, Munksgaard, 1962; and "Male Homosexuals and Their Worlds," Marmor, editor, *op. cit.,* pp. 83–107; there is much valuable descriptive material in Donald Webster Cory, *The Homosexual in America,* New York: Greenberg, 1951; and in Gordon Westwood, *A Minority: A Report on the Life of the Male Homosexual in Great Britain,* London: Longmans, 1960, as well as elsewhere.

11: The Myth of Mental Illness (pp. 120–131)

1. Freud went so far as to say that: "I consider ethics to be taken for granted. Actually I have never done a mean thing" (Jones, 1957, p. 247). This surely is a strange thing to say for someone who has studied man as a social being as closely as did Freud. I mention it here to show how the notion of "illness" (in the case of psychoanalysis, "psychopathology," or "mental illness") was used by Freud—and by most of his followers—as a means for classifying certain forms of human behavior as falling within the scope of medicine, and hence (by *fiat*) outside that of ethics!

13: The Exchange of Social Rewards (pp. 147–152)

1. "We rarely meet with ingratitude, so long as we are in a position to confer favors." François La Rochefoucauld, *The Maxims,* London: Oxford University Press, 1940, p. 101 (#306).

2. Once a person has become emotionally committed to a relationship, his identification with the other and his interest in continuing the association provide new independent incentives for supplying benefits to the other. Similarly, firm commitments to an organization lead members to make recurrent contributions to it without expecting reciprocal benefits in every instance. The significance of these social attachments is further elaborated in subsequent chapters.

3. Bernard Mandeville's central theme is that private vices produce public benefits because the importance of social approval prompts men to contribute to the welfare of others in their own self-interest. As he put it tersely at one point, "Moral Virtues are the Political Offspring which Flattery begot upon Pride." *The Fable of the Bees,* Oxford: Clarendon, 1924, Vol. I, 51; see also pp. 63–80.

4. Erving Goffman, *Asylums,* Chicago: Aldine, 1962, p. 115.

5. Heinrich von Kleist's story "Michael Kohlhaas" is a pathetic illustration of the foolishness inherent in the insistence on rigid conformity with moral standards in complete disregard of consequences.

6. Kenneth Boulding, *Conflict and Defense,* New York: Harper, 1962, p. 151.

7. For a discussion of game theory which calls attention to its limitations, see R. Duncan Luce and Howard Raiffa, *Games and Decisions,* New York: Wiley, 1957, esp. chapters iii and vii. For other criticisms of game theory, notably its failure to utilize empirical research, and an attempt to incorporate some of its principles into a substantive theory of conflict, see Thomas C. Schelling, *The Strategy of Conflict,* Cambridge: Harvard University Press, 1960, esp. chapters iv and vi.

8. See on this point George C. Homans, *Social Behavior,* New York: Harcourt, Brace and World, 1961, pp. 79–80; and Anatol Rapoport, *Fights, Games, and Debates,* Ann Arbor: University of Michigan Press, 1960, p. 122.

14: The Practice of Law as Confidence Game (pp. 157–168)

1. F. J. Davis *et al., Society and the Law: New Meanings for an Old Profession* 301 (1962); L. Orfield, *Criminal Procedure from Arrest to Appeal* 297 (1947).

D. J. Newman, *Pleading Guilty for Considerations: A Study of Bargain Justice,* 46 J. Crim. L. C. & P.S. 780–90 (1954). Newman's data covered only one year, 1954, in a midwestern community; however, it is in general confirmed by my own data drawn from a far more populous area, and from what is one of the major criminal courts in the country, for a period of fifteen years from 1950 to 1964 inclusive. The English experience tends also to confirm American data, see N. Walker, *Crime and Punishment in Britain: An Analysis of the Penal System* (1965). See also D. J. Newman, *Conviction: The Determination of Guilt or Innocence Without Trial* (1966), for a comprehensive legalistic study of the guilty plea sponsored by the American Bar Foundation. The criminal court as a social system, an analysis of "bargaining" and its functions in the criminal court's organizational structure, are examined in my book *Criminal Justice* (Chicago: Quadrangle Books, 1967).

2. G. Feifer, *Justice in Moscow* (1965). The Soviet trial has been termed "an appeal from the pretrial investigation" and Feifer notes that the Soviet "trial" is simply a recapitulation of the data collected by the pretrial investigator. The notions of a trial being a "tabula rasa" and presumptions of innocence are wholly alien to Soviet notions of justice. . . . "the closer the investigation resembles the finished script, the better . . ." *Id.* at 86.

3. For a concise statement of the constitutional and economic aspects of the right to legal assistance, see M. G. Paulsen, *Equal Justice for the Poor Man* (1964); for a brief traditional description of the legal profession see P. A. Freund, *The Legal Profession,* Daedalus 689–700 (1963).

4. I use the concept in the general sense that Erving Goffman employed it in his *Asylums: Essays on the Social Situation of Mental Patients and Other Inmates* (1961).

5. A. L. Wood, *Informal Relations in the Practice of Criminal Law,* 62 Am. J. Soc. 48–55 (1956); J. E. Carlin, *Lawyers on Their Own* 105–09 (1962); R. Goldfarb, *Ransom—A Critique of the American Bail System* 114–15 (1965). In connection with relatively recent data as to recruitment to the legal profession, and variables involved in the type of practice engaged in, will be found in J. Ladinsky, *Careers of Lawyers, Law Practice, and Legal Institutions,* 28 Am. Soc. Rev. 47–54 (1963). See also S. Warkov & J. Zelan, *Lawyers in the Making* (1965).

6. There is a real question to be raised as to whether in certain organizational settings, a complete reversal of the bureaucratic-ideal has not occurred. That is, it would seem, in some instances the organization appears to exist to serve the needs of its various occupational incumbents, rather than its clients. A. Etzioni, *Modern Organizations* 94–104 (1964).

7. Three relatively recent items reported in the New York *Times,* tend to underscore this point as it has manifested itself in one of the major criminal courts. In one instance the Bronx County Bar Association condemned "mass assembly-line justice," which "was rushing defendants into pleas of guilty and

into convictions, in violation of their legal rights." N.Y. *Times*, March 10, 1965, p. 51. Another item, appearing somewhat later that year reports a judge criticizing his own court system (the New York Criminal Court), that "pressure to set statistical records in disposing of cases had hurt the administration of justice." N.Y. *Times*, Nov. 4, 1965, p. 49. A third, and most unusual recent public discussion in the press was a statement by a leading New York appellate judge decrying "instant justice" which is employed to reduce court calendar congestion ". . . converting our courthouses into counting houses . . . , as in most big cities where the volume of business tends to overpower court facilities." N.Y. *Times*, Feb. 5, 1966, p. 58.

8. R. L. Gasser, *The Confidence Game*, 27 Fed. Prob. 47 (1963).

9. C. W. Mills, *White Collar* 121–29 (1951); J. E. Carlin *supra*, note 11.

10. E. O. Smigel, *The Wall Street Lawyer* 309 (1964).

11. Talcott Parsons indicates that the social role and function of the lawyer can be therapeutic, helping his client psychologically in giving him necessary emotional support at critical times. The lawyer is also said to be acting as an agent of social control in the counseling of his client and in the influencing of his course of conduct. See T. Parsons, *Essays in Sociological Theory* 382 *et seq.* (1954); E. Goffman, *On Cooling the Mark Out: Some Aspects of Adaptation to Failure,* in *Human Behavior and Social Processes* 482—505 (A. Rose ed., 1962). Goffman's "cooling out" analysis is especially relevant in the lawyer-accused client relationship.

12. The question has never been raised as to whether "bargain justice," "copping a plea," or justice by negotiation is a constitutional process. Although it has become the most central aspect of the process of criminal law administration, it has received virtually no close scrutiny by the appellate courts. As a consequence, it is relatively free of legal control and supervision. But, apart from any questions of the legality of bargaining, in terms of the pressures and devices that are employed which tend to violate due process of law, there remain ethical and practical questions. The system of bargain-counter justice is like the proverbial iceberg, much of its danger is concealed in secret negotiations and its least alarming feature, the final plea, being the one presented to public view. See A. S. Trebach, *The Rationing of Justice* 74–94 (1964); Note, *Guilty Plea Bargaining: Compromises by Prosecutors to Secure Guilty Pleas,* 112 U. Pa. L. Rev. 865–95 (1964).

13. For a conventional summary statement of some of the inevitable conflicting loyalties encountered in the practice of law, see E. E. Cheatham, *Cases and Materials on the Legal Profession* 70–79 (2d ed. 1955).

14. Some lawyers at either end of the continuum of law practice appear to have grave doubts as to whether it is indeed a profession at all. J. E. Carlin, *op. cit. supra* note 11, at 192; E. O. Smigel *supra*, note 16, at 304–305. Increasingly, it is perceived as a business with widespread evasion of the Canons of Ethics, duplicity and chicanery being practiced in an effort to get and keep business. The poet, Carl Sandburg, epitomized this notion in the following vignette: "Have you a criminal lawyer in this burg?" "We think so but we haven't been able to prove it on him." C. Sandburg, *The People, Yes* 154 (1936).

Thus, while there is a considerable amount of dishonesty present in law practice involving fee splitting, thefts from clients, influence peddling, fixing, questionable use of favors and gifts to obtain business or influence others, this sort of activity is most often attributed to the "solo," private practice lawyer. See A. L. Wood, *Professional Ethics Among Criminal Lawyers, Social Problems* 70–83 (1959). However, to some degree, large scale "downtown" elite firms also engage in these dubious activities. The difference is that the latter firms enjoy a good deal of immunity from these harsh charges because of their institutional and organizational advantages, in terms of near monopoly over more desirable types of practice, as well as exerting great influence in the political, economic and professional realms of power.

16: Slave Systems in North and South America (pp. 179–188)

1. "In all the category of disreputable callings, there were none so despised as the slave-trader. The odium descended upon his children and his children's children. Against the legal right to buy and sell slaves for profit, this public sentiment lifted a strong arm, and rendered forever odious the name of 'Negro-trader.'" Beverly B. Munford, *Virginia's Attitude toward Slavery and Secession* (New York: Longmans, Green, 1909), pp. 101–2.

2. This may be tested against what did typically happen in cases where restrictions were placed by the seller himself upon the separation of slaves with whom he was obliged, for whatever reason, to part. "In proportion as these restrictions put important limitations on the purchaser's rights and were safeguarded, they lessened the slave's salability." Frederic Bancroft, *Slave-trading in the Old South* (Baltimore: J. H. Furst, 1931), p. 214.

3. *Howard* v. *Howard*, 6 Jones N.C. 235 (December, 1858), quoted in Helen T. Catterall, *Judicial Cases concerning American Slavery and the Negro* (Washington: Carnegie Institution, 1926 ff.), II, 221.

4. Thomas R. R. Cobb, *An Inquiry into the Law of Slavery in the United States of America* (Philadelphia: T. & J. W. Johnson, 1858), p. 246.

5. Quoted in Catterall, *Judicial Cases*, II, 221.

6. The few exceptions—none of which meant very much in practice, except perhaps the law of Louisiana—are discussed in Bancroft, *Slave-trading*, pp. 197–221. "Louisiana, least American of the Southern States," writes Mr. Bancroft, "was least inhuman. In becoming Americanized it lost many a liberal feature of the old French *code noir*, but it forbade sale of mothers from their children less than ten years of age (and *vice versa*) and bringing into the State any slave child under ten years of age without its mother, if living. The penalty for violating either prohibition was from $1,000 to $2,000 and the forfeiture of the slave. That would have meant much if it had been strictly enforced" (p. 197). Louisiana's Spanish and French background, plus the fact that in both the legal and social senses slavery in Latin America generally was very different from slavery in North America, may furnish significant clues to some of the idiosyncrasies in the Louisiana code. See below.

7. *Frazier* v. *Spear,* 2 Bibb (Ken.), 385 (Fall, 1811), quoted in Caterall, *Judicial Cases,* I, 287.

8. "A slave has never maintained an action against the violator of his bed. A slave is not admonished for incontinence, or punished for fornication or adultery; never prosecuted for bigamy, or petty treason for killing a husband being a slave, any more than admitted to an appeal for murder." Opinion of Daniel Dulany, Esq., Attorney-General of Maryland, quoted in William Goodell, *The American Slave Code in Theory and Practice* (New York: American and Foreign Anti-Slavery Society, 1853), pp. 106–7.

9. *State* v. *Samuel* (*a slave*), 2 Dev. and Bat. (N.C.), 177 (December, 1836), quoted in Catterall, *Judicial Cases,* II, 77.

10. The picturesque charge that planters deliberately "bred" their slave women has never been substantiated, and Avery Craven's point that white women bred about as young and as often as their black sisters is a sensible one. But with no law to prevent the separation of parents and children, and with the value of a slave being much in excess of what it cost to rear him, the temptation to think and talk about a prolific Negro woman as a "rattlin' good breeder" was very strong. See Avery Craven, *The Coming of the Civil War* (New York: Scribner, 1942; 2d ed.; Chicago: University of Chicago Press, 1957), p. 84; Stampp, *Peculiar Institution,* p. 249. Frederic Bancroft gives numerous examples of advertisements describing Negro women in just this way. *Slave-trading,* pp. 68–79.

11. Opinion of Judge Crenshaw in *Brandon et al.* v. *Planters' and Merchants' Bank of Huntsville,* 1 Stewart's Ala. Report, 320 (January, 1838), quoted in Goodell, *American Slave Code,* p. 92.

12. *Ibid.,* pp. 89–104.

13. *Ibid.,* p. 88. A substantial number of Negroes did in fact buy their freedom in the ante-bellum South, but this required the full co-operation of their masters. Legally the slave had no claim to the money he may have collected for his own purchase. This highly precarious customary sanction, if such it may be called, should be compared to the fully articulated legal sanction embodied in the Cuban *coartación* (see n. 109 below). For a discussion of hiring-out arrangements which, although not recognized in law, were by no means unfamiliar (and under which the slave appears in practice to have had more initiative than the law theoretically gave him), see Richard B. Morris, "The Measure of Bondage in the Slave States," *Mississippi Valley Historical Review,* XLI (September, 1954), 219–40; see also Part IV, n. 115.

14. Goodell, *American Slave Code,* p. 321.

15. Ulrich B. Phillips (ed.), *A Documentary History of American Industrial Society* (Cleveland: Arthur H. Clark, 1910), I, 115.

16. *Ibid.,* p. 127.

17. Quoted in Goodell, *American Slave Code,* p. 334.

18. Hurd, *Law of Freedom and Bondage,* I, 42–43. Such language would lead one to suppose that slavery was a condition which, by its very nature, at all times and in all places, should partake of the same legal and social necessities. But the usage of the ancient world, in which slavery was everywhere prevalent, was

bound by no such necessities. Nor was slavery defined either with great clarity or great rigidity. There were so many degrees between "total" freedom and "total" slavery that the two tended to lose much of their meaning as opposites. Moreover, the stigma of slavery itself did not strike nearly so deep as in American slavery; in the latter, a man was either one thing or the other—slave or free. See William L. Westermann, "Between Slavery and Freedom," *American Historical Review*, L (January, 1945), 213–27. The difference that this made in the social attitudes of classical times toward slavery was considerable. "The lack in antiquity of any deep abhorrence of slavery as a social and economic evil may be explained in part," according to Professor Westermann, by the fact that "the change of legal status out of enslavement into liberty, by way of manumission, was as constant and as easy in Greco-Roman life as the reverse transition over the short passage from individual freedom of action into the constraints of nonfreedom, and the methods employed for making either transition were many." *Ibid.*, p. 215.

19. Hurd, *Law of Freedom and Bondage*, I, 303.

20. Four works upon which I have drawn heavily for my material on Latin-American slavery are Frank Tannenbaum's *Slave and Citizen* (New York: Knopf, 1947), Fr. Dieudonné Rinchon's *La traite et l'esclavage des Congolais par les Européens* (Wetteren, Belgium, 1929), Sir Harry Johnston's *The Negro in the New World* (London: Methuen, 1910), and Fernando Ortiz, *Los Negros esclavos* (Havana: Revista bimestra cubana, 1916).

21. "In the Cuban market freedom was the only commodity which could be bought untaxed; every negro against whom no one had proved a claim of servitude was deemed free. . . ." William Law Mathieson, *British Slavery and Its Abolition* (London: Longmans, Green, 1926), pp. 37–38.

22. Johnston, *Negro in the New World*, p. 89.

23. What I have said in this paragraph is virtually a paraphrase of the information which Mr. Tannenbaum has collected and so skilfully summarized on pp. 50, 53–54, 57–58 of *Slave and Citizen*.

24. Johnston, *Negro in the New World*, p. 42.

25. "The master of slaves must not allow the unlawful intercourse of the two sexes, but must encourage matrimony." Spanish slave code of 1789, quoted in *ibid.*, p. 44. Although slaves were allowed "to divert themselves innocently" on holy days, the males were to be kept apart from the females. *Ibid.*, p. 44.

26. Freyre, *The Masters and the Slaves*, p. 85.

27. Johnston, *Negro in the New World*, pp. 44–45. A diocesan synod of 1680 in Cuba issued weighty regulations on this subject which were supposed to supplement and have equal force with civil law. "Constitution 5 established that 'marriage should be free' and ordered that 'no master prohibit his slaves from marriage, nor impede those who cohabit therein, because we have found that many masters with little fear of God and in grave danger of their consciences, proscribe their slaves from marrying or impede their cohabitation with their married partners, with feigned pretexts'; and also prohibited 'that they go away to sell them outside the city, without that they take together husband and wife.' "

Ortiz, *Los Negros esclavos,* p. 349. The church even made some concessions here to African tribal marriage arrangements, to the extent that a slave with multiple wives might—if the first-married wife's identity could not be ascertained—pick out the one he preferred and have his marriage with her solemnized under the sacraments. *Ibid.,* p. 349.

28. Tannenbaum, *Slave and Citizen,* p. 56.

29. Johnston, *Negro in the New World,* p. 45.

30. The sentence, however, was apparently to be executed by the master. *Ibid.,* p. 45.

31. *Ibid.,* pp. 45–46. The code does not make it clear whether the penalty would be the same against the slave's master as against another person. But in any case the murderer, master or other, was liable to prosecution.

32. *Ibid.,* pp. 45–46. The liberal code of 1789 was not uniformly enforced at first; Ortiz, indeed, insists—contradicting the earlier historian, Saco—that it was widely evaded until well into the nineteenth century. The colonists, however, eventually had to succumb to pressure from the Spanish government, and by the 1840's the code had been written into local police regulations in Cuba. Ortiz, *Los Negros esclavos,* pp. 363–64, 70. A full translation of the code in its municipal form is in *British and Foreign State Papers, 1842–1843,* XXXI (London, 1858), 393–99.

33. It was not even uncommon for ex-slaves who had thus acquired their freedom to become actual slaveholders on their own account. Johnston, *Negro in the New World,* p. 90.

34. *Ibid.,* p. 44.

35. Tannenbaum, *Slave and Citizen,* pp. 58–61.

36. *Ibid.,* p. 55. A practical application of this contractual aspect of slavery was the institution of *coartación* which developed in Cuba in the eighteenth century. This was an arrangement whereby the slave might buy his freedom in instalments. He would first have his price declared (if he and his master disagreed, the local courts would determine it), whereupon he made his first payment. After that point, the price could not be changed, and he could at the same time change masters at will, the new master simply paying the balance of his price. See Hubert H. S. Aimes, "Coartación: A Spanish Institution for the Advancement of Slaves into Freedmen," *Yale Review,* XVII (February, 1909), 412–31.

37. Fr. Cipriano de Utrera, "El Concilio Dominicano de 1622, con una introducción histórica," *Boletín eclesiástico de la Arquidiócesis de Santo Domingo,* 1938–39, p. 40.

38. Johnston, *Negro in the New World,* p. 43. Herbert Klein's excellent monograph, "Slavery in Cuba and Virginia: A Comparative History of the First Hundred Years" (M.A. thesis, University of Chicago, 1959), provides a wealth of detail and specific examples, all of which tend to confirm, in a case-study setting, the general assertions of the present work as well as those of Tannenbaum and Johnston. This is particularly true with regard to the ways in which royal and ecclesiastical power was exercised in the Spanish colonies.

39. *Life in Brazil, or the Land of the Cocoa and the Palm* (New York: Harper, 1856), p. 267.

40. King, "The Colored Castes and American Representation in the Cortes of Cádiz," p. 59. See also Irene Diggs, "Color in Colonial Spanish America," *Journal of Negro History,* XXXVIII (October, 1953), 403–26.

41. Tannenbaum, *Slave and Citizen,* p. 106.

18: Theory of Sexual Politics (pp. 202–212)

1. I am indebted here to Ronald V. Samson's *The Psychology of Power* (New York: Random House, 1968) for his intelligent investigation of the connection between formal power structures and the family and for his analysis of how power corrupts basic human relationships.

2. "Domination in the quite general sense of power, i.e. the possibility of imposing one's will upon the behavior of other persons, can emerge in the most diverse forms." In this central passage of *Wirtschaft und Gesellschaft* Weber is particularly interested in two such forms: control through social authority ("patriarchal, magisterial, or princely") and control through economic force. In patriarchy as in other forms of domination "that control over economic goods, i.e. economic power, is a frequent, often purposively willed, consequence of domination as well as one of its most important instruments." Quoted from Max Rheinstein's and Edward Shil's translation of portions of *Wirtschaft und Gesellschaft* entitled *Max Weber on Law in Economy and Society* (New York: Simon and Schuster, 1967), pp. 323–24.

3. No matriarchal societies are known to exist at present. Matrilineality, which may be, as some anthropologists have held, a residue or a transitional stage of matriarchy, does not constitute an exception to patriarchal rule, it simply channels the power held by males through female descent—, e.g. the Avunculate.

4. Radical democracy would, of course, preclude patriarchy. One might find evidence of a general satisfaction with a less than perfect democracy in the fact that women have so rarely held power within modern "democracies."

5. Hannah Arendt, "Speculations on Violence," *The New York Review of Books,* Vol. XII No. 4, February 27, 1969, p. 24.

6. The social, rather than the physical sciences are referred to here. Traditionally, medical science had often subscribed to such beliefs. This is no longer the case today, when the best medical research points to the conclusion that sexual stereotypes have no bases in biology.

7. "The historians of Roman laws, having very justly remarked that neither birth nor affection was the foundation of the Roman family, have concluded that this foundation must be found in the power of the father or husband. They make a sort of primordial institution of this power; but they do not explain how this power was established, unless it was by the superiority of strength of the husband over the wife, and of the father over the children.

Now, we deceive ourselves sadly when we thus place force as the origin of law. We shall see farther on that the authority of the father or husband, far from having been the first cause, was itself an effect; it was derived from religion, and was established by religion. Superior strength, therefore, was not the principle that established the family." Numa Denis Fustel de Coulanges, *The Ancient City* (1864). English translation by Willard Small (1873), Doubleday Anchor Reprint, pp. 41–42. Unfortunately Fustel de Coulanges neglects to mention how religion came to uphold patriarchal authority, since patriarchal religion is also an effect, rather than an original cause.

8. In some of my remarks on the family I am indebted to Goode's short and concise analysis. See William J. Goode, *The Family* (Englewood Cliffs, New Jersey, Prentice-Hall, 1964).

9. Family, society, and state are three separate but connected entities: women have a decreasing importance as one goes from the first to the third category. But as each of the three categories exists within or is influenced by the overall institution of patriarchy, I am concerned here less with differentiation than with pointing out a general similarity.

10. J. K. Folsom makes a convincing argument as to the anomalous character of patriarchal family systems within democratic society. See Joseph K. Folsom *The Family and Democratic Society* (New York: John Wiley, 1934, 1943).

11. Bronislaw Malinowski, *Sex, Culture and Myth* (New York, Harcourt, 1962), p. 63. An earlier statement is even more sweeping: "In all human societies moral tradition and the law decree that the group consisting of a woman and her offspring is not a sociologically complete unit." *Sex and Repression in Savage Society* (London, Humanities, 1927), p. 213.

12. Goode, *op. cit.*, p. 74.

19: Social Movements (pp. 213–225)

1. Attention is called, in passing, to spatial movements, such as nomadic movements, barbaric invasions, crusades, pilgrimages, colonization, and migrations. Such movements may be carried on as societies, as in the case of tribal migrations; as diverse peoples with a common goal, as in the case of the religious crusades of the Middle Ages; or as individuals with similar goals, as in most of the immigration into the United States. Mechanisms of their collective operation will be dealt with in the following discussion of social movements. In themselves, such movements are too complicated and diversified to be dealt with adequately here.

2. C. A. Dawson and W. E. Gettys, *Introduction to Sociology* (Rev. ed.; New York: Ronald Press Co., 1935, chap. 19).

3. There are political as well as religious sects. The difference is that the political sect seeks to bring about political revolution as well as change in the fundamental philosophy of life.

4. This discussion may appear to be contradicted in the area of clothes fashions by the existence of a large fashion industry which depends heavily on massive, well-organized promotional campaigns. The appearance is delusory. Tastes may be manipulated but only within limits. The fashion industry serves the process; it does not create it.

20: The Role of Ideology in Political Power (pp. 228–236)

1. Joan Robinson, *Economic Philosophy*, Doubleday and Co., Garden City, New York, Anchor Books edition, 1964, p. 12.

2. Harold Lasswell, *Politics: Who Gets What, When, How,* World Publishing Co., New York, Meridian Books, 1958, p. 169.

3. Lasswell, *op. cit.,* pp. 33–34.

4. Lasswell, *op. cit.,* p. 31.

Notes

Notes

Notes

Notes

Notes

Notes

Notes